WHY STUDENTS RESIST LEARNING

WHY STUDENTS RESIST LEARNING

A Practical Model for Understanding and Helping Students

Edited by Anton O. Tolman and

Janine Kremling

Foreword by John Tagg

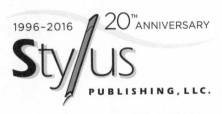

1996–2016   20TH ANNIVERSARY

Stylus

PUBLISHING, LLC.

STERLING, VIRGINIA

Published by Stylus Publishing, LLC.
22883 Quicksilver Drive
Sterling, Virginia 20166-2102

Library of Congress Cataloging-in-Publication Data
Names: Tolman, Anton O., editor. | Kremling, Janine, 1977- editor.
Title: Why students resist learning : a practical model for
understanding and helping students /
edited by Anton O. Tolman and Janine Kremling;
foreword by John Tagg.

Description: First edition. | Sterling, Virginia : Stylus Publishing,
LLC, [2017] | Includes bibliographical references and index.
Identifiers: LCCN 2016016804 (print) |
LCCN 2016025331 (ebook) |
  ISBN 9781620363430 (cloth : alk. paper) |
  ISBN 9781620363447 (pbk. : alk.   paper) |
  ISBN 9781620363454 (library networkable e-edition) |
  ISBN 9781620363461 (consumer e-edition)
Subjects: LCSH: College student development programs. |
Education, Higher--Psychological aspects. |
Learning, Psychology of.
Classification: LCC LB2343.4 .W555 2017 (print) |
LCC LB2343.4 (ebook) | DDC 378.1/98--dc23
LC record available at https://lccn.loc.gov/2016016804

13-digit ISBN: 978-1-62036-343-0 (cloth)
13-digit ISBN: 978-1-62036-344-7 (paperback)
13-digit ISBN: 978-1-62036-345-4 (library networkable e-edition)
13-digit ISBN: 978-1-62036-346-1 (consumer e-edition)

Printed in the United States of America

All first editions printed on acid-free paper
that meets the American National Standards Institute
Z39-48 Standard.

Bulk Purchases

Quantity discounts are available for use in workshops and for
staff development.
Call 1-800-232-0223

First Edition, 2017

10   9   8   7   6   5

CONTENTS

FOREWORD

In this book, Tolman, Kremling, and their colleagues address what is perhaps the greatest challenge colleges and universities must face if they hope to achieve their purpose of providing an education of real value to their students. This challenge, student resistance to learning, has long been an excuse for inaction and an explanation for failure in higher education. This book turns that problem around and makes it an arena for progress and an apparatus for understanding.

The authors grapple with what is one of the core paradoxes of education: Students are the medium and agents of education; if they don't learn, education hasn't happened. But students are also the single greatest barrier to education, because if they won't learn, the best efforts of educators are wasted. We have too long spoken of education and teaching as if they were things we could do to students. But the harsh fact is that if students don't do the learning, and especially if they fight the learning, then the best we can do is conceal the fact or ignore it and play pretend. But if we whitewash or ignore the problem, the ivory tower becomes a Potemkin village, a papier-mâché façade, colorful and pretentious, behind which is . . . not much.

Ask a representative sample of teachers from nearly any college or university why students don't learn more in their pursuit of a bachelor's degree and many—I suspect most—of the responses will converge in identifying the chief culprits: the students themselves. Different faculty members formulate the complaint differently—some will see many students as lacking the requisite skills, others will see them as short on motivation, and a few will find entire generations deficient in focus and attention. Such perceptions are hardly new—we have good evidence that Abelard and his successors were disappointed with their budding clerks back in the 1100s, before the University of Paris formally existed. Indeed, there seems to be a predictable pattern at work: Just as every college president announces that this year's graduating class is the greatest ever, most of the faculty, in private conversations, bemoan that it is worse than in the good old days.

In our own day, however, much good work has been done to awaken the hidden learner in the apparently grade-grubbing, indolent, and slacking student. We know now (and if we do not know it, then we aren't paying attention) that it is possible to inspire and cultivate a deep approach to learning, to prompt students to more engagement and better results.

It used to be common to think of *teaching* and *learning* as separate activities, and those who still think that way find it irritating that the two terms are so often linked together. The transformative insight is that teaching and learning are more like ballroom dancing than piano playing. You can play the piano by yourself, but it proverbially takes two to tango. If you don't have a partner, you just can't dance. It takes at least two for the teaching-learning transaction to happen. If nobody is learning, you aren't teaching, even though you may be practicing the steps in your private studio in front of the lecture hall.

Of course, the dancing analogy is a bit flattering to teachers. The relationship is not purely reciprocal. You can't teach without learners, but you can learn without teachers—as many of us confirm every day of our lives. The only really indispensable participant in the learning transaction is the learner. Without the engagement of the student, learning will never happen. Seen in this light, students who resist learning are not just an inconvenience. They undermine the central mission of the college. Many a professor has had the disheartening sense, after an unmistakable encounter with student resistance, of spinning her wheels. The question arises repeatedly in the teacher's mind: Am I wasting my time? And the answer is, if the student successfully resists real engagement with the learning process, yes, you are wasting your time. And the student's. And the resources and energy of the college.

One of the great attractions of the "traditional" class in which the teacher does the talking and little of the listening is that it is a wonderful way of concealing the results. In a large lecture hall, filled with the instructor's voice and image, with the students sitting silently, heads lowered to their notebooks or laptops, we have a pedagogy of opaque failure. The one-way mode of teaching makes it very likely that many students will resist learning but do so passively, by quiet withdrawal—into their laptops, their phones, their daydreams. Nobody actually knows what they're doing. So you can hope.

But now we know. We know that any pedagogy that asks students to do something on an ongoing basis is better than any pedagogy that does not. Teaching that asks students to talk, write, draw, act, manipulate widgets, design experiments, select and criticize the products of others, tell stories, or argue with one another is better almost always than teaching that just asks them to listen to somebody else talk. We know the ones who need to listen to someone else talk are the teachers. As technology has transformed education, this lesson has, if anything, become more vivid. Whether the class is in person or online, simultaneous or asynchronous, teachers need to find out what the students are thinking and doing. And when teachers do, everything works better, and more learning happens; these teachers are experiencing the difficulties rather than ignoring them, handling the problems rather than sweeping them under the rug. Active learning works.

But as Tolman and Kremling bring vividly to our attention, when you move the students from passive to active roles, they often resist. They do not take their medicine just because it is good for them. They often complain that a contract has been broken, an unwritten rule transgressed: "But you're supposed to teach me!" "Why do I have to do all the work? You're getting paid for it!" "My other teachers don't make me do this!" "I never had to do this in high school!" And so it goes.

The irony is blatant and really quite agonizing if we dwell on it. What works to get students to learn, to learn resiliently, to learn what they can use and when to use it, is something students do not naturally like nor are necessarily drawn to. They fight what's good for them. We have the cure for what ails them, but they resist the treatment.

This student resistance feeds the preexisting faculty resistance to doing what works for education and creates the temptation to revert to the previous norm, to go back to lecture and multiple-choice tests, to hide our failures behind the curtain again. The problem with active learning is that the active learners don't like it, so we have to give them their way. Resistance can breed withdrawal and retrenchment, can make teachers afraid to really teach. This kind of resistance is therefore a major barrier to the progress of higher education and its students.

This book takes the challenge head on. It directly addresses the great and central problem: student resistance to active learning. And it addresses that problem in the right way. The wrong way, which—as suggested previously— we have been practicing in one form or another since the twelfth century, is to simply blame the students, as if education were a zero-sum game in which it is either your fault or my fault. The right way, the way Tolman and Kremling do it, is to recognize that student resistance is a systemic problem: Students do what they do for a reason, and that reason is often their experience of schooling. As we see in the following chapters, the reasons for student resistance are many and varied. Some students resist because of problems they bring with them to college, some because of their college experiences, some because of their experiences with teachers or other students. But student resistance is not magic. If we can understand the reasons for students' behavior, we can change it. That is the central project of this book: to understand why and how students resist taking a deep approach to learning so that we can take a deeper approach to designing a curriculum and a pedagogy that can help them to grow, rather than let them shrink into their protective cocoon of resistance.

This is not the first book to address student resistance. However, as far as I can tell, this is the first book to address the phenomenon systematically and in a way that brings together a variety of perspectives and disciplines that can help to explain it. We can find anecdotes about student resistance sprinkled liberally through books and periodicals on college teaching and learning. What I, at least, have not encountered before is an attempt to construct a systematic and multidisciplinary theory that integrates what we know about psychology, pedagogy, and learning science to construct a framework for recognizing, diagnosing, and addressing such resistance. The anecdotes are important—and this book is full of them—because they help ground our understanding and make the phenomenon real and concrete. But if we stop our analysis with anecdotes, we run the risk of producing colorful complaints rather than solutions. So many of the stories we can tell treat the resistant student as a quirky anomaly. Of course, every student is an individual. But they are individuals whose behavior can tell us much if we will look for the patterns and pull in from disparate disciplines the wisdom that bears on choices and motivations. Tolman and Kremling tell the stories to find the patterns and give us an apparatus for solving the problems rather than just to blame the students.

The authors provide not only a design and framework for analyzing and addressing student resistance but also a role model for interacting with it. As suggested previously, the central move in pedagogy from poor teaching to good learning resides not in telling so much as in listening. Many of Tolman and Kremling's colleagues and coauthors are also their students. They not only listen to their students but also let us listen in, and the students share what it looks like from their perspective, the one that matters most. In reading the book, we are not being preached to; we are practicing what we need to do in order to understand how to proceed.

In his splendid book *Visible Learning: A Synthesis of Over 800 Meta-Analyses Relating to Achievement*, John Hattie (2009) summarizes the result of his meta-analysis of over 800 empirical studies on learning—what works and what doesn't. He summarizes the overall conclusion of this research by emphasizing the vital principle of transparency:

> What is most important is that teaching is visible to the student, and that the learning is visible to the teachers. The more the student becomes the teacher and the more the teacher becomes the learner, the more successful are the outcomes. (Hattie, 2009, p. 25)

In this book, the teachers become learners, the learners become teachers, and thus they make visible to all of us what goes wrong, and how it can go right, in teaching and learning. If you are a teacher or care about what teachers do, you have much to learn.

John Tagg
Professor Emeritus
Palomar College
San Marcos, California

Reference

Hattie, J. (2009). *Visible learning: A synthesis of over 800 meta-analyses relating to achievement.* New York, NY: Routledge.

ACKNOWLEDGMENTS

Anton O. Tolman

Let me begin by thanking my wife, Patricia, for her love, support, and ongoing encouragement for me to finish this book. She knows how much this work has meant to me, and she has nudged and pushed me along when I struggled to get parts of it done. I couldn't have done it without her. Thank you, honey!

I also want to thank my colleague and coeditor, Janine Kremling. She and I met at a Lilly West conference after I had presented my ideas and data on the instruments I developed to encourage student process metacognition. She was very interested in these new tools and began to use them in her own classrooms. We have collaborated on multiple presentations and research projects, and her input, feedback, and ongoing commitment to student learning helped convince me of the value of these ideas.

A fond thank-you goes out to John Tagg, whom I met while I was director of the former Faculty Center for Teaching Excellence at Utah Valley University (UVU). I had sponsored a reading circle on his wonderful book *The Learning Paradigm College* and was struck by the depth of his thinking on how to improve higher education; he and his colleague Robert Barr had also been responsible for launching a national discussion about the shift from an institutional focus on teaching to a focus on student learning back in 1995, a discussion that in many ways continues today. John and I have kept in touch since he came to speak as keynote at UVU's annual faculty convocation many years ago. John also, without being asked, contributed copy editing to many of the chapters and gave excellent input and feedback. Thank you, John, for your insights, friendship, and willingness to write the foreword for this book.

To my colleagues Christopher Lee and Trevor Morris, I express my appreciation. I realized as Janine and I started on this book that we would not be able to handle all of this material on our own. I sought out Chris Lee, with whom I had published a chapter on sharing power with students in the classroom and who had been an active participant and leader of our teaching academy, and Trevor Morris, who was on my staff at the Faculty Center for Teaching Excellence and who is more enthusiastic about psychology than most. Their eager willingness to take part in this project and to work with students on their chapters (that was a stipulation) helped make this project feasible.

A thank-you also goes to David Yells, dean of the College of Humanities and Social Sciences at Utah Valley University, who, as I note in the preface, was the inspiration for pulling a group of students together and working with them on the book. He supported my work with a creative way to accommodate workload demands, and I am grateful for it. Likewise, the unflagging support of my department colleagues and department chair, Kris Doty, as well as the work of several teaching assistants, helped me to manage my teaching as we finished the book.

I could not have completed this project without the many students who contributed their time, anxiety, effort, and ideas to the book. Their names are on every chapter (together with the students Janine worked with), and their ideas and writing are embedded herein. The original excitement of the group of students I pulled together for this project shifted into anxiety once they realized the scope of what we were trying to do and the amount of work that was involved, but they shouldered their assignments and produced significant contributions to this work. Their perspectives and stories bring my integrated model of student resistance to life. Thank you to each and every one of you, especially to those who have maintained contact with me even after graduation and assisted with reviewing subsequent drafts and changes.

Last, I am grateful for Stylus Publishing and John von Knorring. This book was delivered to John more than a year later than we had initially agreed. As we were working toward finishing the book over a year ago, I was diagnosed with cancer and began chemotherapy; a stem cell transplant and post-transplant recovery quickly followed. This threw the entire project into question for a while and, as the reader may imagine, created significant delays in getting everything done. John and Stylus have been incredibly supportive and understanding of this whole process, and while I still struggle with finding a way to live in spite of cancer, the unflagging support and genuine concern expressed by John gave me encouragement to finish the book. I could not have asked for more, and now I can cross this item off my bucket list!

Janine Kremling

First of all I would like to thank Anton O. Tolman for his incredible determination to finish this book. His commitment to the needs of students, his belief in students' abilities, and his patience are admirable. The fact that the book is on his bucket list demonstrates his desire to make a difference in students' and professors' lives. Anton has certainly made a difference in my life and my thinking about student learning. I met Anton when I was a second-year faculty member, trying to improve my teaching skills. The key to my goal was to learn about the way people think, mindsets, and metacognition. When I heard Anton's presentation at Lilly West on metacognition and student learning, it clicked, and we have worked together on presentations and research ever since.

I would also like to thank the Teaching Resource Center (TRC), and especially Kim Costino, for encouraging me and enabling me to attend teaching conferences, hold workshops, and participate in think tanks on high-impact practices. Without the support of the TRC, I may not have participated in Lilly West, met Anton, or had the opportunity to work on this book. Many opportunities for faculty and students depend on institutional support, and this is an issue we have stressed throughout the book.

Finally, I would like to thank John von Knorring and Stylus Publishing, who have been so supportive in the past two years and gave us the confidence that we would finish this book despite all the challenges. Support of and confidence in others is a key factor to success, and I am grateful to have had the opportunity to work with Anton and John, who have given both.

PREFACE

What Makes This Book Unique

Anton O. Tolman

S ince I entered the academy many years ago, every professor I have known has demonstrated concern for student learning. As experts, we care deeply about our fields, and we truly want students to understand the value of these disciplines to enrich their understanding of the world. As Boyer (1990) discovered a while back, even most professors whose work is primarily focused on scholarship rather than teaching at major research institutions still have the same desire. In the words of Barr and Tagg (1995), "For many of us the Learning Paradigm has always lived in our hearts" (p. 13) even if it has not necessarily lived in our minds and the way we work.

This is what can make our regular encounters with student resistance to learning so frustrating. Many years ago, about the second day in an abnormal psychology course, I was explaining to students the collaborative learning methods we would be using in the class and my intention not to lecture very much throughout the semester. My enthusiasm for this approach ran into an obstacle when a student, obviously frustrated, raised his hand and then stated in a loud voice that he objected to this approach. He stated that he was paying for my salary and that he wanted me to teach instead of making them have to learn everything for themselves. A bit flustered, I attempted to use a medical metaphor to explain why my approach was better, but the student was not buying that argument. Although this was not the only experience I have had with student resistance, it was significant because I had been making ongoing changes in my pedagogies to promote more active learning, and this was the first instance of active resistance that I had encountered after having adopted collaborative learning approaches. After that class, I continued to ponder what I could do differently to shape that initial classroom environment to achieve better results.

That pondering initially led me to the idea of student readiness to change based on the clinical theory of the transtheoretical model of change (TTM; Prochaska & DiClemente, 1992) and to the development of metacognitive instruments to help students better understand their own approaches to learning, and their readiness to become more effective learners (e.g., see Tolman, 2011a). This also led me to develop the integrated model of student resistance (IMSR; see Tolman, 2011b) as I began to connect metacognition to other aspects of resistance. I realized that although much work has been done in separate areas, all of which has revealed important facets of resistance, I could not find any discussion or description that was comprehensive or integrated that brought these facets together into a coherent whole. That is the goal of this book.

However, what sets this book apart is not only the creation and elaboration of an integrated vision of student resistance in an academic sense but also the dedication to being of practical value to everyone who reads it. As we describe the elements of the model, we will also discuss ideas and practical suggestions for how instructors can use the concepts to assess the students in their classrooms, to better understand where students are with respect to those concepts. We will also suggest ways that instructors can intervene, take proactive steps to reduce student resistance, and enhance student learning in ways that benefit the instructor, students, and society. In addition to instructors, the book has much to offer faculty developers, department chairs, deans, and administrators in considering the context of higher education and the ways our systems often exacerbate or contribute to elements that trigger or encourage student resistance to learning. We hope that some of our suggestions and ideas will be of value in improving our systems of higher education to reduce student resistance and increase engagement. We encourage our readers to test out some of these strategies and adapt them to their own unique contexts. Understanding student resistance is only useful inasmuch as it informs our ability to help students learn.

This book is also unique in another important and highly relevant way: It integrates the thoughts, efforts, and reflections of a superb team of undergraduate students who have made direct contributions to the book. They are listed as coauthors in the relevant chapters. I teach at Utah Valley University, which has a teaching mission centered on core themes of student engagement, rigor, inclusiveness, and student success. I saw the need to publish this book and share the idea of the IMSR with a wider audience, but I did not have sufficient time to get the book written. I went to my dean and asked if I could reduce my course load to accomplish this. He pondered this for a moment. Then he smiled and said, "What if you write the book as a class with a team of students?"

This was a brilliant suggestion, and I am a bit ashamed that I did not think of it myself. We created a two-semester class and recruited a team of students who were excited to participate and contribute. It is not unusual for professors to write articles or books that include student authors and contributors, but by and large these coauthors tend to be graduate students. Indeed, my coeditor from California State University, San Bernardino, Janine Kremling, wrote her sections of chapter 10 with the collaboration of a graduate student. However, most student authors in this book were under-graduates at the time the book was written. Furthermore, because of the very topic and scope of this book, these students have been immersed in a diverse literature related to student learning and higher education in ways that have changed their perceptions of themselves. Becoming aware of the elements of the IMSR has enabled them to identify their personal sources of resistance and to think differently about their role in their own education. As we have written this book together, each of them has shared and integrated his or her own personal experiences with resistance into its chapters. I know of no other book right now that has such a powerful infusion of student voices and reflections, and I am proud to be a part of it.

References

Barr, R. B., & Tagg, J. (1995). From teaching to learning—a new paradigm forundergraduate education. *Change, 27*(6), 12–26.

Boyer, E. L. (1990). *Scholarship reconsidered: Priorities of the professoriate.* San Francisco, CA: Jossey-Bass.

Prochaska, J. O., & DiClemente, C. C. (1992). Stage of change in the modification of problem behaviors. In M. Herseon, R. M. Eisler, & P. M. Miller (Eds.), *Progress on behavior modification.* Sycamore, IL: Sycamore Press.

Tolman, A. O. (2011a). Creating transformative experiences for students in abnormal psychology. In R. L. Miller, E. Balcetis, S. R. Burns, D. B. Daniel, B. K. Saville, & W. D. Woody (Eds.), *Promoting student engagement* (Vol. 2, pp. 136–145). Washington, DC: Society for the Teaching of Psychology. Retrieved from http://teachpsych.org/resources/e-books/pse2011/vol2/index.php

Tolman, A. O. (2011b, December 16). *Understanding and working with student resistance to active learning* [TLT Friday Live! webinar]. Retrieved from http://tltgroup.roundtablelive.org/event-365557

DEFINING AND UNDERSTANDING STUDENT RESISTANCE

Anton O. Tolman, Andy Sechler, and Shea Smart

As Hollywood would say, the following narrative is based on a true story. In a coffee shop in the student union of a southern U.S. university, two professors waited their turn at the order counter. One professor turned to the other and loudly stated, "They [students] think they are more intelligent than they are." His colleague more than agreed, saying things like "Yeah, they're really dumb." As the professors continued this interchange, grousing about student performance and behavior, the students around them became increasingly angry. The students standing in line both in front and behind this academic duo reported to another professor about their feelings in this situation. One said, "How can you help students when deep down you feel they aren't worth it? You can see I am still pissed hours later." Another student stated, "Who do they think they are? Do they think they are better than us? . . . And they're teaching us when they don't believe in us? . . . If they weren't professors I would have turned around and told them to go to hell. It was easy to see who the dumb ones in line really were" (Schmier, 2012).

Although it might seem obvious to explain this situation as the result of two arrogant professors (i.e., jerks) behaving in an insensitive manner, this unfortunate scenario presents an opportunity to explore the systemic nature of student resistance and the ways it can affect student learning, including the

1

reciprocal impact of professor and student behaviors. Certainly, the students in the coffee shop were expressing resistance to being labeled by the professors, and it is conceivable that a wariness or reluctance to engage in other classes could result from this encounter. One common error that faculty often make when discussing student resistance is to assume that resistance is a *student* behavior. Although there is some truth to this—the students are the ones who are manifesting resistant behavior—the etiology of resistance is more complex. As we will demonstrate in the coming chapters, student resistance is the outcome or result of a confluence of forces, including institutional context, faculty attitudes and behaviors, faculty reactions to student behaviors, and powerful forces that drive and shape student expectations and reactions.

Unfortunately, these systemic elements and interactions are not immediately visible to an instructor; they are not as attention grabbing as a student complaining in one's office or refusing to participate in a class activity. Manifestations of student resistance to learning are a frequent source of conversation among faculty, much of it not very positive or uplifting. Yet in reviewing the multifaceted literature on resistance, one is struck by the similarity to a famous comment from Justice Potter Stewart of the U.S. Supreme Court regarding the difficulty of legally defining *pornography*; the justice noted that it is difficult to articulate a clear definition, but "I know it when I see it" (*Jacobellis v. Ohio*, 1964). Similarly, the teaching literature does not provide a specific definition of *student resistance*; instead, specific behavioral examples of resistance are often provided along with suggestions for understanding resistance and tips for working with it. Some good cases in point include Felder and Brent (1996), who noted that enthusiasts of student-centered or learner-centered instruction are in for a "rude shock" (p. 43) when they begin to actually implement updated pedagogies in the classroom. Felder and Brent advocated for this shift in teaching, but they also wrote that although these approaches offer significant benefits to students, such benefits are "neither immediate nor automatic" (p. 43). They explained that instructors need to be prepared for negative student reactions as they work with students to implement engaged teaching.

Similarly, Doyle (2008) wrote about resistance as the "biggest challenge" (p. 17) facing instructors. He provided a list of reasons why students may resist, including what he refers to as "the powerfully entrenched teacher-centered view of learning these students possess" (p. 17), but he never defined *student resistance* in any cogent way. Weimer (2013) focused an entire chapter in her widely read book on learner-centered teaching on student resistance. She explained that often students respond negatively to changes in course design in ways that may discourage teachers, sometimes by using behaviors that instructors may experience as personally offensive or disrespectful. She proposed four major reasons why students may resist and suggestions for what to do. Although these observations and tips are useful, they do not necessarily advance a nuanced and coherent understanding of what student resistance is, how it works, or where it comes from nor ways to systematically assess and intervene to benefit instructors, students, and society.

Student resistance is not an outcome that we can afford to discuss in general terms any longer. It is time to grapple with it in a comprehensive and detailed way. The purpose of this book is to provide classroom instructors, faculty developers, administrators, and interested others with a conceptual framework, a model that explains why student resistance occurs and offers ideas for assessment and intervention. Through better understanding of student resistance to learning opportunities, instructors can react in ways that do not increase or contribute to it and can become empowered to change their teaching designs or approaches to reduce student resistance and improve learning. Institutions can more effectively develop new policies and strategies that reward and encourage a shift toward learner-centered pedagogies in classrooms throughout institutions of higher education. Let us begin by providing what the existing literature does not: a definition of what we are talking about.

What Is Student Resistance?

As a starting point, we define *student resistance* as follows:

> Student resistance is an outcome, a motivational state in which students reject learning opportunities due to systemic factors. The presence of resistance signals to the instructor the need to assess the systemic variables that are contributing to this outcome in order to intervene effectively and enhance student learning.

Given this definition, our goal in the upcoming chapters is to explore the systemic factors that interact and contribute to resistance and to provide a practical framework for understanding resistance that we hope will make this definition meaningful.

As we progress toward this goal, we want to begin with some points of clarification. Resistance is a motivational *state* and an outcome of multiple interacting factors; it is not a *trait* that endures over time or exists as part of a student's personality or genetics. Our definition implies that resistance is dynamic and fluid, influenced by ongoing interactions and situations among the student, the professor, and student peers. It can even change within a single class period depending on what happens. Consider the following example: A student who normally demonstrates a low level of resistance to class participation and assignments misses more answers on a quiz than she expected. She becomes defensive and softly complains to her peers sitting nearby about the quiz and the professor making the class too difficult. At least for the moment, this situation increases the student's low level of resistance to a higher level and may make her more likely to resist learning new information or participating actively in a class assignment or activity.

Thus, student resistance can fluctuate in reaction to events going on both in the students' lives and in the classroom. Although some students may manifest resistant behaviors from the beginning of the course and remain fairly consistent over time, the example of the reactive student informs us that resistance is not limited only to those students whom faculty might characterize as "unmotivated" (a trait characterization). Resistance can and does occur even in the "best" students, those who sincerely want to learn the material. In all cases of resistance, we suggest that causes of resistant behaviors may be more complex than instructors tend to assume.

It is also probably helpful to consider student resistance as a *signal* that something is happening in the classroom and/or within the students. Too often, instructors react to manifestations of resistance as though they are noise, background static that disrupts the "communication" signal the faculty member is trying to get across, usually content. Like road noise in our cars when we are listening to music or pop-up ads on our laptops, this purported "noise" is often responded to with frustration and a desire to just bypass it and move on to the "important stuff." However, what if the resistance *is* the important stuff? In the field of psychotherapy, there has been growing recognition that a patient's resistance to the suggestions and direction provided by a counselor is a signal of an underlying issue that must be addressed if progress is to be made. Similarly, if instructors can learn to recognize when resistance is occurring, or increasing, it might be worth dedicating time to figuring out what forces are leading to this outcome and taking steps to acknowledge, assess, and reduce the resistance.

Students have the same problem, often ascribing external factors in their lives or at school to their own motivation to resist learning. Students' ability to recognize their own resistance and to evaluate the sources that are contributing to it may also help them to interact more effectively with their instructor and peers, enhancing their learning. When students, and especially professors, mislabel the resistance as noise instead of as signal, they perpetuate a status quo in which students are not learning; such a stance may even lead to increased resistance.

The last point of clarification emphasizes the distinction between motivation and behavior. As noted in the definition, we consider *resistance* to be a motivational state rather than a grouping of behaviors. Without a model, a framework, for understanding the forces that contribute to and generate resistance, it is easy to equate resistance with behaviors because these behaviors are salient, easily visible in the teaching environment. However, if resistance is the same as behavior, how do we explain the various and complex manifestations of different behaviors that have been labeled in the literature as *resistance?*

In their seminal work, Kearney and Plax (1992) noted that historically student resistance was considered equivalent to student misbehavior, almost universally characterized as rebelliousness. In contrast, they argued that resistant behaviors could be either constructive or destructive. They also claimed that constructive resistance enhances student on-task behavior, although they acknowledged that it may be difficult for instructors to accept this idea. These investigators and their colleagues (see Burroughs, Kearney, & Plax, 1989) further subdivided resistant behaviors into teacher-owned and student-owned behaviors. With respect to these investigators and their significant contributions, especially the idea of constructive resistance, we believe their classification system ignores the motivational basis for student behaviors. Resistance is a type of motivation that shapes and guides behaviors. Table 1.1 illustrates our conceptualization and provides some specific examples of behaviors.

In Table 1.1, the columns represent two major types of motivational strategies. In the first, a student is focused on asserting her own autonomy. Such motivation could arise from a reaction to or interaction with many factors, including professor misbehaviors, embedded racism in society or the classroom, or the personal experiences of the student growing up (e.g., family pressure to attend college). The student resists learning opportunities because she sees them as part of an oppressive system trying to force her into a way of thinking she does not accept or to meet capricious requirements with no real rationale behind them. Thus, the student rejects external demands whether they come from the university's requirements to take a specific course (e.g., general education or program prerequisite) or a professor's required homework. Common emotional responses that accompany this motivation are frustration or anger. The oft-heard student complaint about perceived "busywork" is an expression of this frustration.

The second motivation occurs when a different set of forces interacts. For example, a student may have been raised to please authority, or perhaps he believes he is a carrier of his family's hopes for economic advancement. He may be overwhelmed and stressed, juggling classes, a full-time job, and finding time for his wife and children. He could be struggling with a disability or mental disorder and is focused on trying to pass his classes. Possibly, he feels

TABLE 1.1
Forms of Student Resistance Matrix

	Asserting Autonomy *Pushing against external influence* *Emotions: anger, frustration, resentment*	*Preserving Self* *Trying to accommodate an external influence* *Emotions: anxiety, fear*
Active Resistance	• Arguing or disagreeing with professor in the classroom • Repeatedly asking for the rationale for assignments • Saying they paid for the class and want it taught how they like • Inciting other students to rebel or not collaborate; disrupting class activities • Complaining to higher authority	• Repeatedly asking for detailed clarification of grading criteria • Taking over group assignments to ensure an adequate grade • Arguing with the professor over grades received; seeking additional points or consideration • Focusing on surface approach to learning
Passive Resistance	• Refusing to come to class • Refusing to participate during in-class exercises (does not get into groups; does not comply with assignment tasks) • Failing to turn in or being consistently late with assignments • Complaining about the professor to other students	• Expressing concerns about working with others • Avoiding conflicts and refusing to resolve situations or bring them to the professor's awareness • Minimally participating in class (withdrawn, does not speak or give feedback, lets others make all decisions)

unprepared for college, is unsure of his capabilities, and is focused on trying to "just get through" his classes to achieve a degree. Even a student with goals for high achievement may experience this type of motivation, viewing any threat to a high or perfect grade as a personal risk to his self-esteem or, alternatively, as endangering his future (e.g., getting into medical school, supporting his family, getting off welfare, or validating his competency as a person). The emotional responses that accompany this form of motivation tend to be related to anxiety or fear. These students may try to avoid complex assignments, challenges to what they already know, or course requirements that push them beyond their comfort zone in order to maintain their sense of security in achieving their goals.

These two basic forms of motivation may then be expressed in different ways, depending on the student's background or possibly the institutional culture, including the classroom. Some students may express their motivations using assertive or direct action, including confrontation, or they may be passive in that they do not engage in direct interaction with the professor. The self-preservation motive may also involve specifically avoiding direct interactions with peers such as peer reviews or collaborative learning. Thus, it is possible for students to assert their autonomy and to push back against external influences using passive behaviors to achieve their goals. Kearney and Plax (1992) have given good examples of 19 "student resistance techniques" (pp. 91–92) that easily could be included in the forms of student resistance matrix. They also noted that their data indicated that most students tend to prefer more passive strategies, a conclusion that fits with our own observations. Given that instructors hold the power to control grades, many students are reluctant to engage in direct confrontation with an instructor out of concern that it could have a detrimental effect on achieving a degree.

Some authors in fields such as the sociology and psychology of education describe resistance in a more complex way that includes specific aspects of motivation. For instance, Kim (2010) summarized the neo-Marxist critiques of previous theories of education by explaining that student resistance could be seen as a rejection of the social status imposed on students by society. Later authors have pointed out motivational aspects related to a student's ethnicity, gender, or other characteristics (see Kim, 2010). In educational psychology, Brown and Gilligan (1992) described resistance as a healthy coping strategy for females and classified resistant behaviors as either psychological or political. Looking across these various classification systems, there is recognition of the role of motivation in understanding student resistance; furthermore, despite the various disciplinary perspectives that created them, the definitions of *resistance* we are aware of appear to fit reasonably well into the resistance matrix.

Regardless of the ways that various fields categorize resistant behaviors, the ultimate message for instructors is that student resistance is *communicative* (see Kim, 2010); the manifestation of either active or passive resistant behaviors signals the instructor that there is an underlying motivation and that multiple factors are contributing to that resistant behavior. We are not implying that students resist in order to communicate a specific message to the professor, although this could happen; in most cases, students are likely unaware of why they are resisting learning opportunities. It is also important to acknowledge that in some cases, especially with passive resistance, students may emit signals that are intended to disguise or conceal resistance, such as appearing to be taking notes on their laptop while actually reading Facebook posts.

This type of obscured signal is more likely to occur in lecture-focused classrooms or in large classes where anonymity is easier to achieve and where the students are not personally and directly involved in a learning activity. It is also more difficult to hide in an active learning classroom, such as one using team-based learning (Michaelsen, Knight, & Fink, 2004), where students are involved with each other and the professor is actively facilitating team learning and interacting with students. However, in those environments professors need to be aware that passive resistance can still occur, but it may take different forms, such as not speaking or contributing to a team's discussion.

Regardless of the specific form resistance takes, when instructors accept that resistant behaviors signal important aspects of a student's motivation and the presence of important underlying forces, they can adapt their own behaviors and the structural elements of their courses (e.g., assignments, timelines, use of class time) to reduce that resistance and enhance learning of both content and key life skills. Resistant behaviors tell us, as instructors, some very important things about our students, and by seeking to better understand and elicit that communication signal, we can become more effective teachers.

Moving Toward a Systemic Understanding of Student Resistance

Now that we have defined *resistance*, we are better able to "know it when we see it." However, in the quest to avoid becoming the coffee shop instructors, we need to move toward a conceptual model, a framework for understanding not just the student motivation for resisting but the underlying forces and interactions that are generating it. In order to help the reader better understand the need and benefits of moving from more simplistic explanations of student resistance to more systemic explanations, we will use an overarching framework borrowed from a giant in education, John Dewey. Long ago, Dewey and Bentley (1949) provided useful ways to categorize and evaluate most of the approaches we have discussed and will discuss.

As summarized by Abowitz (2000), Dewey and Bentley (1949) described three modes of inquiry for understanding an event or a given behavior: self-action, interaction, and transaction. Self-action explanations assume that the origins of a behavior can be found in the individual—or in the words of Abowitz (2000), "Things are viewed as acting under their own power" (p. 878). In education, this means that instructors interpret or explain student resistance according to the assumption that students are acting on their own, under their own power; the choice to resist is grounded in an individual decision by a student for personal reasons. As an example, consider an instructor who, early in the semester, asks students to get into collaborative groups, whereupon a student throws up his hands and then states loudly, "When are you going to start really teaching instead of making us do all of the work?"

From a self-action perspective, one could conclude that this student is choosing to resist group work and has decided to express his concerns in a confrontational manner. He could be seen, or labeled, as a stubborn student who does not really want to learn, is lazy, or is concerned mostly about his grade (tell me what will be on the exam). All of these explanations share an assumption that the student's behavior is emerging from internal sources; he is acting according to his own agenda and choices, conscious or not. This type of explanation is probably common among faculty, and there is a temptation for the instructor to jump to one of these explanations. However, this interpretation omits contextual factors that may also be influencing the student's behavior, including the influences of his peers, the institutional context of his college, and the instructor's own behaviors. Omitting consideration of these other influences and relationships makes the task of explaining the student's behavior faster and simpler, and it excuses the instructor from worrying what she may have done to contribute to the behavior. However, adopting a self-action explanation might lead the instructor to respond in such a way that the student's resistance may continue or even increase. Giving some thought to the influences of others on behavior leads us to the interaction perspective.

In the interaction inquiry mode (Dewey & Bentley, 1949), an object can cause or influence another object to behave in specific ways, such as those described by Newtonian laws of motion. This type of interaction is also present in human relationships. We do not act solely on the basis of intrinsic motives (self-action). We often react directly to the behaviors of others, both emotionally and behaviorally. The interaction inquiry mode has been widely used by resistance theorists (see Abowitz, 2000; Kim, 2010) as a way to understand the dynamics of resistance in education. To these theorists, resistant student behaviors (mostly characterized as asserting autonomy) may denote a challenge to attempts by the dominant society to train students to behave according to their appointed social roles or status, represented by instructor behavior or institutional policies.

For example, a teacher's offhand or even unintentional racist comment might trigger a student to argue with a point the teacher is making regardless of the content. In an effort to assert autonomy, the student may begin to dismiss other course elements as irrelevant or biased. Alternatively, if a student, to complete an assignment, requests using a different path to the same learning outcome and is told by the professor that there are no exceptions and that she needs to do the work as assigned, she may begin to manifest resistant behaviors in a wide variety of situations. These examples illustrate how resistance may signal an attempt to assert one's autonomy against the dominant power of the instructor.

Communication theorists have also revealed some important ways that professor-student relationships shape learning and resistance. In this literature, *immediacy* refers to the amount of interpersonal warmth and social connection that an instructor demonstrates toward students. Burroughs (2007) found that students manifested less resistance with immediate instructors versus nonimmediate instructors. Other investigators (see Kearney, Plax, Hays, & Ivey, 1991) have evaluated the role and impact of teacher misbehaviors, primarily incompetence, offensiveness, and indolence, on student reactions and classroom resistance.

By understanding that sometimes students may be reacting to *our own* misbehaviors, including not adequately preparing students for tasks or not helping them understand the reasons for assignments (see Doyle, 2008), we may discover opportunities to alter our behavior to enhance student learning. By understanding the important role that immediacy plays in fanning or dampening student resistance, we can seek to develop our social connection with students. The interaction perspective gives us a lens to see new opportunities to become more effective mentors of student learning.

Last, consider the transactional perspective. This perspective is systemic, subsuming both the self-action and the interaction perspectives and expanding the explanation beyond the individual or the immediate interactions between one or more persons. The transactional perspective gives us a broader view of what is happening in the classroom because it reminds us that history and cultural forces are present in the classroom at all times. Take the case of the disgruntled student who views group work as a waste of time and an abdication of a professor's responsibility to "teach." Many students who resist group work do so because of a history of prior negative experiences with study groups or class teams; out of fear for their grades, some may have shouldered disproportionate (and stressful) responsibility for assignments because peers were socially "loafing." Group meetings, such as study groups, may have been mostly exercises in social posturing and relaxation rather than on-task, focused activities. Thus, students' personal histories, their own experiences with a type of "learner-centered pedagogy," have actually given them reason to reject it as a useful approach to learning.

To be honest, some of the valid reasons that students reject group or collaborative work may be the fault of professors who have not prepared or structured these activities to enhance the probability of success or have not prepared students adequately to use these methods. An instructor who is unaware that students may embody a history of negative experiences might not realize that taking time at the beginning of the semester to explain how to be successful in study groups or teams and provide structure to enhance success is vital for these learner-centered activities to be effective (see Oakley, Felder, Brent, & Elhajj, 2004; Sibley & Ostafichuk, 2014).

This extended example illustrates a complex, systemic interaction of forces, including the student's own personal history and experience, the experiences of others on his assigned team, their combined skills in social interaction, and the professor's design and structure of the course as well as her degree of immediacy and time spent preparing students to participate. Other forces might also influence the outcome, including the student's level of cognitive development, his personal inclinations and preferences for social interaction, the degree to which he feels welcome and a part of the institution and the class, and his own awareness of his role and part in any negative experiences with previous teams.

Additionally, some students, especially those who are first generation, at risk, or culturally disadvantaged, may have experienced rejection or marginalization from peers and authority figures like professors. Unfamiliar with the academic environment, they may not understand how to succeed or access available resources that might enhance their chances of success. They may feel socially isolated and anxious about looking incapable by asking for help. These cultural and historical forces may then interact with professors and *their* own level of awareness of cultural issues and diversity. Some instructors may understand these issues, recognize their manifestations, and demonstrate acceptance of the reality of students' lives, whereas others may not recognize how these forces may be present and might make the situation worse by either denying these realities or blaming the students, even unconsciously, for their difficulties in adapting to the classroom environment.

This level of awareness or understanding is not achievable if we focus on explaining resistance mostly at the level of self-action or even at the level of interaction. In contrast, the transaction or systemic perspective accepts all these factors as part of the explanation for the student's resistance while maintaining the ability to separate these elements and address them individually. The transactional perspective was foundational in the creation of the integrated model of student resistance (IMSR; Tolman, 2011).

A Coherent Model for Understanding Student Resistance

As its name suggests, the IMSR was created to integrate a diverse literature on student resistance into a coherent understanding of the factors leading to student resistance. It consists of five separate elements that are divided into external social and cultural forces and situations that affect students' expectations and performance and internal forces originating within the students themselves (see Figure 1.1). Although each of these five elements is grounded in its own literature and has its own connections to student resistance, it is also clear that these elements interact actively with one another, shaping for good or ill the intensity of student resistance. External factors include situations and pressures that may interact with student characteristics or may directly shape student expectations, generate or create stress, and/or compete for student attention and resources. They include environmental and cultural forces such as family history, cultural identity, social class, disabilities, and other forces; the contextual influences of institutions of higher education on both faculty and students that affect behavior and the way classes operate; and the students' own prior negative classroom experiences that influence how they view active learning approaches. Internal forces are divided into a cognitive development element that frames how students perceive education and knowledge and that affects their ability to perform and a metacognitive element reflecting students' understanding and awareness of how they learn and their readiness to adopt more effective learning strategies. As indicated in Figure 1.1, all elements of the IMSR are part of a *system*, meaning that they interact either to generate student resistance or to reduce it.

In a system, individual elements contribute to the whole (resistance), but they are simultaneously *interdependent* so that something that affects one element (e.g., sexist comments) also affects the system as a whole, leading to the aphorism of the whole being greater than the sum of its parts (or less in the case of negative interactions). In the case of student resistance, students' personal biases, specific gender or ethnicity, previous and current classroom experiences, level of cognitive development, and degree of metacognitive awareness of their own learning and mastery and the background cultural context of the institution they attend (e.g., teaching institution or research institution, party school, etc.) all interact and shape the degree of student resistance to learning. For example, negative interactions with a professor in class, perhaps one who is low in immediacy, who controls all aspects of the learning environment, and who is focused mostly on research rather than teaching, can increase the perceived relevance and validity of a student's preexisting expectations and increase the student's fears of failure, leading to increased resistance. These elements affect the student's willingness to believe that he is capable of becoming a more effective learner and may make it more difficult for him to develop cognitively; this can also affect future resistance, especially in active learning environments in other classes. Even worse, the instructor may become increasingly frustrated with student resistance and not know how to act to reduce it.

Figure 1.1. Integrated model of student resistance.

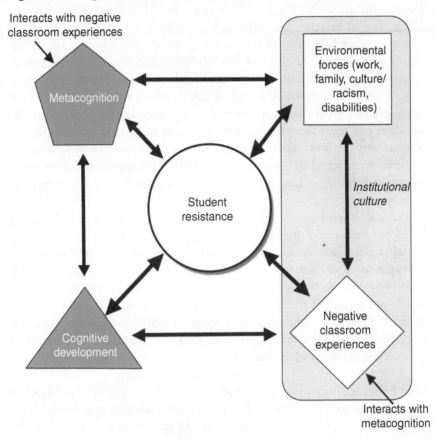

The flip side of this example is that of a warm and caring instructor who designs a learning environment that promotes students' metacognition of their own learning; acknowledges their uniqueness due to gender, cultural background, and previous experiences; and involves students in critical learning decisions. Such an instructor could have a significant influence on reducing student resistance and promoting cognitive development. Because systemic or transactional interactions are interdependent, interventions do not need to target every single element in the system to achieve a change. An instructor who has access to a coherent, systemic model of resistance, such as the IMSR, is better able to assess the elements of the system in students, recognizes that each student is different in the factors that may be contributing to resistance, and may intentionally select effective targets for intervention.

The IMSR is necessary because the literature does not currently offer a comprehensive framework. A reading of teaching-related publications suggests that the topic of resistance is being addressed more explicitly (e.g., Dembo & Seli, 2004; Doyle, 2008; Sibley & Ostafichuk, 2014; Weimer, 2013), but although these authors have offered useful information and strategies, they have not offered an integrated systemic model for understanding resistance. For example, Doyle (2008) described student resistance to learning as due to eight different causes: old habits die hard, high schools remain teacher centered, learning is not a top reason students give for attending college, students do not like taking risks, learner-centered teaching does not resemble what students think of as school, students do not want to put forth the extra effort that learner-centered teaching requires, students' mindsets about learning make adapting to learner-centered teaching more difficult, and many students follow the path of least resistance in their learning.

Although some items on Doyle's list acknowledge the social and cultural impact of high school on student thinking, most of these purported causes are self-action statements: The problem lies within the students. To be fair, in his explanation of these causes, Doyle (2008) described the role of intrinsic versus extrinsic motivation in how schools shape student behavior. However, he did not do justice to the role of interactions among students, peers, and instructors; the influence of the environment within the college itself (not just what it inherits from high schools); or the way that multiple influences interact and build on each other.

Other work of relevance to understanding student resistance has also been published—for example, Claude Steele's (2011) summary of his work on stereotype threat and its influence on the emotions and behaviors of minorities or Nelson's (2010) description of nine common "dysfunctional illusions of rigor" often held by college professors that shape instructor attitudes and behaviors, often interacting in subtle ways with cultural forces. For example, Nelson described the first of these dysfunctional illusions as the idea that difficult courses should exist to weed out unprepared students and that student failure in these courses is largely due to inadequate preparation, insufficient effort, or lack of ability in the subject. He then illustrated the fallacy of this approach using a study by Triesman (1992) that found a 60% rate of D, F, or withdrawal of black students enrolled in calculus at the University of California, Berkeley. Closer examination revealed that struggling students were following a common instructor recommendation to study two hours out of class for every class hour and were studying alone. Triesman changed the pedagogy by inviting these poorly performing students into *honors* homework sections requiring group work, with the outcome that only 4% of these students ultimately finished with a D, F, or withdrawal. Nelson's (2010) point was that the failure of these students in this "rigorous" course was actually due to poor pedagogy and not to student lack of ability or preparation.

In a more recent report, Savini (2016) described student behaviors in her classes that most professors would assume express resistance. She went on to describe how taking the time to inquire and learn more about the students' specific situations opened her eyes to the reality of how mental health situations, especially anxiety and depression, can affect student behaviors and performance in class and to suggest strategies that professors could adopt to support students as they struggle to learn. She noted that in order to do this, she had to alter her conception of the meaning of academic rigor and wrote, "After . . . more than a decade of teaching, I realized that my idea of the good student was standing in the way of good teaching" (para. 1). This insight and the intentional ability to assess the situation through a new lens demonstrate the power and value of a conceptual model and the need for transactional explanations of resistance.

These published reports are valuable for those who have been exposed to them, but this work has not been well integrated into the teaching literature in regard to student resistance even though there are clear links between them, and these explanations are not systemic in that they do not take into account a more comprehensive range of systemic elements. In contrast, the IMSR can effectively explain and integrate the findings discussed previously and add relevant elements that are missing from these other explanations in a way that leads to practical application.

In using the IMSR, we suggest instructors consider the model as a whole but begin with the elements they encounter most in their classrooms or institutions. This can give a productive starting point for making adjustments to courses and teaching practices that can be expanded as the instructor's understanding and experience increase. For example, instructors teaching introductory or general education courses might benefit especially from considering cognitive development and environmental forces, whereas those who teach upper division courses might consider negative classroom experiences and ways to enhance student metacognition. Administrators might benefit from focusing on the institutional culture element and then expanding their understanding of how it influences other environmental forces and negative classroom experiences. At the same time, it is important to recognize that systems themselves often resist change and attempt to restore equilibrium, so interventions should be intentional, be persistent, and involve continuous learning. The best path might be to adopt the mantra of a nurse manager of a facility where Tolman once worked: When asked how he would achieve a change in the nursing culture, he said, "Gentle persuasion, relentlessly applied."

With a comprehensive framework such as the IMSR in her head, an instructor is better positioned to apply that gentle persuasion via assessment of the sources of resistance in her particular students and to implement effective interventions by escaping the clutches of the human biases that beset all of us. In other words, the IMSR not only can improve our interactions with our students and promote their learning but also may save us all from becoming the focus of angry students in a campus coffee shop.

We also note that the IMSR has undergone a few changes following its creation, most notably the brilliant addition of the institutional context element suggested by Janine Kremling, coeditor of this book, as well as other tweaks based on input from the students who participated in this project. The model has been presented in several venues (Tolman, 2011, 2012; Tolman, Lee, Blair, & Smart, 2014; Tolman & Sorensen, 2012, 2013) in order to receive further feedback and to refine the nature of the interactions in the model. We are grateful for those who have clarified and helped us make the model more useful.

The Road Map for This Book

The first three chapters of this book are introductory. Chapter 2 consists of the reflective stories of the student authors who participated in writing this book as well as commentary on the stories. The students describe situations that affected their own resistance to learning and the ways their research and contributions to this book increased their awareness of, and their ability to learn from, that resistance. These stories are a testament to the power of metacognition in shaping students' thoughts, feelings, and behaviors. Student experiences and reactions are the heart of the book, and in this chapter, readers get to hear from them directly.

In chapter 3, the authors describe several key obstacles that often prevent instructors, students, and administrators from recognizing resistance. These obstacles are usually grounded in powerful patterns of human biases that can be changed but only through awareness and intentional effort. Once we can see past our biases, we can begin to acknowledge the urgent need to deal with the issue of resistance and recognize the cost to individual students and society if we continue to ignore it or accept simplistic individualized (mostly self-action) explanations. Resistance is not just a concern for a student's grade in a particular class; the failure to identify and reduce student resistance is vital for everyone to understand, whether they are involved in higher education or not.

The specific five elements of the IMSR will be explored in detail in chapters 4 through 9. As shown in Figure 1.1, these five elements are environmental forces, negative classroom experiences, institutional culture, cognitive development, and metacognition.

In the IMSR, both environmental forces and negative classroom experiences are embedded in a matrix of institutional culture. This represents how these elements are shaped and influenced by the culture of the institution. From the time when students first interact with the campus, the values, mission, and culture of an institution begin to shape their expectations and behaviors. How they are treated by others (peers, staff, and faculty) and whether they feel a part of the college may confirm or threaten their self-efficacy beliefs. Even aspects of institutional culture that are hidden from view, such as an emphasis on research productivity above teaching or financial considerations that drive decisions affecting professors and/or the physical environment, can have a powerful emotional and learning impact on students. Institutional culture is discussed in depth in chapter 4.

Due to the complexity involved, chapters 5 and 6 break down the element of environmental forces. Chapter 5 focuses primarily on external societal and environmental forces that affect student desire to learn and provides examples of race, class, and gender and the ways these intrinsic aspects of personality and identity interact with the social learning environment. Chapter 6 examines how identity as well as societal elements are internalized, shaping student attitudes, expectations, and beliefs about their own capabilities to learn as well as the role and purpose of education. These environmental forces are important because they can be overlooked or minimized by faculty who are primarily concerned with content delivery and assume that all students enter college on an equal playing field.

In chapter 7, the authors expand on the preliminary discussions regarding how a history of negative interactions among students and their instructors and peers can affect student learning. Some of these interactions are shaped and influenced by environmental forces as well. Students often carry forward these negative experiences as expectations into future classrooms, increasing resistance to active pedagogies and potentially contributing to additional future negative experiences for both instructors and students.

The authors of chapter 8 focus on how students' current level of cognitive development affects their perceptions of the purpose of education and their ability to understand the rationale behind course assignments and design. The emphasis in the chapter is on understanding where students are in this developmental process and how a student's level of development shapes resistance to learning. This perspective can help an instructor recognize why one student may strongly resist a type of assignment whereas another may embrace it. The authors review the major contributions in this area from Perry (1970), King and Kitchener (1994), and Baxter Magolda

(1992) and discuss ways that an instructor can assist students in their cognitive maturation and reduce resistance.

Chapter 9 describes the last element of the model and focuses on the role of student metacognition in resistance. Although investigators have documented the foundational role of metacognition in student learning (see Bransford, Brown, & Cocking, 2000), many instructors do not intentionally include this element as a core part of their teaching or course design. Building primarily on the work of Dweck (2000), findings from neuroplasticity, and assessment methods developed to help students become aware of their learning patterns, including innovative new instruments developed by Tolman (e.g., Tolman & Kremling, 2011; Kremling & Tolman, 2011), the authors describe how promoting student metacognition can reduce student resistance to learning and enhance students' depth of understanding of themselves and of course content.

Chapter 10, the concluding chapter, suggests the use of the IMSR as a model for institutional change and strategic planning. By understanding what aspects of institutional culture may be increasing or reducing student resistance, faculty, staff, and administrators can make decisions to benefit student learning and motivation to succeed. The authors propose six broad strategies for institutional change and link them to the elements of the IMSR. In this way, the IMSR provides a new perspective, an alternative way to view institutional efforts to achieve key outcomes such as student learning, retention, and persistence to graduation.

References

Abowitz, K. K. (2000). A pragmatic revisioning of resistance theory. *American Education Research Journal, 37*(4), 877–907.

Baxter Magolda, M. (1992). *Knowing and reasoning in college: Gender-related patterns in student development.* San Francisco, CA: Jossey-Bass.

Bransford, J. D., Brown, A. L., & Cocking, R. R. (Eds.). (2000). *How people learn: Brain, mind, experience, and school* (Exp. ed.). Washington, DC: National Academies Press.

Brown, L. M., & Gilligan, C. (1992). *Meeting at the crossroads: Women's psychology and girls' development.* Cambridge, MA: Harvard University Press.

Burroughs, N. F. (2007). A reinvestigation of the relationship of teacher nonverbal immediacy and student compliance-resistance with learning. *Communication Education, 56*(4), 453–475.

Burroughs, N. F., Kearney, P., & Plax, T. G. (1989). Compliance-resistance in the college classroom. *Communication Education, 38,* 214–229.

Dembo, M. H., & Seli, H. P. (2004). Students' resistance to change in learning strategies courses. *Journal of Developmental Education, 27*(3), 2–11.

Dewey, J., & Bentley, A. (1949). *Knowing and the known.* Boston, MA: Beacon Press.

Doyle, T. (2008). *Helping students learn in a learner-centered environment: A guide to facilitating learning in higher education.* Sterling, VA: Stylus.

Dweck, C. S. (2000). *Self-theories: Their role in motivation, personality, and development.* New York, NY: Psychology Press.

Felder, R. M., & Brent, R. (1996). Navigating the bumpy road to student-centered instruction. *College Teaching, 44*(2), 43–47.

Jacobellis v. Ohio, 378 U.S. 184 (1964).

Kearney, P., & Plax, T. G. (1992). Student resistance to control. In V. P. Richmond & J. C. McCroskey (Eds.), *Power in the classroom: Communication, control, and concern* (pp. 85–100). Hillsdale, NJ: Erlbaum.

Kearney, P., Plax, T. G., Hays, E. R., & Ivey, M. J. (1991). College teacher misbehaviors: What students don't like about what teachers say and do. *Communication Quarterly, 39*(4), 309–324.

Kim, J. (2010). Understanding student resistance as a communicative act. *Ethnography and Education, 5*(3), 261–276.

King, P. M., & Kitchener, K. S. (1994). *Developing reflective judgment: Understanding and promoting intellectual growth and critical thinking in adolescents and adults.* San Francisco, CA: Jossey-Bass.

Kremling, J., & Tolman, A. O. (2011, April 16). *Assessing the validity of three metacognitive instruments: TTM Learning Survey, R-SPQ, and LSSA.* Paper presented at the 14th CSU Symposium on University Teaching, California State University, Channel Islands.

Michaelsen, L. K., Knight, A. B., & Fink, L. D. (Eds.). (2004). *Team-based learning: A transformative use of small groups in college teaching.* Sterling, VA: Stylus.

Nelson, C. E. (2010). Dysfunctional illusions of rigor: Lessons from the scholarship of teaching and learning. In L. B. Nilson & J. E. Miller (Eds.), *To improve the academy* (Vol. 28, pp. 177–192). San Francisco, CA: Jossey-Bass.

Oakley, B., Felder, R. M., Brent, R., & Elhajj, I. (2004). Turning student groups into effective teams. *Journal of Student Centered Learning, 2*(1), 9–34.

Perry, W. G. (1970). *Forms of intellectual and ethical development in the college years: A scheme.* New York, NY: Holt, Rinehart and Winston.

Savini, C. (2016, May 4). Are you being rigorous or just intolerant? How to promote mental health in the college classroom. *Chronicle of Higher Education.* Retrieved from http://chronicle.com/article/Are-You-Being-Rigorous-or-Just/236341/

Schmier, L. (2012, October 18). Re: Responding to student resistence [sic] [Electronic mailing list message]. Retrieved from https://listserv.nd.edu/cgi-bin/wa?A2=ind1210&L=POD&T=0&X=398130135F966FE4AB&Y=anton.tolman%40uvu.edu&P=104039

Sibley, J., & Ostafichuk, P. (Eds.). (2014). *Getting started with team-based learning.* Sterling, VA: Stylus.

Steele, C. M. (2011). *Whistling Vivaldi: How stereotypes affect us and what we can do.* New York, NY: W. W. Norton.

Tolman, A. O. (2011, December 16). *Understanding and working with student resistance to active learning* [TLT FridayLive! Webinar]. Retrieved from http://tltgroup .roundtablelive.org/event-365557

Tolman, A. O. (2012, May 4). *Strategies for overcoming student resistance to active learning, Part 2* [TLT FridayLive! Webinar]. Retrieved from http://tltgroup .roundtablelive.org/event-464528

Tolman, A. O., & Kremling, J. (2011, March 12). *Using metacognitive instruments to reduce student resistance to active learning.* Workshop presented at the 23rd Annual Conference of the International Alliance of Teacher-Scholars (Lilly West), Pomona, CA.

Tolman, A. O., Lee, C. S., Blair, R., & Smart, S. (2014, June). *Why students resist learning: Strategies and ideas to help college instructors.* Seminar presentation at the biannual conference of the International Consortium for Educational Development (ICED), Stockholm, Sweden.

Tolman, A. O., & Sorensen, U. N. (2012, October). *Winning them over: Helping faculty overcome student resistance.* Preconference workshop presented at the Annual Conference of the Professional Organizational Development Network (POD), Seattle, WA.

Tolman, A. O., & Sorensen, U. N. (2013, January). *Foundations for meaningful learning: An integrated model of student resistance.* Paper presented at the International Conference for Higher Education Teaching & Learning (HETL), Orlando, FL.

Triesman, U. (1992). Studying students studying calculus: A look at the lives of minority mathematics students in college. *College Mathematics Journal, 23*(5), 362–372.

Weimer, M. (2013). *Learner-centered teaching: Five key changes to practice* (2nd ed.). San Francisco, CA: Jossey-Bass.

2

STUDENT VOICES

Discovering Resistance

Averie Hamilton, Andy Sechler, Colt Rothlisberger, Shea Smart,
Anton O. Tolman, Matthew Andersen, Rob Blair, and Amy Lindstrom

The preface of this book described the genesis of Tolman's integrated model of student resistance (IMSR), which led to recruiting a group of undergraduate students to participate in developing the ideas, connecting them to the literature, integrating concepts across diverse fields, and then writing—lots of writing. The first chapter provided a definition of *student resistance* and laid out the IMSR model itself. This chapter adds to that discussion by including an element that is usually missing in the academic literature: the voices and perspectives of the students who, by and large, are the subject of that literature. In this chapter, we share our stories and experiences of times we have witnessed student resistance or have expressed it ourselves, along with commentary (including input from Tolman) on how these experiences illustrate parts of the IMSR and lead to ideas about intervention and prevention.

The countless hours we spent researching, discussing, exploring, writing, and reviewing the material for this book readjusted the lens by which we viewed our own resistance to learning and enabled us to recognize student resistance going on around us. We not only evaluated and witnessed resistance in our present experiences in classrooms (including the one in which we worked on this book) but also began to reflect on the past with a new perspective. For the team members who contributed to this book, in-depth study and discussion of student resistance led us to a variety of *meta-moments*, including contemplation of the roots, results, and potential resolutions for that resistance.

As noted in chapter 1, no instance of student resistance is rooted in a single cause; our experiences illustrate that the nature of resistance is dynamic. It is our hope that reading about our experiences can give faculty and administrators additional insight, from the inside out as it were, of the forces that affect students every day. These stories also teach us that helping students to become aware of their own resistance, through a framework such as the IMSR, can be a powerful tool for helping students to enhance their own learning.

Student Experiences

Matthew Andersen

I experienced some resistance in a mediation class. There were these assignments due every week for which we had to write reflections on unpleasant interactions between people we had observed. The concepts we had to use to describe these interactions were very similar, and after a while, it seemed like many of us didn't want to write them anymore. The writing felt really redundant, and I felt like I wasn't learning anything from the assignments. The assignments themselves were also not worth much, relative to all of the other work in the class. I learned that many students stopped caring to turn the papers in on time; they would turn them in later and received docked points. It seemed like the student resistance was a product of the assignments feeling unproductive and not worth many points.

Matthew's story illustrates mostly passive resistance on the part of students that appears to have stemmed from a desire to assert their own autonomy, to resist the instructor's mandate that these assignments be regularly completed. The instructor's perspective on this assignment is not present in this description, but it seems clear that the students did not understand the value or purpose of the assignment in the same way that the instructor probably did. By putting off doing the assignment, students passively demonstrated that they were not just going to go along with what the instructor was asking them to do.

Matthew's comments also demonstrate a theme that is common in evaluating student resistance and that will be mentioned in other chapters: Unless students understand and accept the larger picture or see the relevance and value of the course objectives and assignments, they tend to be primarily concerned with receiving a passing (or good) grade rather than grasping and understanding the content of the course. This is especially true for a repeated assignment that may echo previous "busywork" assignments that students have experienced in classes before. The story does not clarify this, but it is likely that past negative experiences may have led to resistance that built over time toward following assignments of a similar nature.

By changing the structure of the assignment, it is possible that the instructor could have decreased the amount of student resistance in this situation. Matthew calls out for deeper learning, particularly from course content: "I felt like I wasn't learning anything from the assignments." Engaging content fosters a deeper level of learning within students. A central problem here seems to be that the same concepts were being linked to the assignment over time—there was no progression into more advanced content to match progress through the course. By altering the prompts or reflective questions required as the students progressed through new concepts in the course, the instructor could have helped keep the assignment fresh.

The instructor could also have recognized that the increasing numbers of students turning in these late assignments was a signal of resistance and acted by having a discussion with the class about what was happening. It is highly likely that the quality of the responses also decreased over time, becoming more superficial, another signal that something was going on and needed to be addressed. Dealing with this issue openly could have increased student awareness of their own resistance and improved the student-instructor relationship.

Early communication with students regarding the course objectives and the value and contribution of the assignment to those objectives might also have helped to enhance student motivation. Helping students to recognize that the assignment was contributing to key professional skills or helping them to recognize abstract concepts in real-world settings might have made a significant difference.

Rob Blair

My form of resistance demands autonomy rather than rejects it. I often challenge professors when they make black/white statements, and I bring up alternative possibilities for how class activities can be structured. When I feel assignments are unclear or seem unproductive, I tend to vocalize those feelings. Some professors seem to honestly appreciate this. Others seem irritated.

When professors are irritated by this approach, I tend to hush up and disengage. I will often just disengage from the get-go if I'm studying a topic that I have no real interest in. In my recent statistics class, for example, I did less than half of the homework, attended fewer than half of the classes, and did other work on my computer during the class periods I did attend. I self-directed my learning outside of class. It's easy enough to say this makes me a "bad" student (it probably does), but I'm aware enough of my own learning styles that it allows me to grasp the materials without the boredom or frustration of going through the sort of busywork that is ineffective for me. As I got 99% on the class final and 94% on the department final, these statements of mine may even be slightly more than just arrogance on my part.

Rob's experience is fascinating because it demonstrates that a student does not manifest only one type of resistance to a course or assignment; students may vary in their individual reactions to a course, but an individual student's resistance can be dynamic, shifting between active and passive forms depending on the environment. Rob acknowledges that his initial reaction to specific triggers tends to be to assert his autonomy by emphasizing a desire for complex thinking and deeper learning and suggesting pedagogical strategies that may be more effective in helping him learn. If these are accepted, his trust in the instructor likely grows, and his resistance would probably decrease. However, if his input is rejected and the professor becomes irritated or annoyed by his attempts to assert autonomy, he shifts into a passive form of resistance, probably out of desire to protect his grade in the class as is indicated by his final comments. This strategy appears to have helped him to retain a sense of himself as a deep learner and to complete course and degree requirements successfully.

His ability to shift between forms of resistance is almost certainly based on the outcome of prior negative experiences, possibly with both peers and instructors, and his attempts to adapt to them. It is also a manifestation of his own metacognition regarding how he learns, and in this sense he may be more advanced in this area than many of his peers. He may also be dealing with personal concerns that are influenced by social forces and labels as well as potential external stressors (work, financial aid, etc.) that also shape his behavior. Rob's story also serves to remind instructors that resistance is complex and systemic and that the nature of the relationship between professor and student can either increase resistance or decrease it. Enthusiastic attitudes and intrinsic motivation can lead students to challenge instructors when the students believe that the learning environment they are providing could be improved on, redesigned, or altered. This enthusiastic attitude exhibits itself as resistance—not to learning the content but to learning it in the manner and method the instructor has chosen.

Instructors could profitably perceive this form of resistance as an opportunity to review curriculum and course design rather than as a nuisance or disruption of the class. Recognizing the resistance as an expression of autonomy and desire for deep learning, rather than considering it a personal attack or evidence of a lack of desire to learn, can lead to growth and development, and prevent the negative resistance that often forms because of an instructor's unwillingness to negotiate and collaborate. It may be helpful to meet with the student individually in order to better understand the social forces and previous experiences that are shaping his or her behavior. It is important to note that the irritation exhibited by some professors who avoid working with resistance, possibly influenced by institutional culture, could result in an increase in student resistance in later courses. Through inviting and discussing student input to course and instruction design, professors could prevent or resolve resistance.

Averie Hamilton

The other day I was discussing the lunar eclipse with a male friend who is currently completing medical school and intends to go into neuroscience. I was explaining how much I enjoyed the opportunity not only to witness a recent lunar eclipse but also to research background information on lunar and solar eclipses before the event. This was purely for leisure; when I told my friend how much I enjoyed having a learning experience "for fun," he simply replied, "Says the dame to the doctor." As a female, I felt extremely stereotyped by his comment; he apparently felt that a "dame" wasn't capable of higher-level thinking and thus took pleasure from any form of scientific learning. The following weeks, I found myself particularly motivated in my neuroanatomy class (originally taken simply for the fun of it) and slacking in my psychology classes. I felt I needed to prove my friend wrong, that I was capable of not only enjoying the sciences but also mastering them. I felt ashamed of my social sciences courses and resisted any effort at high-level learning in them for a little while because of my new outlook. I had originally planned on going into neuroanatomy early in my college career, and I began to reconsider my decision to replace it with industrial-organizational (IO) psychology. Did studying the social sciences make me such a "dame"? I thought, "I don't want to appear stupid, so I'm just going to do what I need to do to get an A in psych courses." I then realized, due to our recent discussions of the effects that social expectations can have on student resistance, the root of my resistance. I was consciously manifesting cultural expectations that intelligence is defined by a demonstration of excellence in mathematics or the biological sciences, and that men are dominant in these areas; thus, women are less capable of higher level understanding. I wanted to prove this stereotype wrong with every fiber in my soul, even if it meant channeling my intelligence into a subject I was less passionate about than IO psychology.

After I had received an A in neuroanatomy, I realized I was just as intellectually capable as "the doctor," but my dedication to statistics and workplace improvement didn't communicate a lack of intelligence. I rereviewed the concepts

I ignorantly had skimmed over while resisting in my psychology classes and renewed my efforts for deeper learning in all my classes.

Averie's story is a significant contrast to Rob's in that her passive resistance to learning in her psychology courses had little to do with those courses themselves; instead, it was based on social stereotypes and expectations that were triggered by a peer's comments. This illustrates the power of these preexisting social and gender roles in student learning. It is noteworthy that the cultural expectation or stereotype—that women underperform in STEM fields (science, technology, engineering, mathematics)—began to play a significant role only when Averie believed that her friend considered it to be true. Her behavior changed as she attempted to "fight back" or assert her autonomy against that social expectation, shifting her energies and focus to one course and adopting a passive role in the others.

The power and influence of social expectations and stereotypes is pernicious and can be difficult to detect in some of its manifestations. For some students, the internal impact of these social forces is large; for others, these forces may not be as intense, or the students may have developed effective coping mechanisms. The influence of social forces can also manifest in other types of passive resistance, such as dropping a class, feeling overwhelmed, or experiencing resentment when asked to do things in specific ways. It seems likely that as the number of marginalizing characteristics in a student increases (e.g., gender, race, economic, first-generation status), the number of interactions among them may also increase, leading to stronger potential resistance.

Though these existing social forces cannot be eliminated, instructors can become aware of their impact and alert to situations in which they might be triggered, including by peers in the classroom who may make insensitive or rude remarks. Instructors can seek to understand their students' backgrounds early in the semester so they can provide support and encouragement if needed, specific advice about how to be successful in the class, or referrals to mentors, advisers, or counselors if necessary. There is also a wealth of information about effective study strategies that students could be pointed to or that instructors could post online via their learning management system.

Also important in Averie's story is self-efficacy, the set of beliefs people hold about their capability to accomplish things in a specific domain. Instead of allowing gender stereotypes to define her self-efficacy, she set a goal to be successful in her neuroanatomy course. However, the concluding statement about her success highlights the fact that she was experiencing stereotype threat (see Steele & Aronson, 1995; see also chapter 5), a situation in which the pressure to avoid confirming social stereotypes disrupts student learning

Instructors should learn to be aware of situations such as stereotype threat and the effects these situations can have so that they can intervene. Through discussions related to writing this book, Averie became conscious of this pattern in her performance and thinking and acted proactively to disrupt it. Other students may need assistance from instructors and others in achieving this same level of metacognition.

Nelson (2010) has offered great examples of common obstacles to faculty recognition of student characteristics that can affect student performance. For instance, he summarized some studies by Triesman (1992) and others about black students at Berkeley who were doing poorly in a calculus course, probably due to stereotype threat. The students were aware of social expectations that they would not do well in such a course and were attempting to reject that pressure by following the stated advice of their professors to study individually two hours for every hour of class (an almost standard form of academic advice), but it was not working. In contrast, when they were required to do collaborative group work as part of an honors course, the drop-fail rate among these students went from 60% to 4%. Similarly, Nelson noted how many professors either implicitly or explicitly assume that entering students have already mastered a range of different skills and do not need assistance in adapting to the higher education environment. He provides examples that demonstrate how changes in pedagogy result in significant improvement and success in student performance.

It is easy to imagine how instructors might overlook, as the calculus professors did, the social causes of student struggles and resist making the pedagogical changes that would reduce student stress, failure, and resistance. The failure of black calculus students could only lead to increased future resistance to such courses via confirmation of the social stereotype.

Andy Sechler

This semester, before a class in political sociology, I asked a few people how their term research paper had been going. Someone said he hadn't even looked at the prompt yet, and I asked if he was aware that it was due the next class period. Several students looked like deer in headlights, and one of the students suggested that they all band together to ask for an extension on the project. They argued that "the professor can't turn all of us down if we demand an extension." I think at least eight students did band together to ask for an extension at the end of that class. The professor acquiesced but emphasized that taking academic deadlines seriously is paramount. Sadly, at least eight students crammed what should have been weeks of research into a weekend to "BS" their way through a paper, as students say. I believe that this form of resistance falls into the category of students demonstrating that they will be playing by their own rules and also doing the minimum amount of work necessary to pass a course. It shows a great lack of responsibility on the part of the students.

Most of the stories shared in this chapter reflect passive resistance on the part of students. This is likely the more common form of resistance, given the authority and social power possessed by professors, although this would make a good question for empirical investigation. Andy's story reflects on a group of students who actively collaborated on resisting elements of a course (i.e., deadlines for work that they had been informed of at the beginning of the semester). It could be argued that this active resistance was caused by a buildup of previous resistance to the assignment; over time the students had avoided thinking about the assignment and neglected the preparatory work necessary to succeed. When it was no longer possible to avoid dealing with the situation, the students banded together to "demand" an extension.

In this way, resistance can build over time, beginning with more passive behaviors regarding small aspects of the course and then gradually increasing. For example, passive forms of resistance, such as complaints made to other students and delays in responding to instructor e-mails, could build up over the course of a semester until a student loudly exclaims in class after asking a question, "Why can't you just give us an answer? Why do you just keep asking us more questions?!" Thus, previously passive resistance has now changed form and emerged publicly as a critique or indication of frustration or anger with the instructor.

It is helpful for instructors to be aware of subtle indicators of passive forms of resistance early in the semester (e.g., grumbling when asked to get into teams, requests for more lecture, delayed responses to required assignments) so that students may be approached in order to determine whether the student is facing individual obstacles (e.g., illness, work stress) or whether the student is reluctant to engage in the learning environment. By using proactive interventions, instructors may be able to head resistance off at the pass by demonstrating concern for student learning, explaining the rationale for the course and assignment, and offering support. This gradual escalation of resistance also emphasizes the importance of engaging with the class in discussion at the beginning of the semester about the reasons for the course design, the importance of the skills being focused on, and the relevance of course material to students' personal and professional lives. Instructors might benefit from considering the use of specific activities to obtain student buy-in for active learning environments such as those described by Smith (2013). These activities include discussing the purpose of education (learn facts, apply knowledge, or gain lifelong learning skills), connecting course objectives to what employers are looking for in graduates, the acquisition of relating expertise outside education to useful skills in the classroom, asking students to identify and reflect on solutions to the perceived disadvantages of group work, establishing team roles and responsibilities that rotate over the term, and asking teams to regularly evaluate their own performance as a team. Other resources for ideas on how to "frame" or introduce an engaged classroom environment to students are available for a variety of disciplines from the Science Education Initiative (n.d.) of the University of Colorado.

Shea Smart

Many students in my introductory English composition class were disengaged throughout the semester. The resistance was almost entirely passive; when students were unclear about assignment details, for example, they tended to just not do the assignment. Even when they were told to write a paper about topics that mattered to them, many students were unresponsive. Some of the students I spoke with declared an absolute uncertainty about what they could write about. I would prompt them to tell me what they cared about; one student, as an example, responded by saying that he liked bikes. I asked him what sort of bikes, and he proceeded to detail some of the extreme sports that he was interested in. I questioned why he didn't write about that, and he didn't have an answer; what seemed apparent to me was that students are routinely trained to dismiss ideas that seem "personal" rather than "academic." It seems counterproductive to me to segregate personal interests from academic pursuits, as I find that I often solidify course concepts when they are integrated into my everyday life. I am also reminded of those concepts later when I engage in my personal interests.

Shea's bike-loving peer in the class he describes could be resisting for a variety of interacting reasons, one being a consumerist attitude based on social expectations and stereotypes of higher education (see chapter 6). As a consumer at a university, the student might expect all course-related information to be provided to him; he should not have to inquire about what is expected in the assignment. If assignment details are unclear, if attendance isn't deemed "necessary," he and similarly minded students might resist anything beyond what they interpret as clearly required assignments. This attitude may have been fueled by negative experiences in the classroom and the reaction of previous teachers or peers when he asked for clarification or tried to bring up personal experiences or concerns.

The passive resistance described by Shea could reflect the student's anxiety that asking about the requirements for an assignment would confirm his own fear that he is unintelligent and unable to navigate a college environment, a pattern linked to a "fixed mindset" (see chapter 9). Students' passive pushback on these assignments could also be a reflection of their level of cognitive development (see chapter 8). Some students may see the purpose of education as providing correct answers or learning facts and concepts rather than as the development of skills, including communication and critical thinking or problem-solving skills. Students at this level of dualistic thinking about the world (e.g., right answers versus wrong answers) may not understand the purpose, rationale, or value of assignments that ask them to share their own experiences. Reasoning that they are not experts in writing, they do not see how writing about their own lives or experiences serves any useful purpose or can enrich their own or others' writing.

Clearly, instructors need to ensure that adequate time at the beginning of a semester is spent "getting students on board." By accepting the reality of negative prior experiences (especially in writing or math) for many students and by understanding how cognitive development and mindsets influence student perceptions of their role in learning, instructors can devise early assignments, discussions, and activities to highlight student responsibility for learning, demonstrate respect and curiosity about students' personal experiences, and explain the significant value of core skills in students' personal and professional lives. Shea's conclusion demonstrates that his ability to connect subject concepts to his personal experiences, rather than trying to learn them in a vacuum, led him to deeper learning. These steps may require instructors to take a hard look at how they cover content, but this early effort is necessary to increase the chances of reducing student resistance to assignments and course activities. Breaking the ice by increasing collaborative work in class may be another way to increase students' willingness to share information and to enhance their ability to critique their own and others' work, leading to a greater sense of responsibility and better chances for success.

Colt Rothlisberger

One of my biology professors would complain in frustration that students did not participate in class. After having heard this complaint several times, few if any students felt motivated to participate in class. One student tried answering a question posed by the professor to test our knowledge as students. The student was incorrect. The professor got right in the student's face (he was sitting in the front row) and shouted, "No, no, no! Don't you understand? You need to think and know this stuff!" The entire classroom was uneasily quiet as all of us felt bad and embarrassed for this young man who tried answering the professor's question, but we dared not say anything as any one of us could be the next one to be yelled at. The students remained quiet for the rest of the class period. As the professor asked for final comments and questions at the end of class, he ranted about how we need to participate and ask questions. He asked, "I don't know; what can I do to get you guys to start taking this seriously?" I was shocked that he didn't seem to understand what he had done to make us afraid to say anything in class. We couldn't win!

Colt's horrific story is an example of the impact of teacher misbehaviors on student resistance (see chapter 3). In a course where a commonly stated learning outcome is to develop the capacity for raising questions, generating hypotheses, and understanding the scientific method, the instructor's behavior dramatically increased the amount of anxiety experienced by students in the class. This pushed them toward passive resistance, mostly to protect themselves; students avoided class participation and kept their heads down, focusing on passing the class rather than learning the material. Such behaviors by professors alienate students from content and, combined with a history of other negative experiences, increase resistance in other courses.

Amy Lindstrom

When I was in second grade, I spent a lot of time in time-out, which consisted of a closet with a closed door and the light off. My mom was PTA president at the time and remembers coming to my class one day and not being able to see me in the classroom. She asked my teacher where I was, and the teacher told her that she had put me in the closet for a time-out. My mom said that she opened the door and found me in this dark closet crying. My teacher was vocal about her dislike for kids and teaching.

When I was in third grade, my teacher told me I was a horrible student multiple times. He constantly punished me by having me write a page out of the dictionary, because I didn't understand the concept of borrowing in subtraction, and he was frustrated that I couldn't understand the way he was explaining it to me and that I kept asking for help because I didn't understand. He also told me, on multiple occasions, that I had a "dumb math brain" and that I wasn't good at it.

I had multiple experiences like this. In junior high my art teacher laughed at a drawing I did, which I felt really proud of, and told me that art isn't for everyone. These negative classroom experiences caused me to lose all sense of self-efficacy, and I stopped trying because I accepted that I wasn't a good student. It took a lot of life experience and self-motivated learning to get me to the point where I decided to come back to school. Now I absolutely love it. I enjoy feeling my brain make connections and learning new things.

It wasn't until I began to succeed, and even excel in school, that I realized that the labels given to me in my early education did not actually define me. When I started school, and even before, I wore these negative experiences as a badge of who I was, and because I never believed I could be successful, I feared confirming these "truths" to myself. I feel that a lot of the credit for helping me shake off the burden of these harmful self-beliefs belongs to a Learning Strategies class; it opened my eyes to embracing my own methods of learning and adapting them to a multitude of situations throughout my academic journey. It served as a new kickoff point for me. When I find myself resisting, I think back to the lessons I learned in that class, reflecting on how far I have come and the difficult tasks I was able to not only complete but also do extremely well in. This reflection has helped me stop my cycle of resistance.

Amy's story is an important illustration that teacher misbehaviors are not limited to higher education; more than that, it demonstrates how harsh feedback from instructors over time can shape and influence a student's adoption of a fixed mindset (see chapter 9), in this case Amy's conclusion that "I wasn't a good student." This sense that she was not competent in academic settings haunted her for years until she gradually learned from her life experiences and her Learning Strategies course that she was more capable than she had been led to believe. She arrived at that conclusion mostly on her own, and it is a shame that her instructors did not recognize her withdrawal as evidence of passive resistance and take the opportunity to help her learn how to become an effective learner much sooner.

Unfortunately, several of Amy's teachers implicitly endorsed the idea of "weeding out," that some students are suited for specific fields whereas others are not or that some students are more capable than others and therefore deserve greater attention and support, is a form of a fixed mindset that is also present in higher education. When instructors approach student learning with this attitude (consciously or not), they reinforce prior negative experiences, only adding to the difficulty that many students have with actively engaging in learning. Instead of concerning themselves with self-identifying those students they deem worthy of continuing in their field, instructors would be of greater benefit to society if they recognized the resistance in their students (whatever its form) and provided the support necessary for all students to learn and succeed. The skills developed through active engagement and interaction benefit all of us.

Amy's story also illustrates the staying power of these early negative experiences on a student's life and self-perception in ways that continue to manifest years later. Amy is a nontraditional student, married with a family and a job, who returned to complete her education. Although it is laudable that she was able to overcome these negative early experiences, it was a long time coming. Instructors need to recognize how important it is to eliminate their own misbehaviors and create positive experiences in the classroom, but they also need to be aware that the passive resistance and anxiety they observe may have deep roots.

Colt Rothlisberger

I got to see firsthand a student progress from dualism to multiplicity [early levels of cognitive development explained in chapter 8] *in my English class. She was very religious and was reluctant to see others' perspectives. Anything that fell in a moral gray area frustrated her. When she was frustrated and started being a little loud, the professor patiently validated her view and calmly explained an alternate view. The student resisted for about the first half of the semester but then slowly started understanding that other people had good reasons for thinking differently. At the time I did not have the knowledge to understand how well the teacher's handling of the situation helped to encourage the student to move to a higher level of cognitive development, but I recognize it now.*

Here Colt identified the interaction between a person's level of cognitive development and her degree of resistance. As explained in detail in chapter 8, William Perry has described different positions along a continuum of cognitive development. Dualist thinkers tend to look at the world in terms of black and white, good and bad, right and wrong. Colt's peer clearly was in this stage in the way she began the course. However, the instructor handled the situation very well by gently nudging and encouraging the student to develop to a point where she could begin to acknowledge the reality that there can be different ways of viewing the world and that viewpoints different from her own are not necessarily "wrong" or incorrect. Colt also nicely demonstrates his own increased level of metacognition from participating in this book through his newfound appreciation for the skillful intervention of the instructor.

Andy Sechler

Just before midterms, as I walked down the halls through campus, the strategically placed digital screens had an ad playing that piqued my interest. This ad brought to mind what I have been studying about learning-centered teaching and student resistance. The ad displayed a concerned student below the words "It's midterms. Do you have the grade that you want?" Then, on the bottom of the screen, another admonition read, "Talk to your professors and make sure that you have the grade that you want now." Another ad displayed a worried student along with a caption that read, "I thought I was turning in A work, but was surprised to wind up with a C after finals." I believe the intention of these ads was to encourage students to work hard and take responsibility for their performance. However, the ads stressed a grade focus over learning. They also subtly encouraged grade entitlement and perhaps slightly demanding behaviors on the part of the students. I jotted down my thoughts about this so that I could include them [in this chapter] and then forgot about the ad for a while.

However, about two weeks later, after midterms, I witnessed a student asking the professor about his grade as I waited in line to turn in a paper. The professor replied that the student had been meeting the requirements of the course and was probably on track for an A. To my surprise, this bright and insightful student largely stopped coming to class after this exchange. He would show up only on days that assignments were due, chime in to the class discussion to make his presence known (participation points), and then leave after asking a nearby student to turn in his work. It didn't take long for the professor to start commenting about this. The professor would express discontent with students doing minimum work to "get a grade." This being a political sociology course, the professor thought that learning was especially important. In my mind, the ads played over again. It seems that the ad motivated the student to behave in this way. The student seemed to believe that his "verbal agreement" about grades with the professor absolved him of responsibility and learning in general. I believe this highlights an example of student resistance to learning on many levels.

This story demonstrates the interaction among institutional culture, student consumerist attitudes (chapter 6), and resistance. Chapter 4 describes how institutional priorities and goals often influence faculty efforts to improve the learning environment. Andy may be right that the ostensible goal of this advertising campaign was retention, to encourage students to think about their grades ahead of time and work toward improving performance, but in reality these types of institutional efforts may backfire because of preexisting attitudes that many students have toward education. The campaign emphasis on grades rather than learning could easily reinforce the expectations of students like Andy's peer, who see a surface approach to learning as a useful strategy for getting what they want for the least amount of effort. However, the solution to helping students get past these attitudes is probably not achieved by complaining in the classroom about the problem. Genuine and concerned discussions with students about the value of their education, the link between course activities and skill and knowledge acquisition, and the transparency of course design would probably bear better fruit.

Shea Smart

"How does he expect me to learn? I'm not here to teach myself. That is why I pay tuition, so that he will teach me the information for the exam. If I could just go to class, have him tell me all the answers, and leave, we could both save ourselves a lot of time and frustration. He is so stupid!" These were the words, verbatim, I

overheard from a peer as I was waiting outside Dr. Tolman's office to discuss the chapter on student resistance I was working on. I felt angry at the student's arrogance as I am sure most professors feel when they hear similar comments. Unfortunately, I hear conversations like this regularly on campus; however, after learning more about student resistance, I began to feel pity for the student instead of anger. It was sad to think that a person in his 20s did not understand the purpose of an education, especially considering the amount of time he had spent in school. I thought of the many complex factors causing him to think and, more important, act the way he was. This student clearly had unrealistic expectations for college. He believed that college would reflect previous years of schooling during which he probably learned primarily through lecture-style teaching. I thought of how I would feel if I had paid for something and was disappointed in the product. I would probably try to get my money back and get angry at the person who had sold it to me. I am not saying that education is like other products we purchase; however, this student and others may feel that they have wasted their money, and therefore they become angry. In this way it became less about blaming the professor or the student for being "stupid" and more about how we can understand the position that each is in.

Several stories in this chapter demonstrate the value of helping students become aware of resistance, its manifestations, and the connection to systemic factors. Shea and his fellow authors learned this through their own research, our discussions, and their reflections. However, this raises the issue that it might be useful to increase student metacognition regarding their own resistance as part of many courses, especially when it is manifest. In Shea's story, the complaining student demonstrated a consumerist attitude (see chapter 6) and expectations for lecture-based pedagogy, expectations that were violated. However, Shea's ability to use the IMSR as a tool to understand the student's behavior led him to a more compassionate stance—less about blaming and more about understanding. This is the antithesis of the two professors in the coffee shop described in chapter 1 and highlights the real value of the IMSR model.

Shea Smart

Having read academic journals and articles as I worked on this book, I would like to think that I don't resist learning; however, I know I still do. I am more aware now of my behaviors that impair my own learning, and I am working harder at changing my own resistance. It is so much easier to just have a professor lecture me on exactly what will be on a final than to teach myself through reading the material. That, at times, can be frustrating for me.

For example, this semester I have two hybrid classes, half online, half face-to-face. Because of the nature of these classes, much of the learning is done on your own time, and you have to stay self-motivated to learn. My professors have little involvement in these courses, and due dates are not concrete. With only a week left in the semester, there are many students who haven't taken the exams or started the homework. At times I wish we just had more face-to-face communication so that I could simply ask a question and get the answer instead of having to watch lecture videos and read the books. With a face-to-face course structure, I know I have a standard day and time when I come into class. This is part of my routine. However, with the online portion of the class, I don't have to study. I could spend time watching TV or doing whatever I want. It makes it hard because I choose when to study, which at times doesn't happen. Being in this class and helping write this book has helped me to notice when I am resisting learning. It helps me to stop resisting and start learning on my own.

Andy Sechler

Once I had the option of either working in a group to complete a long paper or researching and writing the paper myself. I chose to write the paper myself and avoid group work, which is a form of resistance. In some ways that was easier, and in some ways it was harder, but it was certainly another instance of avoiding an opportunity to develop collaboration skills that I will need in my future career. It was not until I took a course with Dr. Tolman involving a high degree of collaborative learning that I realized I was resisting important elements of my education. In choosing to avoid group work, I was losing the opportunity to learn from my peers. I also lost the opportunity to develop my skills in communication, in delegation of responsibility, and in helping those who are struggling. Scheduling meetings with other busy adults can be difficult, but I am sure that I will face those challenges for the rest of my life. It is important to figure it out now. Dr. Tolman helped me to realize that, and I have been making an effort to engage in group work and do my best in collaborating with my peers since.

In these last stories, Shea and Andy turn the mirror on themselves. Their stories illustrate several key issues discussed so far, including the deep-seated human tendency toward being miserly with cognitive effort: People generally prefer not to expend mental energy if they can avoid it (see chapter 3). Just as almost anyone would probably purchase the same good for a cheaper price given the opportunity, people generally seek to conserve resources. These two stories are a reminder that this is true of even high-performing students who are in school for all the right reasons and who take responsibility for their learning. The high-structure, spoon-feeding model of education exists for a reason: It is easier and less energy intensive, for both students and instructors. However, as chapter 3 will describe, that convenience comes with a cost, and the price associated with that cost is rising.

If students, instructors, and administrators are to accept the value of active student participation in their own learning, it is vital to connect the dots. A few years ago, John Tagg delivered a keynote address related to the importance of engaged teaching and learning. He shared a concept embedded in his writing (Tagg, 2003) that we need to help students see the long-term value of committing to their own deep learning and gave the example of his use of a rental car to get from the airport to campus. Renting a car was a short-term proposition. It would last only a few days, and Tagg would not own the car when it was over, so he had very little commitment to taking good care of that rental car, of investing his time and energy into it.

On the other hand, if he were to visit multiple car dealers with the intent to purchase a new vehicle, he would invest a substantial amount of time in comparing prices and options and evaluating the best model to meet his needs. Once the purchase occurred, he would be significantly more committed to the care and maintenance of that vehicle. Buying his own car would entail a long-term commitment that had personal meaning and would validate the effort involved. To many students, education is a rental car; they are in it for the short term (the few weeks of a semester), and they value mostly the diploma rather than the courses that led to it, which they view as externally imposed requirements, so they have little reason to commit their time and energy to it. They prefer to select options that require less investment on their part. If an instructor, or much better, a group of instructors over the trajectory of students' experiences in college, repeatedly help those students to see the personal long-term value of education to their lives, their family's lives, and their careers, they become more committed and willing to put in the time and effort to obtain that value. Some student resistance arises because of human nature; by accepting this fact, instructors and administrators responsible for encouraging campus-wide development of active learning environments can turn the mirror on themselves and, like Shea and Andy, overcome their own resistance and take responsibility for helping students to succeed.

Final Word

Our stories shared in this chapter represent a view from the trenches, they provide the perspectives and experiences of students who have achieved, we hope, a deep understanding of their own resistance and who can share what they have learned. Our stories have demonstrated that resistance is complex and interactive, that it plays out across time, and the commentaries have shown how our experiences fit with the elements of the IMSR. We hope we have provided a chance for professors and administrators to learn more about the day-to-day reality of students in higher education, a window that promotes increased compassion and understanding and, by utilizing the IMSR, creates new opportunities for improvement.

References

Nelson, C. E. (2010). Dysfunctional illusions of rigor: Lessons from the scholarship of teaching and learning. In L. B. Nilson & J. E. Miller (Eds.), *To improve the academy* (Vol. 28, pp. 177–192). San Francisco, CA: Jossey-Bass.

Science Education Initiative. (n.d.). *Resources.* Retrieved from http://www.colorado.edu/sei/fac-resources/framing.html

Smith, G. A. (2013, November). *Selling active learning to faculty requires a student purchase, too.* Workshop presented at the annual conference of the Professional and Organizational Development Network in Higher Education (POD), Pittsburgh, PA.

Steele, C. M., & Aronson, J. (1995). Stereotype threat and the intellectual test performance of African Americans. *Journal of Personality and Social Psychology, 69*(5), 797–811.

Tagg, J. (2003). *The learning paradigm college.* San Francisco, CA: Jossey-Bass.

Triesman, U. (1992). Studying students studying calculus: A look at the lives of minority mathematics students in college. *College Mathematics Journal, 23*(5), 362–372.

3

OBSTACLES, BIASES, AND THE URGENT NEED TO UNDERSTAND THE SOCIAL COST OF RESISTANCE

Anton O. Tolman, Andy Sechler, and Shea Smart

Andy Sechler

There have been many times that I have witnessed an instructor pose questions (both closed and open-ended) to a classroom full of students without receiving any response or participation. I have even witnessed an instructor pose question after question in a class period, only to be met with blank stares and silence. It has been so bad at times that I have been forced to wonder if my university is filled with exceptionally apathetic students or if this is a problem that affects higher education around the country and the world. I had a class this semester in which the professor threatened to lower everyone's grade a full letter if students did not begin to actively participate. This tactic (silence) maintains the status quo by forcing the professor to continue lecturing and take most of the responsibility for student learning.

The first chapter of this book defined *student resistance* and introduced the integrated model of student resistance (IMSR) as a practical tool that can be used to better understand the origins of student resistance and the interactive elements that can generate it. According to the resistance matrix in chapter 1, the behaviors of Andy's peers would be classified as passive resistance, although the underlying motivation is unclear. Andy reports that one professor's attempted solution to the problem was to threaten to punish students if they did not participate, a strategy that might produce some immediate results, but we suspect that the long-term results would not be favorable. It also seems likely that the silent students did not think of their behavior in terms of resisting learning, and many of the probably frustrated professors in Andy's classrooms may not have thought of it in that particular way either. This brings us to the central questions of this chapter: Why is it sometimes difficult to recognize resistance when we see it, and why is it so important that we recognize it? What would happen if professors, faculty developers, and administrators just ignored this entire book and continued on as they have been doing so far?

The short answer to these questions has been hinted at in the previous chapters analyzing student behaviors, professor misbehaviors, and the impact of these behaviors on student learning. In this chapter, we go into these situations in more detail. There is a widely understood adage in psychotherapy that one cannot change what one cannot see; without a recognition that resistance is occurring, the ability to assess its causes and to take steps to ameliorate or prevent it is obstructed. Instead, instructors and students use partial or inadequate explanations for their behavior, which frequently result in "interventions," such as student silence or instructor threats, that may actually make the situation worse. Similarly, without an understanding of the significant negative cost of student resistance to both students and society, we cannot understand the urgency of the situation that is before us and the need to act.

We begin with an analysis of some of the most common forms of biases and obstacles that prevent students, faculty, and administrators from recognizing resistance, and then we explain the urgent need to change this situation.

Human Biases and Assumptions

Cognitive Misers

To varying degrees, most human beings are cognitive misers, relying on heuristic processes to conserve mental energy; these processes promote quick decisions when demands on attention are high (Stanovich, 2009). Heuristics are mental shortcuts that help us make "good enough" decisions, at least some of the time. Instructors and students act as cognitive misers when they make choices or come to conclusions that are easier and more comfortable than would be the case if they invested significant amounts of time and energy in a task, particularly if they are not convinced that the task is strongly deserving of their time. The tradeoff is that their unquestioned assumptions and heuristic judgments can produce negative interactions and increase resistance.

Faculty manifest cognitive miserliness when they are reluctant to make changes to improve their courses, especially if those changes require planning, thought, and perceived additional effort; it takes more energy and time to implement these changes than to update existing slides or lecture notes. It also takes less effort to conclude that students are lazy, unmotivated, or uncaring than it does to assess *why* students are resisting and to reach out to them or make substantive changes to reduce that resistance.

Students act as cognitive misers in a number of ways, most commonly when they focus on memorizing only information they believe will be on an exam; this requires low levels of effort. This superficial approach leads to expectations for instructors to deliver targeted information, and it increases resistance when the instructor moves away from content-delivery lectures. Resistance can be manifested passively via dropped courses or complaints about busywork or actively by lobbying the professor to change course or assignment requirements. It also shows up when students quickly answer questions without much thought during discussions, assignments, and exams. Exam or quiz questions requiring more effort and thought such as application or contrast questions may challenge a student's self-efficacy or sense of entitlement and increase resistant behaviors.

We note that even intrinsically motivated students may seek to reduce cognitive effort because of multiple demands, such as exams or pressures from home or work. Sometimes the best students in a course may increase their own stress by taking more classes and participating in more extracurricular activities than are feasible; they do this because they assume that they *can* succeed with this strategy by putting out low levels of effort in most courses while still achieving high grades. After all, this pattern has been effective in the past for them; it has been positively reinforcing.

Fortunately, it is possible to become aware of one's cognitive miserliness and to mitigate the negative outcomes. Waller (1999) pointed out that cognitive misers are not often intrinsically motivated to think deeply, whereas *cognizers* enjoy deep thought. Unfortunately, an educational system based primarily on extrinsic rewards, namely, grades, tends to reinforce miserly behavior more than cognizing. Deliberately developing deep learning skills, especially early in the curriculum, and scaffolding this process throughout a major or program increases the capacity for deep thinking, decreases reliance on cognitive biases, and aids in reducing student resistance. Otherwise, students may see these efforts in isolated classrooms as tangential to content and grade acquisition; they do not transfer the use of the skills automatically to new environments. As Doyle (2008) and Tagg (2003) have argued, deeper learning is facilitated when students recognize the *personal relevance* of their learning as a "long-term investment" rather than a short-term concern. Instructors can further reduce student resistance by examining their own cognitive biases, understanding the factors leading students to act as cognitive misers, and designing their courses to specifically address these issues in collaboration with their colleagues.

Actor-Observer Effect

The actor-observer effect is another cognitive bias that affects resistance in higher education. Robins, Mendelsohn, and Spranca (1996) wrote that the effect occurs when the actors (the persons behaving, such as students) explain the causes of their own behavior in situational terms whereas observers (the instructors) explain actors' behaviors as due to personality traits or dispositions (e.g., lazy, unmotivated, distracted). Humans tend to focus attention on other humans' behavior as more *salient* or vital in comparison with situational or systemic factors. The student's behavior is the "figure," and the other influences are the "ground" and tend to be ignored. However, when *we* are the actors, situational forces are most salient to us, and so we explain our behavior using situational context or demands.

As actors, students may explain their resistance to learning in terms of situational pressures and norms such as the expectation to get good grades and to appear competent to their peers and instructors, along with the challenges of juggling many, possibly new, responsibilities. For example, students may resist challenging and open-ended work, stating they do not have the time required, or may resist collaborative work, claiming that it threatens their ability to maintain high grades. Situational explanations might also focus on perceived instructor "misbehaviors" or the effects of cultural factors (e.g., racism or labeling).

Central to these situational explanations is the opportunity to avoid responsibility for performing up to the standards that deep learning requires. Situational reasoning obscures or inhibits students' awareness of their own anxieties about falling short in performance, their frustrations with a learning curve, or their fears of appearing incompetent in front of peers and instructors, all of which are dispositional traits. Acknowledging the *interaction* of both situational forces and their own dispositional origins of resistance empowers students to take responsibility and to face learning challenges more directly.

The actor-observer effect can also increase resistance in the context of collaborative work. In a collaborative team, students are actors but also observers and may attribute a classmate's behavior to personality, making it easier to dismiss the work and input of others. In doing so, students fail to acknowledge the pressures that all members of the collaborative team are likely experiencing. Unfortunately, Green and McClearn (2010) pointed out, this cognitive bias is more likely when others are seen to be different from oneself. When students perceive themselves as *disconnected* from others, their resistance will increase and learning will decrease. However, if students challenge their cognitive biases and find meaning and benefit from the input of others, their resistance will decrease. Professors can support student growth by ensuring that collaborative work is based on best practices such as teacher-formed teams, use of accountability practices (e.g., effective peer-rating systems), and clear explanations (possibly demonstrations) of the rationale and benefits of collaborative learning strategies (see Sibley & Ostafichuk, 2014).

Conversely, instructors may increase resistance by assuming that student behavior is due to dispositional traits, such as occurred in the coffee shop example in chapter 1. In class, acting on dispositional assumptions can lead to frustrated behaviors, such as Andy described, that alienate students from the professor; they can also occur in subtle ways, influencing grading decisions, instructor responsiveness, and willingness to work with students who struggle. Accepting the reality of situational factors, such as students' level of cognitive and social development, lack of preparedness for some entering the university, social and institutionalized racism and gender bias, and the many pressures on time that students face, will assist instructors in better understanding resistance. It will become easier to manage and overcome resistance as instructors increase student responsibility and learning in incremental steps and ensure a developmental trajectory in the acquisition of course skills and content (see Weimer, 2013).

As actors, instructors may overemphasize the situational pressures they experience, including the need to obtain positive student evaluations, deal with frustrated or stressed students, and manage institutional pressures of workload and expectations for grant or scholarly productivity. In spite of these real challenges, a strong focus on situational explanations of their own behavior prevents instructors from accepting and dealing with their own subjectivity (e.g., this is how I was taught, so they will learn it the same way), potential misbehaviors, reluctance to learn new teaching approaches, and other dispositional realities. As in the case of students, there are intersecting truths from both the situational and dispositional sides. The productive route out of these cognitive bias traps is to practice seeing both sides of the issue by recognizing the need to improve one's own dispositional issues while doing what is possible to manage the situational forces and steering away from simplistic explanations for student behaviors as well.

The Curse of Knowledge

Bransford, Brown, and Cocking (2000) summarized the distinctions between expert and novice thinking, noting that differences are not due to memory, intelligence, general abilities, or problem-solving strategies. Instead, expert knowledge is "conditionalized": Experts see problems, data, or situations as examples of core concepts and frameworks in the discipline. Lacking expertise, novices struggle, focusing on superficial aspects of the data and situations rather than relating them to core principles or disciplinary frameworks. For example, when asked why they grouped two physics problems together, students said both were block and incline plane problems whereas experts described these same problems as conservation of energy problems (Bransford, Brown, & Cocking, 2000). Experts "chunk" or group together features of a situation and access relevant information from memory quickly and easily; for students, this process takes significant mental effort because they have to actively search through memory or other sources to identify relevant information. The novices do not chunk the features of the same situation and do not recognize the existing patterns. These differences have been demonstrated across fields as diverse as math (e.g., Schoenfeld & Hermann, 1982), management (e.g., Hinds, Patterson, & Pfeffer, 2001), categorization of species (e.g., Shafto & Coley, 2003), and even competitive Scrabble (e.g., Halpern & Wai, 2007). To instructors, concepts that seem obvious and simple can seem to students abstract and confusing, requiring a lot of effort to learn. This negative side of expertise has been called the curse of knowledge (see Heath and Heath, 2007).

Birch and Bloom (2007) explained that the curse of knowledge can become so entrenched that it biases one's perspective and makes it difficult to understand the struggles of those new to the field. This can lead to instructor frustration when the students resist moving past the basics; it also may be difficult for the instructor to understand why students are struggling. This frustration can emerge in offhand comments, praise for students who "get it" (implying that those who don't are deficient), or other behaviors. This bias may exacerbate the viewpoint that students are lazy and not very intelligent or want to be spoon-fed. When students sense this perspective, or even hear an instructor explicitly state it, they may become upset and resist the relationship with the professor and learning in general as they assert their autonomy or give up, retreating to protect their sense of self and grades. Heath and Heath (2007) pointed out that as an instructor's knowledge becomes more sophisticated and refined over time, this disconnect between the instructor and students may only increase.

Hinds, Patterson, and Pfeffer (2001) explained that experts frequently use abstract language and advanced concepts when teaching novices. Experts also have difficulty remembering their own novice experiences and may rely on recent experiences from their own work in an attempt to estimate what students need to know. These curse-of-knowledge behaviors impair novice learning of new material and skills, but Hinds and colleagues (2001) reported a more constructive approach based on a study they conducted. They found that student "beginners" at a task used more concrete statements and better tailored their instruction to novices than did expert students; as a result, the novices learned the task more effectively when taught by beginners than by experts. However, expert use of abstract and advanced concepts facilitated knowledge transfer to a separate but related task later on. Although expert bias toward abstraction and advanced thinking may be difficult to eliminate, recognizing the need to learn from students through careful observation and solicitation of specific feedback may help professors to be more concrete and specific in their language and use of concepts early on; professors can also ensure that they design a developmental pathway for students to follow toward more complex thinking, leading to improvements in learning and knowledge transfer.

Anton O. Tolman

In my faculty development work, I often encouraged new faculty to adopt the mantra "Our students are not us." This can become a helpful lever for shifting one's perspective. We need to acknowledge the many ways we are different from our students in terms of cultural differences, life experiences, and level of expertise instead of assuming that because we learned a specific way or had a passion for our subject that students naturally will, or should, follow that same path. Reminding ourselves that many, if not most, of our students are not going to become professors (or writers or physicists) can ground us and help us discover new ways to reach out to students. It also emphasizes the invaluable role of formative assessment in evaluating what students know and the necessity of "scaffolding" or creating a supportive developmental path for students to learn the material and skills at the core of the course.

Sibley and Ostafichuk (2014) made an observation in the context of team-based learning that applies to higher education in general: The question is not whether student resistance will occur; the question is when it will start and how intense it will be. They explained that planning for resistance, orienting and preparing students for the learning environment, remaining positive, and responding effectively to student concerns are keys to success and quoted a faculty member who concluded that "it takes you two or three rounds to get to the point where you say, yeah, that's okay" (p. 179).

   This discussion has illustrated that if the goal is to reduce student resistance and enhance learning, it is a vital first step for instructors to clear their own heads of biased reasoning, to understand the complex interactions of expert versus novice knowledge, to accept the reality of human desires for achievement at reduced cost, and to acknowledge that resistance is not a clear sign of failure on their part or bad behavior on the part of students. By taking this first step, instructors are enabled to see student resistance in its complexity through the lens of the IMSR and to work on promoting constructive strategies for dealing with these learning obstacles.

Negative Situations and Interactions

So far we have focused on understanding some common biases and expectations that lead faculty and students to become frustrated and that enable a quick jump to blaming the other side for the problem, increasing student resistance to learning. If self-awareness of one's biases is the first step to reducing resistance, then the second step is the ability to recognize situations or interactions between professor and students that tend to escalate tension and increase resistance, regardless of the origins of the situation. As with biases, both instructors and students contribute to these negative interactions.

Instructor Contributions to Tension in the Relationship

In a typical classroom, the professor, as the expert, has all the power, and knowledge flows from her the way a faucet spews water. Whenever students need knowledge on a subject, they can ask her to turn on the water. This can create a subtle pattern in which students become dependent on instructors for answers to their questions or for help on assignments instead of relying on their own abilities to learn or gather information. If the instructor is preoccupied, unavailable, or unable to respond quickly, students may feel they have no access to essential resources, especially first-generation students and those in lower division courses. Some students may fall into a repeating pattern of learned helplessness and frustration, increasing resistance.

This cycle of tension between instructors and students may escalate as the semester progresses, leading to even more resistance and frustration on all sides. The subtle part of this interaction is that the instructor may not realize that by making herself the focus of power and decision-making in the class, she is actually contributing to the dependency of her students and increasing her own frustration.

There may be other negative effects on students when instructors act as knowledge dispensers. For example, when students feel they have little or no control or input into their own education, students may experience lower self-esteem (Boswell, 2012). If the instructor holds all power, students may feel afraid to contribute to a discussion, worried that their thoughts do not fit with the lesson plan or trajectory of the instructor. This may explain, in part, Andy's silent classroom at the start of the chapter. Students may be concerned that their comments could undermine the authority of the professor or they may doubt the validity of their comments because they are not the "expert." These anxieties stop the student from contributing valuable insights that could assist or enrich other students or the instructor. Rob Blair's story from chapter 2 about the reactions of some of his instructors when he spoke up or assertively requested clarification or changes, are another great example of the impact of these instructor behaviors on students. In these ways, students' emotional and educational growth may be compromised when instructors are perceived as the sole gatekeepers of knowledge.

Dependency on the instructor may also hinder students' metacognition, their ability to evaluate their mastery of knowledge (content metacognition) and the effectiveness of their learning strategies (process metacognition; see chapter 9). For example, a student may ask about *negative reinforcement*. If the instructor just provides a definition or refers to a page in the text, this communicates that knowledge is fixed and comes only from authoritative sources. Presenting knowledge as a set of facts to be memorized rather than encouraging the use of skills to find answers hampers students' abilities to reflect on how well they are learning the subject. On the other hand, if the instructor effectively uses questions, discussion, reflective writing, application of concepts to new situations, or collaborative learning, the student will have multiple opportunities to compare answers with peers, think through questions posed, and recognize her mistakes and strengths. It is this reflection that gives students an opportunity to think about how they can learn and solve problems in the future.

Roberson and Franchini (2014) have given several good examples of how preexisting beliefs and a desire to maintain professional identity may produce instructor behaviors corrosive to positive instructor-student relationships. These examples are given in the context of team-based learning, but these behaviors could easily occur in almost any classroom. In one of these examples, a professor assigned a prequiz based on required readings; students took this quiz prior to class discussion or lecture. This "readiness" quiz was followed immediately by students taking the same quiz again as a team. The students were highly engaged with each other, arguing for their positions using the readings and writing team appeals for missed questions. However, as soon as this engaged process finished, the instructor spent the next 30 minutes of class going over each question, explaining why the right answer was correct. In the words of an observer, "I watched the enthusiasm drain from the room" (p. 170).

Roberson and Franchini (2014) described this scenario as common and potentially destructive of the instructor-student relationship. The instructor violated the premise of student autonomy and responsibility for learning basic content on their own. A similar violation occurs in lecture courses when the instructor requires students to read the text but then repeats the content during lecture. She has also reminded them that she is the expert, the authority, who knows all of the right answers. Over time, students may resent how this quiz process has become a coercive exercise to get them to read, and she risks her behaviors being construed as insults to students' intelligence and work ethic, increasing distrust between students and the professor. Roberson and Franchini (2014) pointed out that some professors may assume that undergraduate students are incapable of acquiring knowledge effectively on their own without input from the expert. Other common obstacles to power sharing with students have been described in detail by Tolman and Lee (2013), who also suggested other potential remedies for faculty to consider.

This team-based learning example demonstrates how power dynamics and behaviors interact in ways that can decrease motivation, increase resistance, and result in greater relationship tension even when the professor is making a good faith effort to create a supportive learning environment. An initial foray into a method designed to *increase* student intrinsic motivation stalled due to behaviors and assumptions that encouraged students to fall back into patterns of *extrinsic* motivation and lack of responsibility for their own learning. If instructors could recognize these situations when they occur, they could alter their behaviors to support and maintain intrinsic learning again. Learning from one's own mistakes is a critical part of progress for both students and faculty. Roberson and Franchini (2014) have emphasized the importance of being flexible, accepting the change in role from expert to facilitator or guide, having faith in students' capacities, removing one's own ego from the situation, and embracing the reality that engaged learning environments are "emotional journeys" for both instructor and students.

Shea Smart

Early in my academic career I anticipated listening to lectures and taking notes. However, I quickly learned that this method of teaching was not used in many of my courses. In my challenging classes there were expectations for me to contribute. One such class was my first course as an honors student. On acceptance into the honors program, I remember thinking that there had been a mistake, that I didn't belong; I was a charlatan. The honors program was for the "gifted" students, and I was not one of those. In this class, the final assignment was to write about any modern novel and analyze the thesis. We weren't told which novel to choose, nor given the thesis. I was somewhat panicked as I was unsure exactly what I should write about. I remember it took me much longer to write this paper than previous ones. However, when I was finished, I received some of the best praise I had ever received on a paper. I felt that my paper could contribute in some way to the discussion of modern novels and that I did in fact belong in this classroom and in the honors program. My confidence was increased, and I continued to do well in my classes, in part because of this newly increased confidence.

Student Contributions to Tension in the Relationship

The previous sections have dealt mostly with instructor choices and attitudes that affect their relationships with students. However, student attitudes and behaviors can also contribute to relationship tension. Some students may see themselves as "victims" in the classroom power structure. Others may view homework assignments and tests, especially if challenging, as hindrances to a degree and professors as potential roadblocks to their future careers. Due to cultural or family standards, students may define *success* as achieving high grades, even if little learning has occurred. Grades serve as "proof" of the student's intelligence and hard work to parents, peers, and imagined future employers. Conversely, parents and peers may issue criticism, or ridicule, when high grades are not achieved. In order to avoid being labeled as inferior, or even average, students may choose the easier path.

These behaviors do not result just from cognitive miserliness. Students may genuinely fear being labeled unintelligent. It becomes emotionally rewarding to take easier classes to sustain an image of intellectualism to others and possibly to themselves. This cycle of both positive and negative reinforcement continues as students work to avoid drops in GPA, a pattern that represents the intersection of learned behaviors and a fixed mindset by which one sees oneself dichotomously as either intelligent or not (see chapter 9). There are also practical consequences of lower grades; students know that high grades help to secure scholarships, obtain entry into graduate programs, and maintain financial aid. The promotion of pseudo-intelligence is also the motivation for some students to blame instructors for their own shortcomings, a pattern leading to a common form of resistance called *academic entitlement* (described in more detail in chapter 6 in the context of social and cultural identity).

Faculty may misinterpret academic entitlement as a form of student laziness. A better definition of *entitlement* might be the tendency for an individual to expect academic success without a sense of personal responsibility for achieving that success (Chowning & Campbell, 2009). Academic entitlement has been shown to have a negative relationship to metacognitive development (Ciani, Summers, & Easter, 2008). Students scoring higher on scales of academic entitlement believe they have less control over their learning (Sparks, 2012). For example, an entitled student might ask, "What is the answer to this question?" whereas a better question would be "Can you help me understand this concept?" The latter question asks for guidance in helping the student discover the answer while still allowing them to develop their own reasoning skills.

Entitlement makes it easier for students to blame instructors for their own struggles or failures. Ginsberg and Wlodkowski (2009) described a blaming cycle that students and instructors fall into that begins when a student is not performing well. She becomes frustrated and may feel entitled due to expectations of academic success. The instructor tries to assist by describing traditional learning methods (e.g., flash cards, studying two hours per hour of class time) to help the student who may resist taking advantage of these or who may not know how to properly implement such strategies. This method of prescriptive learning may cause both student and faculty to push back against change, as they reach a critical point of blaming. The student blames the teacher for providing ineffective methods of learning. The instructor blames the student for not knowing how to use or refusing to use these methods. By blaming the other, each reduces his or her own anxiety about feeling responsible for the situation. The student feels unable to influence the classroom environment and loses motivation to work hard.

At the same time, by labeling students, instructors feel relieved because the problem is not *their* fault. Rationalization is useful here because if it is the students who are truculent or lazy, then even the world's best instructor would be ineffective. Finally, instructors have no need to change what they are doing when the fault is the students'. Furthermore, hundreds of other students have done just fine in their courses. So why should they change? The answer to this rhetorical question is that many students are likely *not* doing well in their classes, and until the instructor can acknowledge this and strive to improve, this pattern will continue.

Labeling and blaming for both parties lead to self-fulfilling prophecies. The student and instructor may become hostile or withdrawn from each other, and stereotypes of each are further confirmed and cemented by the "evidence" of observable behaviors. This cycle is obviously extremely counterproductive to the goals of both the instructor and the student. Instead of working together, they actively work against one another (Ginsberg and Wlodkowski, 2009).

Setting realistic expectations for students can help them to overcome initial expectations of entitlement. Faculty should begin at the start of the semester by explaining that their courses require direct student involvement, genuine student choices, and work beyond mere content acquisition. Smith

(2008, 2013) proposed specific questions that can be raised for discussion at the beginning of the semester as well as other reflective activities to help students evaluate their reasons for taking a class and the potential benefits that can accrue from full participation. For instance, he asks students to vote on which of the following outcomes is most important: (a) acquiring factual knowledge, (b) learning how to use knowledge in new situations, or (c) developing skills to continue learning after college. Most students opt for either choice (b) or (c). He acknowledges that knowledge is necessary for (b) and (c) to occur, but he asks them to revisit the goals and to indicate which of these they can make the most progress on without help, outside of class, and which would be better focused on in class. Students usually acknowledge they can gain factual knowledge on their own and agree that they need help with application and skills. This naturally leads to a productive discussion about how an active learning environment will help them to achieve those goals.

Of course, instructors need to put "their money where their mouth is" by consistently following up and not falling back into a pattern of pure content delivery. Weimer (2013) emphasized that instead of "covering" content, instructors should "use" content to teach important or core principles within the discipline. Content becomes the *mechanism* or *process* that leads to the development of the core skills (e.g., communication, critical thinking, teamwork) as it is infused into collaborative learning, inquiry, and engaged class activities. This also relates to grading schemes because students may not understand the purpose or rationale behind the instructor's grading plan. By linking grades to professional attitudes and skill development rather than purely to factual-level content knowledge and by providing rubrics or skill ladders to help students self-evaluate, metacognition and cognitive development can be enhanced. As students develop greater depth of understanding of content through these activities and assignments, and as this issue is discussed openly in the class, students will gain a greater appreciation for the approach being used and their resistance will decrease. Developing students to become intrinsically motivated and powerful scholars begins with setting their expectations correctly and providing a learning environment that promotes personal responsibility.

The Social Cost of Resistance

The previous discussion has focused on identifying and exploring the obstacles that make it difficult to recognize resistance for what it is: a form of communication, a message that something is going wrong in the learning process. Human biases, expectations, and patterns that develop, usually defensively, in the relationship between instructor and students not only contribute to and exacerbate resistance but also obscure it. These obstacles serve to make it easier for both instructors and students to blame each other and to avoid taking responsibility for their own part in student resistance to learning. However, as John Tagg noted in his foreword to this book, student resistance to learning is possibly the greatest challenge to the effectiveness of institutions of higher education. As he notes, if students are not learning, then the financial, moral, and emotional costs of higher education have no value. If we, collectively as professors, staff, administrators, and students, are to make the difficult commitment to change our behaviors, to improve our classes and our institutions, we need to truly understand *why* this issue is so important and so central.

Although it has become almost trite to say it, the world really *is* a global village. When persons in the middle of uprisings or turmoil around the world can post messages or video of what is happening and organize collectively through modern technology, it is clear that people and nations are intricately connected. Cleveland-Innes and Emes (2005) have argued that the changing nature of the global economy requires highly skilled workers capable of lifelong learning because the pace of change will not slow down and the problems that confront societies will most likely be improved only through the efforts and innovation of a globally conscious workforce. Higher education has an imperative to accommodate the changing needs of students in ways that benefit them and society as well.

Hains and Smith (2012) and many others (e.g., Beers, 2005; Cornelius-White, 2007; Crouch & Mazur, 2001; Garside, 1996; Hake, 1998; Tiwari, Lai, So, & Yuen, 2006) also found that active teaching approaches were superior to traditional pedagogies in producing students with improved content knowledge and globally relevant skills such as critical thinking and problem-solving. Other evidence supports the conclusion that active teaching practices also enhance school persistence, leading the Association of American Colleges and Universities (AAC&U) to identify a set of these practices as "high impact" (Kuh, 2008). A more recent survey of employers by the AAC&U and Hart Research Associates (2013) concluded that employers are generally dissatisfied with students' critical thinking, written and oral communication, problem-solving, and applied knowledge skills in real-world settings, lending an ongoing sense of urgency to implement and sustain these new pedagogies across the curriculum.

Therefore, when students resist these "new" approaches, resist developing critical skills in exchange for a less anxiety-provoking learning environment, the outcomes ripple out to the global level. The industrial, social, ethical, political, environmental, and educational dilemmas that characterize the contemporary world must be met by highly educated workers who can effectively communicate with one another, problem-solve, and innovate. These skills are not developed in learning environments that reinforce individualistic, passive, surface approaches to learning. Resistance not only impedes an individual student's learning but also negatively affects the ability of the coming generation to make progress on the problems that plague us today. Preparing students for the future and to make significant contributions to society and the world has always been the noblest aim of higher education. If that is to continue to be true, we must confront and reduce student resistance and engage students more directly in their own learning, for the sake of all.

A key part of this noble aspiration has been the conviction that college prepares students to become informed citizens in a democracy through application of the skills discussed. Yet the traditional classroom with its focus on individual effort, memorization of content, and satisfaction of the demands and expectations set by an authority figure arguably embeds students in an environment antithetical to this very goal. Yilmaz (2009) wrote,

> Democracy, as a means of co-existing both within and outside the school environment, must inform and shape the educational experiences of students, teachers, and administrators alike if the democratic ideals and values are to be attained and practiced in . . . society. (p. 34)

Only by altering the power dynamics and the relationship between instructor and students can a more democratic environment, one in which student autonomy is recognized and respected and in which student responsibility for learning is the norm, be realized (see Tolman & Lee, 2013); such an environment cannot be created without accepting and working with student resistance.

The complex natures of national and global societies require that citizens be informed and able to participate in democracy, even when such participation can be messy and, at times, arduous. Similarly, an instructor's struggle to design for, address, and resolve resistance may be messy and, at times, arduous for both instructors and students. An active learning environment helps students to develop the skills of listening respectfully to opinions different from their own, judging their own level of understanding and need for additional information, critically·evaluating sources, supporting their position with evidence, and reaching consensus on how to address a problem or situation. These skills counter the trend of a population that is frequently uninformed or misinformed and increasingly polarized. Furthermore, when individuals do not feel motivated and empowered to shape their world or do not know how to reach out and work with others, political apathy or polarization may become even more widespread.

Active learning environments that promote egalitarianism, responsibility, and inclusion are powerful ways to challenge the inequalities that affect so many people. Engaged classrooms become learning laboratories for students of all backgrounds to work together while helping avoid intellectual and social isolation. In engaged classrooms, learning communities are built, sometimes consisting of an entire class, sometimes of small teams, and students can feel understood and work together to succeed. If these experiences are structured effectively, students can come to realize that teams frequently produce better outcomes than individuals working alone and appreciate the value of input from other perspectives. When students resist, they bow out of opportunities to hear, interact with, and learn from those with different ideas and experiences than their own. Instead, they focus on their own agendas and concerns and never learn the value that comes through the rigorous exploration of ideas or ways to amicably and effectively engage with others.

Both the local and the campus communities may also be affected by student resistance to active learning environments. Potter and Meisels (2005) have suggested that active learning courses tend to provide instructors and students with opportunities to shape course content and activities around locally relevant events and needs. For example, at Utah Valley University a learning community course combined a general education English class with a stress management class that assigned a service-learning project chosen by students. The class was made aware of the needs of international refugees who were living in the state, something few of them had any prior knowledge about. Together, they identified the needs of this community, devised ways to assist, and carried out the project while linking this activity to the course objectives for learning to write and managing stress. These types of engaged learning opportunities, which push students to apply or integrate course content with experiential learning opportunities, are central to deep learning and link directly to civic engagement at the local level. Resistance to these opportunities restricts students' understanding of the purpose and value of education and limits their growth in understanding local community needs.

Andy Sechler

I took a political sociology course that required attendance at two meetings of local government, and I chose to attend two city council meetings. After the meetings, I had to write about my observations and experiences and to critically reflect on the functioning of local government. The intent was not only to participate and apply skills learned within the context of the local community but also to investigate how well the local officials were doing in ensuring that citizens had access to relevant information and were given ample opportunity for participation. This activity quickly offered a taste of real-world interaction and left me feeling inspired and empowered to use my developing knowledge and skills for the betterment of the community.

Although the results were largely positive, I admit to initial resistance to the project. I believed the project would be time-consuming, and it felt like it was extra work, unnecessary on top of reading, research, writing, and attending lectures. I noticed some of my classmates felt this way as well. One classmate sat near me at a city council meeting making sarcastic remarks about how great that he thought democracy was and what a waste of time this assignment was for him. I am not sure how my classmate's experience wound up, but I had a change of heart going to the meetings, particularly because I was in the midst of doing research for this book. As I listened to concerned neighbors working for the betterment of the community, I began to relate to their positions, and I recognized that a significant part of my education is for the very purpose of participating in the world from an informed perspective, specifically in contexts just like this local government meeting. This engaged assignment made my education feel more integrated and relevant to my future real-world work and life. It also demonstrated the stress, time constraints, and resistance that students will almost universally face in their education. More important, the project showed me my own ability to work with resistance as I opened up to the bigger view of education, development, and civic participation.

As in the case of Andy's peer, student resistance can have significant, often subconscious effects on students, such as a decrease in motivation to learn skills related to lifelong learning. Derting and Ebert-May (2010) found that active learning courses contribute to students' ability to engage in lifelong learning. Due to the rapid pace of change in technology, professional knowledge bases, and careers, it is vital for students to continually learn on the job, especially as they shift careers over time. Student resistance to acquiring cognitive skills in favor of mostly factual learning could reduce employability or perceived competence, or at least curtail opportunities to advance in one's chosen field. Lifelong learning is also central to civic participation, especially in regard to significant problems faced by society; the advent of the Internet and access to significant amounts of information require citizens to sift and critically evaluate that information and to continue learning, even, for example, in regard to their own health. By resisting opportunities to develop these skills in the practice environment of an active learning classroom, students impair their own long-term development.

When students resist learning, they tend to retain, at best, a superficial understanding of the material. Goodboy and Bolkan (2009) reported that resistance also influences student affective outcomes, or their feelings about the professor, the classroom, learning, and their own motivation to work. The more that students resist, especially if the instructor does not effectively address that resistance, the more likely they are to feel a sense of negativity about the process of education and the more reluctant they are to take on the challenges of accepting increased responsibility for directing their own learning. This negative impact on student motivation is important not only for its immediate effects in a particular class but also because it can interact with students' perceptions of the value of education and their desire to continue in school, issues of relevance to an increasingly complex society and economy.

As noted previously, the consequences of resistance are not limited to the student's own life. Freeman and colleagues (2014) have noted that the President's Council of Advisors on Science and Technology has called for a 33% increase in the number of science, technology, engineering, mathematics (STEM) degrees in the United States. This call has become urgent in order to increase and sustain American competitiveness in the world. In support of this effort, Freeman and his colleagues carried out the largest and "most comprehensive" meta-analysis in the field, evaluating more than 200 studies and comparing lecture-based courses with active learning environments. Their results indicated that students participating in active learning STEM courses, across disciplines, were significantly more likely to learn better and that the risk of failure was 1.5 times greater for students in lecture-based courses. They concluded that one way to increase the number of successful STEM graduates to serve the national need would be to abandon traditional lecturing in favor of active learning in all STEM courses. These conclusions build on earlier work that demonstrated the value of engaging students in their own learning.

Sundberg and Dini (1993) investigated the differences between sections of an introductory biology course oriented toward science majors and sections oriented toward general education nonscience majors. The majors sections emphasize rigorous student acquisition of foundational knowledge to enable movement into upper division courses. The nonmajors courses featured a less intense focus on content, emphasizing an understanding of core concepts in biology and making that content more relevant to students' lives. In comparing pre- and posttests of *content knowledge*, the investigators were shocked (their word) that at the end of the semester the science majors did not perform any better on these tests than did the nonmajors. In fact, while students in the majors courses had significantly *higher* scores on the pretest, the nonmajors' gains in knowledge of biology exceeded by about 50% the gains of students in the majors sections; in some sections of the exam, the nonmajors outperformed the majors.

Although there is insufficient information to accurately link these results to any specific form of pedagogy, the nonmajors' courses clearly used more active learning methods than the traditional content-heavy, lecture-based science major courses. The nonmajors course design focused on making content more relevant to students and promoting understanding of core concepts, patterns that would tend to reduce student resistance to learning. Sundberg and Dini (1993) also reported that nonmajor student attitudes toward science also improved to a reasonable degree as measured by teacher course ratings. This result is consistent with the findings of Stage, Muller, Kinzie, and Simmons (1998), who reported that science majors were *less* enthusiastic about their field following completion of a traditional lecture-based science course whereas nonmajors participating in a more active learning course emphasizing relevancy and engaged activities had more positive views of science, with some students more willing to now consider a major in the field.

Although not specifically addressing the issue of resistance, these examples demonstrate that student resistance focused on maintaining the classroom as a place that fits expectations of passive learning and expected routines is counterproductive to student learning and, as Freeman and colleagues (2014) pointed out, may actually slow down urgent national priorities. These examples also demonstrate that classroom environments that promote relevance and engage students actively not only enhance learning, presumably at least in part by reducing resistance, but also improve student motivation to learn and possibly to participate in different career options as a result.

Conclusion

Anton O. Tolman

When I was about 12 years old, my parents took me to see an eye doctor; it was the first time I remember seeing one. I wasn't sure why we were there. Several weeks later, when I got my first glasses, I put them on and was shocked by the colors around me and the beauty of the mountains that surround Albuquerque. I had known there were mountains there but only in the abstract. With my eyes opened, I saw a whole new panorama of the world, and my appreciation for its beauty intensified. It gave me a love for the environment that has endured to this day.

As we said in the beginning, you cannot change or influence what you cannot see. Perhaps this chapter serves as eyeglasses for some of our readers. For others, it may just strengthen what you already knew. In either case, we hope it has enriched your understanding and appreciation of what happens in your classes. When we recognize and act to reduce our own very human biases, when we can remember our students are not us, and when we pay attention to the nature and quality of our interactions with students, we are taking positive steps forward. Whether students understand their own behaviors as resistant or not, that resistance carries a significant and real cost to their motivation to learn, the depth of their understanding of the material, and the development of critical life skills. In addition it affects their careers, families, local environments, and even our collective national interests. If higher education is to fulfill its potential, if postsecondary learning is to mean anything real, administrators, staff, faculty, and students must work together to understand resistance and to proactively move to create supportive environments in which deep learning occurs.

References

Association of American Colleges and Universities & Hart Research Associates. (2013). *It takes more than a major: Employer priorities for college learning and student success.* Washington, DC: Author.

Beers, G. W. (2005). The effect of teaching method on objective test scores: Problem-based learning versus lecture. *Journal of Nursing Education, 44*(7), 305–309.

Birch, S. A. J., & Bloom, P. (2007). The curse of knowledge in reasoning about false beliefs. *Psychological Science, 18*(5), 382–386.

Boswell, S. (2012). "I deserve success": Academic entitlement attitudes and their relationships with course self-efficacy, social networking, and demographic variables. *Social Psychology of Education, 15*, 353–365.

Bransford, J. D., Brown, A. L., & Cocking, R. R. (Eds.). (2000). *How people learn: Brain, mind, experience, and school* (Exp. ed.). Washington, DC: National Academies Press.

Chowning, K., & Campbell, N. (2009). Development and validation of a measure of academic entitlement: Individual differences in students' externalized responsibility and entitled expectations. *Journal of Educational Psychology, 101*(4), 982–997. doi:10.1037/a0016351

Ciani, K. D., Summers, J. J., & Easter, M. A. (2008). Gender differences in academic entitlement among college students. *Journal of Genetic Psychology, 169*(4), 332–344.

Cleveland-Innes, M., & Emes, C. (2005). Principles of learner-centered curriculum: Responding to the call for change in higher education. *Canadian Journal of Higher Education, 35*(4), 85–110.

Cornelius-White, J. (2007). Learner-centered teacher-student relationships are effective: A meta-analysis. *Review of Educational Research, 77*(1), 113–143.

Crouch, C. H., & Mazur, E. (2001). Peer instruction: Ten years of experience and results. *American Journal of Physics, 69*(9), 970–977.

Derting, T. L., & Ebert-May, D. (2010). Learner-centered inquiry in undergraduate biology: Positive relationships with long-term student achievement. *CBE—Life Sciences Education, 9*(4), 462–472.

Doyle, T. (2008). *Helping students learn in a learner-centered environment.* Sterling, VA: Stylus.

Freeman, S., Eddy, S. L., McDonough, M., Smith, M. K., Okoroafor, N., Jordt, H., & Wenderoth, M. P. (2014). End of lecture: Active learning increases student performance across the STEM disciplines. *Proceedings of the National Academy of Sciences of the USA, 111*(23), 8410–8415.

Garside, C. (1996). Look who's talking: A comparison of lecture and group discussion teaching strategies in developing critical thinking skills. *Communication Education, 45*(3), 212–227.

Ginsberg, M. B., & Wlodkowski, R. J. (2009). *Diversity and motivation: Culturally responsive teaching in college* (2nd ed.). San Francisco, CA: Jossey-Bass.

Goodboy, A. K., and Bolkan, S. (2009). College teacher misbehaviors: Direct and indirect effects on student communication behavior and traditional learning outcomes. *Western Journal of Communication, 73*(2), 204–219.

Green, T. D., & McClearn, D. G. (2010). The actor-observer effect as a function of performance outcome and nationality of other. *Social Behavior and Personality, 38*(10), 1335–1344.

Hains, B. J., & Smith, B. (2012). Student-centered course design: Empowering students to become self-directed learners. *Journal of Experiential Education, 35*(2), 357–374.

Hake, R. R. (1998). Interactive-engagement vs traditional methods: A six-thousand-student survey of mechanics test data for introductory physics courses. *American Journal of Physics, 66*(1), 64–74. doi: 10.1119/1.18809

Halpern, D. F., & Wai, J. (2007). The world of competitive Scrabble: Novice and expert differences in visuospatial and verbal abilities. *Journal of Experimental Psychology, 13*(2), 79–94.

Heath, C., & Heath, D. (2007). *Made to stick.* New York, NY: Random House.

Hinds, P. J., Patterson, M., & Pfeffer, J. (2001). Bothered by abstraction: The effect of expertise on knowledge transfer and subsequent novice performance. *Journal of Applied Psychology, 86*(6), 1232–1243.

Kuh, G. (2008). *High-impact educational practices: What they are, who has access to them, and why they matter.* Washington, DC: Association of American Colleges and Universities.

Potter, R., & Meisels, G. (2005). Enhancing teacher preparation and improving faculty teaching skills: Lessons learned from implementing "Science That Matters," a standards based interdisciplinary science course sequence. *Journal of Science Education and Technology, 14*(2), 191–204.

Roberson, B., & Franchini, B. (2014). The emotional journey to team-based learning. In J. Sibley and P. Ostafichuk (Eds.), *Getting started with team-based learning* (pp. 161–174). Sterling, VA: Stylus.

Robins, R. W., Mendelsohn, G. A., & Spranca, M. D. (1996). The actor-observer effect revisited: Effects of individual differences and repeated social interactions on actor and observer attributions. *Journal of Personality and Social Psychology, 71*, 375–389.

Schoenfeld, A. H., & Herrmann, D. J. (1982). Problem-solving and knowledge structure in expert and novice mathematical problem solvers. *Journal of Experimental Psychology: Learning, Memory, and Cognition, 8*(5), 484–494.

Shafto, P., & Coley, J. D. (2003). Development of categorization and reasoning in the natural world: Novices to experts, naïve similarity to ecological knowledge. *Journal of Experimental Psychology: Learning, Memory, and Cognition, 29*(4), 641–649.

Sibley, J., & Ostafichuk, P. (Eds.). (2014). *Getting started with team-based learning.* Sterling, VA: Stylus.

Smith, G. A. (2008). First-day questions for the learner-centered classroom. *National Teaching and Learning Forum, 17*(5), 1–4.

Smith, G. A. (2013, November). *Selling active learning to faculty requires a student purchase, too.* Workshop presented at the annual conference of the Professional and Organizational Development Network in Higher Education (POD), Pittsburgh, PA.

Sparks, S. D. (2012). "Academic entitlement" leads to reduced student effort. *Education Week, 31*(33), 15.

Stage, F. K., Muller, P. A., Kinzie, J., & Simmons, A. (1998). *Creating learner-centered classrooms: What does learning theory have to say?* (ASHE-ERIC Higher Education Report, Vol. 26, No. 4). Washington, DC: George Washington University Graduate School of Education and Human Development.

Stanovich, K. E. (2009). *What intelligence tests miss: The psychology of rational thought.* New Haven, CT: Yale University Press.

Sundberg, M. D., & Dini, M. L. (1993). Science majors vs non-majors: Is there a difference? *Journal of College Science Teaching, 23*(22), 299–304.

Tagg, J. (2003). *The learning paradigm college.* San Francisco, CA: Anker Publishing.

Tiwari, A., Lai, P., So, M., & Yuen, K. (2006). A comparison of the effects of problem-based learning and lecturing on the development of students' critical thinking. *Medical Education, 40,* 547–554.

Tolman, A. O., & Lee, C. S. (2013). True collaboration: Building meaning in learning through sharing power with students. In O. Kovbasyuk & P. Blessinger (Eds.), *Meaning centered education: International perspectives and explorations in higher education* (pp. 110–121). New York, NY: Routledge.

Waller, B. N. (1999). Deep thinkers, cognitive misers, and moral responsibility. *Analysis, 59*(4), 223–229.

Weimer, M. (2013). *Learner-centered teaching: Five key changes to practice* (2nd ed.). San Francisco, CA: Jossey-Bass.

Yilmaz, K. (2009). Democracy through learner-centered education: A Turkish perspective. *International Review of Education, 55*(1), 21–37.

4

THE IMPACT OF INSTITUTIONAL CULTURE ON STUDENT DISENGAGEMENT AND RESISTANCE TO LEARNING

Janine Kremling and Erikca DeAnn Brown

In the 1960s and, to a lesser extent, the 1950s, campuses were public arenas—platforms for political theater, recruiting grounds for social activists, and often the places where public officials sought judicious expertise when sorting out vexing issues. Today colleges and universities are seen principally as gateways to economic security and middle-class status. Except for the occasional bout with political correctness, almost no one worries about higher education institutions leading young people astray. If anything, the lament is that they have, in their pursuit of market advantage, become dispensers of degrees and certificates rather than communities of educators who originate, debate, and promulgate important ideas

—R. Zemsky, G. R. Wegner, and W. F. Massy, *Remaking the American University*

This chapter begins the analysis of the discrete elements of the integrated model of student resistance (IMSR) by discussing student disengagement and resistance to learning as an outcome of the institutional practices and priorities students experience in their everyday campus interactions, such as those mentioned by Zemsky, Wegner, and Massy (2005). Students are also regularly affected by institutional values, practices, and priorities in areas such as access to classes, tuition, financial aid, teaching practices, and mentorship opportunities that shape their degree of resistance to higher education and learning. Thus, the institution creates a cultural context for student behaviors and can help students, even those with internal and external obstacles, to succeed, but institutional culture can also inhibit students' success by failing to fully engage them in higher education. One aspect of student resistance is represented by withdrawing or pulling back from an educational institution when students feel that they are not a priority. They may feel that the institution thinks of them mainly as sources of income who must be retained either as a means of maintaining financial stability or as graduation statistics for legislative support, rather than as citizens developing the skills to contribute to society.

The IMSR incorporates institutional culture as a rectangle in which are embedded the social and environmental forces that affect the way students view higher education as well as themselves and that shape how students view their interactions with others in the context of an institution and campus (see chapter 1). These social and environmental forces exert pressure on institutions from outside and also are brought onto campus in the heads of the students, shaping their attitudes and behaviors. The institutional culture may either reinforce preexisting beliefs and attitudes, strengthening the status quo, or it may address these issues more directly in constructive ways that may help reduce student resistance. Institutional culture is also obviously a context in which instructor-student interactions occur inside and outside classes; institutional values, policies, and practices often shape or even define the nature of instructor-student relationships and therefore students' experiences of higher education.

McFarland (2001) supported this conceptualization when he argued that student resistance was affected by the formal and informal characteristics of social settings, the campus, and the classroom. In this sense, resistance may be an attempt to assert autonomy in a system that devalues students. Stated differently, students may feel empowered through resistance rather than feeling helpless due to a variety of factors such as low grades, little interaction between students and faculty, lack of access to classes, rising tuition, and the costs of subsequent private loans (Pfaff & Huddleston, 2003; Seidel & Tanner, 2013). For instance, frustration about higher tuition may increase resistance to active learning because students feel that their money pays for "being taught"—that is, lectured to. Asking students to take responsibility for their own learning may be met with protest (active or passive) because they believe they are now paying to teach themselves (Felder & Brent, 1996). It is not rare to see student comments such as "She wasn't teaching us anything; I had to teach myself. I didn't pay money to teach myself" on teaching evaluations when active or collaborative teaching techniques are used. This is true not only for undergraduate students but also for graduate students.

To date, most research on student resistance has focused on the behaviors of students and faculty in the classroom. This emphasis (referred to in chapter 1 as self-action or interaction-level explanations) ignores the importance of the institutional culture that shapes the behaviors and beliefs of students and faculty. The institutional context, including values, policies, practices, and the beliefs and behaviors of faculty and administrators, shapes the environment in which students learn and in which student resistance emerges. Institutions also create the climate in which faculty make decisions about instructional strategies, research, and their priorities in general. This chapter is not an exhaustive assessment of the ways that institutional culture influences student resistance for good or ill; our goal is to illuminate the influence of institutional culture with some specific examples that can serve as entry points for students, faculty, and administrators to begin considering these issues. We start by exploring how institutional values, policies, and practices interact with student expectations and reactions.

Resistance in the Context of Student and Faculty Priorities and Institutional Practices

Research suggests that the priorities of students, faculty, and universities have shifted, with each party pursuing separate goals (Arum & Roksa, 2011; Astin, 1993; Bok, 2003, 2006; Kuh, 2003). Even though these goals, such as learning and research to advance society, may seem complementary, in the reality of university politics this is often not true. In fact, legislatures and national education commissions have taken note of the apparent mismatch between what universities ought to accomplish and what they actually accomplish (Reyes & Rincon, 2008; U.S. Department of Education, 2006). These competing goals among institutions, faculty, and students can often result in negative situations that increase student resistance.

Marketing Versus Reality as Experienced by Students

Looking at the website or marketing materials of most institutions of higher education, one usually sees clearly stated goals for excellence in teaching and learning. These lofty aims may not reflect the reality of daily university operations, however. For some institutions, such as research universities, research has always had a higher priority than teaching, but increasingly the mission statements of other types of institutions have started to conflict with the hidden paradigms that drive actual policies and behaviors.

Administrators, faculty, and students have some goals in common, such as working and learning in a positive environment and achieving the specific goals they each have set. However, the specific goals that these groups are striving to accomplish are different, and some goals are in direct competition with one another. For instance, the personal goal of faculty to accomplish tenure may focus their energies on publishing and working on grants rather than teaching, which may conflict with a student's desire to learn from the most accomplished faculty in the field. Similarly, the goal of students to get high grades with less effort may conflict with a professor's intention to teach students to become independent and deep learners. As a result of these conflicts, the goals of each group may not be accomplished. Many students are aware of the power structure, with administrators on the top, followed by faculty, and then students. This power structure and the relative powerlessness of students may be an important factor in student disengagement and resistance.

Anonymous Graduate Student[1]

When I started my graduate program, every student was required to complete four qualifying exams (later three, and now reduced to two) with three professors as committee members. From the end of 2011 until completion of my last exam in 2013, I spent most of my time recruiting and retaining committee members instead of completing my dissertation and doing research with a mentor who could guide my professional development.

My attempts to recruit committee members for my dissertation were thwarted by professors who left the university, professors who agreed to serve as long as I took a class with them but then rescinded upon my completion of the course, professors whose advising loads were too high or who limited the number of students they were willing to work with, and professors whose professional commitments to their own research agenda prevented them from participating.

Why are students still admitted to a program whose faculty are unable to advise and serve as committee members, especially if graduation rates are important? While in my graduate program, I met all program requirements (i.e., completion of specific classes, satisfactory performance, passing competency assessments, and meeting the institution's financial requirements) sufficient for the institution to provide me with an education and a degree. I entered into a contract with this institution with the assumption that by upholding my end of the bargain, the institution would do the same. However, my inability to secure committee members, through no fault of my own, was a failure of the institution to meet my needs. Having finished my coursework, I enrolled in continuing education units, accruing more debt, but I was still unable to complete my doctorate because of the unwillingness of professors to participate.

This student describes the painful odyssey that some (possibly many) students go through in graduate school. Undergraduates may have similar experiences when they can't enroll in prerequisite or required major classes, can't complete independent study requirements because professors have no time, or are ignored or rejected when seeking advice about career opportunities. Institutional and thus faculty priorities for publication and recognition or tenure often conflict with students' needs for quality instruction or mentoring by faculty members.

Studies have shown that the relationship between students and faculty, especially mentoring outside the classroom, is one of the strongest predictors of student motivation and achievement (Institute for Higher Education Policy, 2011; Nugent, 2009). The lack of faculty and/or staff availability and support in many settings decreases student motivation and ability to complete requirements, leading to increased resistance to working with faculty. The preceding example clearly illustrates the student's feelings, including helplessness, graduation worries, and a certain hopelessness about accomplishing her career goal. Situations like this are a clear example of how some institutional priorities, including recruitment of students through a marketing plan, emphasizing goals of excellence in teaching and learning, and the process of granting faculty tenure or promotion, can actually violate the purported purpose of the institution that serious students accepted and expected when they enrolled. This leads to disappointment, resentment, and increased student resistance.

Student Priorities, Expectations, and Behaviors

Socializing Versus Academic Work

A significant number of students who come to a university are not only underprepared academically (one-third of all college students; National Center for Education Statistics, 2003) but also entering the institution with an emphasis on values that are often contrary to academic commitment and rigor. Students are spending more time on the social experience of college than in the past, and colleges are facilitating this by providing more such experiences, contradicting their own stated commitment to student learning. As tuition has increased, so have opportunities to engage in clubs and other social activities because schools compete for students, and students desire a full social and academic experience to get their money's worth. It's the college experience—the social aspect of it—that matters most to many of them:

The best part of it is not from classes. It's coming from just a whole college experience: Learning to live on your own, learning to take care of yourself, learning to live on your own schedule, learning to budget your time, and learning to meet new people and deal with your relationships and new issues. (quoted in Champbliss & Takacs, 2014, p. 134)

Research on students' academic effort suggests that part of the resistance to learning may be due to the decrease in time students are willing to spend on academic tasks. Babcock and Marks (2011) demonstrated that through the early 1960s students spent about 40 hours per week studying, which signified a full-time academic schedule. Since then there has been a steady decline in actual study time and an increase in time spent on social activities. By 2003 students only spent an average of 13 hours per week on class time and studying. Only 44% of students reported spending more than 20 hours per week on average on academic tasks. Some academics believe that faculty are also spending less time on teaching and mentoring (Boyer, 1990; Jencks & Riesman, 1968; Kuh, 2003). Kuh (2003) even claimed that there exists a "disengagement compact" between many faculty and students:

"I'll leave you alone if you leave me alone." That is, I won't make you work too hard (read a lot, write a lot) so that I won't have to grade as many papers or explain why you are not performing well. The existence of this bargain is suggested by the fact that at a relatively low level of effort, many students get decent grades—B's and sometimes better. There seems to be a breakdown of shared responsibility for learning—on the part of faculty members who allow students to get by with far less than maximum effort, and on the part of students who are not taking full advantage of the resources institutions provide. (Kuh, 2003, p. 28)

This pattern or implicit compact between many faculty and students is one contributing aspect of the oft-heard concerns regarding grade inflation. What is not usually mentioned in discussions about grade inflation is the role that institutional priorities and policies, and student resistance, play in sustaining it, as illustrated in the following student perspective regarding the desire to do well with little effort dedicated to deep learning:

I hate classes with a lot of reading that is tested on. Any class where a teacher is just gonna give us notes and a worksheet is better. Something that I can study and just learn from in five minutes I'll usually do pretty good in. Whereas, if I'm expected to read, you know, a hundred-and-fifty-page book and then write a three-page essay on it, you know, on a test let's say, I'll probably do worse on that test because I probably wouldn't have read the book. Maybe ask the kids, what's in this book? And I can draw my own conclusions, but I rarely actually do reading assignments or stuff like that, which is a mistake I'm sure, but it saves me a lot of time. (quoted in Grigsby, 2009, p. 117)

High-impact practices typically include additional out-of-class assignments for students, which may be met with resistance because they interfere with social or work time and may result in lower grades if the student doesn't invest a substantial amount of time in them.

Student Attempts to Shape the Learning Environment
Students, such as the one quoted previously, in an effort to create time for social or work life, may "train" faculty to give them less work by providing negative feedback in teaching evaluations or on public websites or by avoiding time-consuming classes altogether. These forms of resistance may reflect either student autonomy or a fear of failure. These behaviors may also reduce enrollment in active learning courses, especially if there is no departmental attempt to standardize curriculum across sections of the same course. Some students, once they discover a course will require active learning and increased effort, may drop the course fairly quickly and change to a more passive learning section of the same course. Institutional and/or departmental policies that penalize or add pressure on instructors whose classes are dropped for low enrollment reinforce these student behaviors.

A fear of lower grades due to complex and difficult assignments might motivate students to resist by trying to influence the instructor with the threat that low grades will result in negative student evaluations. Most students are aware that instructor ratings are, in some institutions, the only or primary evaluation measure in contract decisions and faculty reviews for tenure and promotion. Ratings give students a chance to express autonomy by influencing which professors are retained and to promote the learning environment they prefer. This strategy can work because fear of negative teaching evaluations is a salient factor in faculty decisions on whether to use active teaching methods. Untenured faculty and adjunct faculty may be hesitant to risk negative evaluations in institutional environments that overvalue student ratings, especially if their evaluations are generally good using a lecture-based approach. Chapter 6 provides more details regarding student evaluations.

Another resistance strategy used to influence faculty is to go "above" the faculty and complain to the chair of the department or even the dean of the school/college; this approach fits well with a consumerist attitude (described later). Students hope that authority figures will tell the faculty to be more accommodating toward students' needs in order to help increase retention and graduation rates, which have become one of the main goals of universities and state legislatures.

Even though faculty theoretically have academic freedom, this right may be constrained by the threat of negative tenure or promotion decisions and possibly by non-retention. Concerned faculty may "give in" to student requests to prevent negative ratings or administrative complaints, thereby empowering students to continue these behaviors. Faculty may also be deterred from attempting active learning, sometimes even at the recommendation of their tenured colleagues, because existing policies mean that even one really bad evaluation could be interpreted as incompetency. Faculty who attempt active teaching methods and have negative results may not be able to defend themselves effectively against negative reviews and threats to take away their class by the chair of the department. It does not take many instances of success for student resistance to become known as an effective technique to accomplish a goal; what students don't realize is that it may also be very effective in inhibiting actual learning.

Students as Consumers

In chapter 6, the authors explore student consumer attitudes in the context of the larger culture. Consumer attitudes are also created by the institutions themselves, however. Universities are concerned about attracting students, and many act very much like a company trying to attract customers. For instance, universities are building residential halls that include pool areas and other amenities; they are building state-of-the-art student unions with mall-like food courts and Starbucks franchises; they are providing first-class athletic facilities and all-day entertainment. These facilities and opportunities are heavily advertised in hopes of beating out direct competitors for student enrollments. The competition for students and the advertisement of recreational facilities create the impression that students are consumers, who in turn treat the university similarly to the car dealership where they bargain for the car with the most "extras." Very often, once students are actually attending classes, things change. For instance, professors do not typically treat them like consumers. In many state universities, students have to wait to get into required classes. They may not have the access to professors they expected because their professors are busy with research, service, grants, and graduate students. In this situation, students may feel disappointed, cheated, or frustrated and may try to assert their wants and needs by resisting in the classroom.

Professors' Changes in Professional Expectations and Behaviors

Professor behaviors have changed over time for a variety of reasons, including new pressures from the institution, increased consumerism and resistant behaviors by students, and changes in their professional interests. Some scholars suggest that faculty disengagement from teaching may be a response to the shifting of institutional values toward research. This shift affects all types of universities and reflects the perceived increased value of research activity and publications (Arum & Roksa, 2011; Wilshire, 1989). Faculty are concerned about their economic well-being and professional advancement due to the significant amount of time and money spent obtaining their degrees. Financial security and professional advancement depend increasingly on publications, preferably articles in high-ranking journals (Jencks & Riesman, 1968; Price & Cotton, 2006). If a decade ago one or two publications were sufficient to get hired, today it may require four or five. Similarly, even teaching institutions now require on average three to six publications for tenure and more for promotion to full professor (Price & Cotton, 2006). At teaching institutions the type of publication is typically more flexible, including book chapters, textbooks, and second-tier articles. Research universities typically require substantially more publications, all preferably published in the top-tier journals. This increasing attention to research and grants and decreasing time for students or as some have called it, "abandoning students," may not be a fully conscious behavior by faculty but is an adaptive response to changing requirements for tenure and promotion by the institution.

In addition to raising publication and grant expectations, some universities have started to devalue teaching in the tenure decision in general. For instance, faculty may be told that absent horrific teaching evaluations, their teaching record will not substantially affect their ability to make tenure and promotion. Also, even an outstanding teaching record, including teaching awards, will not make up for the lack of publications. A study by Harvard University ("Toward Top-Tier Teaching," 2007) demonstrated the disconnect between faculty enthusiasm and effort in teaching and their strong skepticism that the institution cared about their efforts. In the study a faculty member stated, "In my department, teaching is de-emphasized to an extreme. . . . There's no training or guidance," and graduate students are acquainted with "a silent understanding that you should put as little time into it as possible." A junior faculty member said, "In my six years at Harvard, I have never been given the impression that my teaching is taken into account in promotion decisions" (pp. 1–2).

A major contributor to this growing shift is that measuring the quality of teaching is difficult, if not impossible, with most current student evaluation systems ("Toward Top-Tier Teaching," 2007). Arum and Roksa (2011) concluded that students are satisfied with passive learning and don't appreciate faculty who make them work for their grade beyond taking a multiple-choice test, especially not assignments requiring critical thinking and problem-solving. Thus, even though students may learn a lot and even realize this, the evaluations may show that the students very much disliked the class and the instructor. Even though high scores on the teaching evaluations are not sufficient to get tenure and promotion, very low scores can hurt faculty. In other words, good student evaluations are necessary but not sufficient for tenure and promotion (Boyer, 1990; Price & Cotton, 2006).

There are alternatives to typical student evaluations of teaching quality. These include observation of actual methods used, student learning outcomes, peer reviews, videos, student interviews, and teaching portfolios (Berk, 2005, 2006; Van Note Chism, 1999). These methods are used rarely because of the substantial time investment and because faculty and administrators are often not well versed in pedagogy or assessment of pedagogical quality (Weimer, 2008). The institutional lack of interest in genuine student learning, the use of teaching evaluations by students to modify faculty behavior, and the absence of incentives for effective teaching influence instructional strategies and faculty behaviors in the classroom. There are many institutional disadvantages and disincentives for faculty to implement active learning. Faculty may choose to use a lecture-style class and give good grades for little effort to keep students satisfied and get reasonable teaching evaluations. In this sense, faculty strive to please the students and the institution with good evaluations, even though many of them are fully aware of the general ineffectiveness of the lecture-style, passive learning approach.

Influence of General Institutional Priorities and Practices on Student Resistance

In addition to the institutional effects described previously, we believe it is important to highlight several additional institutional forces that shape a context for resistance. These include institutional emphases on student retention and persistence to graduation and institutional paradigms that reflect change in how institutions view their missions and priorities.

Efforts to Improve Student Retention and Persistence

One of the most discussed concerns of the public, and therefore of institutions of higher education, is the retention rate of students, especially after the first year of college. Institutions across the country, as well as the federal government, have made significant investments of resources to attempt to reduce the dropout rate of students and increase graduation percentages, with mixed success. These efforts have often focused on increasing the support services available through the student affairs side of the institution, and some would argue that this has come at the expense of support for academic affairs and student learning.

One of the primary drivers of current institutional policies and practices regarding retention appears to be the seminal work of Tinto (1975). Tinto's model described 13 elements that he believed were related to a student's decision to continue at a university. Later empirical tests (Braxton, Sullivan, & Johnson, 1997) concluded that only five elements had empirical support in an actual institutional context, and Berger and Braxton (1998) reduced this to four: student entry characteristics (gender, race, etc.), student initial commitment to the institution, subsequent commitment, and student integration into the social community of the college. Berger and Braxton (1998) noted that one problem with Tinto's model was that the key aspect of student integration was not well defined. Many institutions have worked to create environments more open to diverse students (entry characteristics) and to provide supportive social environments with changes to student orientation, increased use of student advisers and counselors, and greater support for student government and recreational activities; institutions have also been changing the physical environment of campus housing, libraries, and student centers to be more inviting. Although these efforts make sense in terms of Tinto's model, helping students feel more a part of the campus culture and thus enhancing their desire to persist, they also may increase resistance when they reinforce or interact with student consumer attitudes. Recent passionate protests on multiple campuses focusing on institutionalized racism, however, also suggest that there is much work still to be done in several of these areas.

Furthermore, in empirically evaluating Tinto's (1975) model, Berger and Braxton (1998) found strong support for the role of specific organizational characteristics in the social integration of students: effective communication of rules and expectations (we would add values), fair enforcement of institutional rules, and encouragement of student participation in campus decision-making. We note that none of these efforts requires significant expenditures in marketing, physical environment, or additional personnel. These organizational characteristics carry down into the classroom, and Berger and Braxton (1998) have suggested that institutions would be well advised to make sure faculty are aware of these characteristics while supporting professional development to assist faculty in implementing these characteristics in the classroom.

A recent example serves as an object lesson for how an institution's purported focus on student retention and persistence may actually serve more superficial administrative goals in ways that alienate faculty and students, increasing resistance. The president of a small liberal arts university launched a new survey and requested that a group of faculty test it in their introductory courses. The faculty agreed, believing that the survey would help students understand their learning styles and thus enhance academic performance. However, e-mails from the president to the provost were leaked to the student paper. These e-mails indicated that the president had set a goal for how many students he wanted to leave the university by the date of announcing retention to the federal government. The president's e-mail is reported to have emphasized a benefit to the university if at-risk students left early. He wrote, "This one thing will boost our retention by 4–5%" (quoted in Mangan, 2016, para. 9). The president also reportedly expressed frustration that faculty had not implemented his suggested "come to Jesus" meeting with students who did not do well on the survey; the faculty refused because they saw this effort as a deliberate attempt to encourage students to leave the university and to artificially inflate retention figures. When a reporter from the student paper asked the president about this, he claimed that encouraging the students least likely to succeed to drop out was the "most humane approach" (para. 3) as it would help them to avoid incurring large amounts of debt "for something they don't want to do" (Mangan, 2016, para. 4). Whatever the ultimate truth behind these behaviors and practices, it seems clear that the president believed his actions would benefit the institution by increasing retention rates while actively discouraging some students from participating in higher education. The faculty reaction illustrates how institutional practices and polices perceived as aiming to achieve superficial goals at the expense of student development and learning can provoke a negative reaction that would be likely to filter down into the classroom. Because this situation was published in the student newspaper, it would likely serve to increase student resistance and disengagement from the university.

Institutional Paradigms

Research has suggested that the following major trends are reflecting changes in the missions of institutions as manifested in administrative practices and priorities: (a) a shift from a quasi-parental to an administrative model and (b) increased focus on research and ranking.

A Shift From a Quasi-Parental to an Administrative Model

In the past, universities perceived themselves as quasi-parents authorized to guide students in regard to academic content, social behavior, and moral development (Arum & Roksa, 2011; Ginsberg, 2011a). Most administrators had been faculty members who had spent many years at the university, who had institutional memory, and who were acting in the spirit of faculty and students because they were closely connected to both (Brint, 2002; Ginsberg, 2011a). More recently, this previous pattern of "homegrown" administrators has shifted toward a nonacademic professionalization; universities increasingly rely on professional headhunters to hire administrators who are familiar with neither the university nor its mission and history and who are increasingly from nonacademic backgrounds (Brint, 2002; Ginsberg, 2011a). This growing practice has shaped the mission in use (as opposed to the stated mission) and the rise of nonacademic services and functions such as advising and financial services at many institutions (Arum & Roksa, 2011; Brint, 2002); it has also likely contributed to the increasing cost of attending college (Ginsberg, 2011a). King (2007) found that one in seven university presidents came from outside academia and the use of professional headhunters had increased from 12% in 1984 to almost 50% in 2007. This trend may be more pronounced in private and research universities, but the trend is also apparent for public comprehensive and teaching universities (Ginsberg, 2011a).

In addition to this change in who leads the university, there has been a significant blowup of administration (Ginsberg, 2011a, b). The rise of the administration appears to be paralleled by the "fall of the faculty," who are losing influence over the institutional mission and over student development, as these roles are performed more often by nonacademic professionals. Whereas the number of administrators has increased, faculty numbers (on a per-student basis) have decreased; moreover, available funding for education has also decreased, forcing students to accumulate student loans that they will struggle to pay off for years or even decades (Ginsberg, 2011a, b). Ginsberg (2011b) demonstrated that, between 1975 and 2005, although faculty numbers increased by 51%, the ranks of administrators grew by 85% and professional staff increased by 240%.

Salary has also been affected. For instance, between 2004 and 2013, the California State University (CSU) system experienced a widening gap between salaries of administrators and faculty. The California Faculty Association (CFA) has calculated that between 2004 and 2014, full-time equivalent faculty throughout the CSU *lost* $9,056 in purchasing power (adjusted for inflation), while CSU campus presidents' average salaries *gained* $22,917 in purchasing power. This increase in salaries is not only true for presidents but also for upper-level administrators. Between 2004 and 2014, CSU expenditures for the salaries of managers and supervisors increased by 48% (CFA, Raise to the Bottom, 2015). Also, in the CSU system, the number of administrative positions increased by 19% whereas the numbers of tenure-line faculty fell by 3%. At the same time, the student body of the CSU system increased, resulting in a higher faculty–student ratio and decreased student access to professors. Instead of hiring tenure-line faculty, CSU started to hire temporary faculty at high rates (CFA, 2015). These temporary faculty may be fine teachers, but the nature of their appointment reduces participation in activities, such as service and mentoring, that are important to student success and faculty shared governance. As the CFA (2015) stated,

> CSU campus presidents have clearly prioritized managers on their campuses over tenure-line faculty in making their decisions. That set of priorities has enormous ramifications for current, and future, students. Not only are students today missing out on a stable faculty workforce over the course of their college careers; future students face an even bleaker prospect. (p. 5)

This "blight of administration" changes the focus of universities from a true liberal arts education to vocational training. This is problematic because departments that are at the heart of a true liberal arts education, such as philosophy, could potentially be pushed out because of a lack of majors. The refocus on profitability of majors limits student learning and can become a serious disadvantage in the global job market. The blight of administration also threatens faculty by lessening shared governance (Ginsberg, 2011a, b). These forces significantly influence faculty motivation and commitment to the institution as well as time available for students and can contribute to student cynicism, resistance, and disengagement.

In addition, the inflation of administration has likely contributed to rising student tuition over the past three decades. Between 1978 and 2008, average tuition and fees increased from $9,903 to $25,143 (College Board, 2008). Students have been relying increasingly on private loans to meet their financial obligations. About 60% of students need private loans to pay their bills, and between 2000 and 2007, the student loan debt increased by 18%. The national student loan debt was recently reported to be $17.6 billion (College Board, 2008).

A growing administration with increasing salaries also means that numbers of tenure-line faculty must decrease because the budget cannot sustain both the administrative growth and the increase in number of students who are entering the university. The lack of tenure-line faculty is compensated for by relying more on adjunct instructors, both full-time and part-time. This is true across all types of universities. According to the American Association of University Professors (2015), both part-time and full-time nontenure positions are increasing. Currently, 76% of all instructional staff at American universities are nontenure positions. Increasing the numbers of part-time faculty and decreasing the actual number of tenure-line faculty have negative consequences for all actors in the university. For instance, part-time faculty are paid only for teaching. They are not paid and do not have time to engage in service to students or the university, whether as advisers or mentors or as thesis, dissertation, or independent study supervisors. In the long run, this will negatively affect retention and graduation rates.

Part-time instructors often work for several institutions and drive from class to class in an effort to make a living. The more part-time faculty in a department, the less advising, mentoring, and involvement of students with faculty can occur, activities that enhance student engagement, reduce resistance, and promote deep learning. Fewer full-time faculty means restricted use of high-impact practices (Kuh, 2008) and teaching approaches that lead to more superficial learning, which only increases student resistance to those courses in which more active learning is promoted. The consequences of these administrative changes for students are very real and contribute to frustration and disengagement.

Anonymous Graduate Student

At this point I have taken all my graduate coursework and completed three research methods courses, but I have not been afforded the opportunity to practice what I have been taught (other than my dissertation). I have never been given real data or been given the chance to practice qualitative and quantitative data analysis. I am actually in the process of collecting data that I don't know how to analyze. I have only read about coding and themes, but I have had no hands-on experience doing it. My lack of knowledge leaves me feeling frustrated and disheartened with the possibility of completing my dissertation, fraudulent as a graduate student, and impotent and ineffectual as a researcher. This lack of guidance, mentoring, or practical knowledge has left me feeling unmotivated to continue on with this program and scared that all this hard work has left me without the requisite skills to do research and publish, which appears to be the main component to a successful career in higher education.

Increased Focus on Research and Rankings

Investigation has suggested that there also has been a shift toward increased research activity across university types (Arum & Roksa, 2011; Wilshire, 1989). The most significant result of a greater focus on research may be a growing faculty disengagement from teaching, with a subsequent increase in student disengagement. State funding of universities has decreased in all but two states (Alaska and North Carolina) in the past decade, and tuition has increased as a means to offset the budget shortfalls. For instance, in California, between 2008 and 2014, the higher education budget was cut by 15.8% per full-time student. During the same time, tuition increased $5,563 to $9,037, leading to mass student protests of outrage. In Arizona, the budget for public universities and colleges was cut by a whopping 48%, and tuition increased from $5,572 to $10,065 (Mitchell & Leachman, 2015).

As state funding for universities drops, financial stability and survival is bound to a good reputation, which is bound to a high ranking in international college ratings and to improvements in student retention. A good research reputation leads to profitable grants and endowments, without which many universities would not be functional (Price & Cotton, 2006). Colleges do not receive high rankings in these college ratings for teaching students valuable skills; instead, reputation is built primarily on research and grant monies. For example, the Quacquarelli Symonds World Academic Ranking (Quacquarelli, 2010) rates colleges according to the following criteria: 40% research quality, 20% citations per faculty, 10% student employability, 20% faculty–student ratio, 5% international student ratio, and 5% international faculty ratio. In this ranking system, 60% of the ranking depends on research productivity. Teaching quality or student learning outcomes are not even measured, although the student–teacher ratio is used as a proxy. Student–teacher ratio, however, says nothing about teaching quality and even less about student learning outcomes. If college ranking agencies give little or no weight to teaching quality and learning, why would institutions promote student learning and reward faculty who engage in high-impact practices?

Not everyone agrees with the point of view that institutions have abandoned student education. Bok (2006) has argued that these criticisms mainly target research universities, but most universities are not research institutions; most faculty work at a teaching or comprehensive university that operates under different conditions and has a more teaching-centered mission. His point of view is partially supported by studies demonstrating that most college seniors have reported a positive experience in their classes and claimed that they have substantially greater intellectual skills than they had before starting college (Pascarella & Terenzini, 1991, 2005). In fact, 77.3% of college graduates state that they enjoyed their college time, learned a lot, and would enroll in the same institution (Astin, 1993). In addition, alumni, especially from Ivy League schools, give much money and resources to their university and feel closely connected to their alma mater (Bowen & Bok, 1998). Thus, Bok (2006) has argued that the negative views of faculty are not supported when considering students' experiences: "These positive results suggest that the critics were too harsh and too one-sided in their judgments" (p. 8).

Bok's (2006) central argument was that higher education is not "broken," although he clearly acknowledged the need for improvement. We would agree with that call for improvement and note that the other data reported previously were based on the self-reports of students who had successfully graduated from college; they were not from those who dropped out in frustration or out of a sense of alienation. We also note that empirical assessments of student learning (e.g., Arum & Roksa, 2011) and ongoing dropout rates suggest that whether

or not many students are pleased with their college experience, a significant
· need for change remains. Institutional values, policies, and practices form a
critical context in which student resistance can be ameliorated or exacerbated.
We will discuss systemic opportunities for improvement in chapter 10.

Conclusion

Students who perceive their learning environment as supportive are more
likely to engage in deep learning and have better learning outcomes (Lizzio,
Wilson, & Simons, 2002). Biggs (2003) found that surface learners hold
more cynical views toward education as compared to deep learners. Poor
teaching and assessment practices are more likely to encourage surface
learning, which may increase cynicism toward the teacher and the university. Thus, students who feel that their education is not as important to the
university as advertised may develop a more cynical view toward education.
Institutional values, policies, and practices are important; they affect how
students are recruited and brought into the campus environment, interact
with student prior expectations, and shape the degree to which students feel
welcome and a part of the institution. Many of the changes in institutions
of higher education over recent decades appear to exacerbate or reinforce
existing problematic social forces, producing additional cynicism through
superficial goals disguised as genuine attempts to help students or society
and increasing pressures on faculty and students that drive tension in the
classroom and disrupt the learning environment.

If we want to change student resistance to learning, it will require more
than just personal alterations to student and professor attitudes and behaviors. It will require a change in how universities operate, how faculty are
being evaluated, and how students are treated. It will require changes to the
faculty–student ratio or to the way faculty workload is allocated to substantially increase professor accessibility, opportunities to mentor students, and
opportunities to do research with them, and it will mean a partial turn toward
a quasi-parental model again. It will require better informed administrators
and staff who understand the institution and its constituencies. It will require
that universities implement high-impact practices in most classes because a
consistent exposure across the curriculum and within programs will reduce
resistance as students come to understand these methods and experience aha
moments of learning. It will require that teaching evaluations rely on actual
teaching quality rather than more or less biased student beliefs or attempts
to influence pedagogy. It will require an honest attempt to measure learning
and increase learning. As students experience these changes toward a more
active learning university, they will become more engaged and less resistant.

The reality is that today's higher education system is not currently pointed in these directions, and students may continue to "academically drift away." Just as dealing with student resistance in our classrooms requires understanding our own biases and misconceptions in order to see what is happening, we need to learn to see the existing problematic institutional assumptions and practices that increase student resistance. We don't have to change all of these things at once—probably an impossible task—but we can identify targets and start working on those we can reach. Because universities are strongly influenced by external forces such as legislatures and other institutions, there is also a vital role in educating stakeholders in order to have a chance for success. And after all, isn't education the primary goal of a university or college?

Note

1. The student referenced gave consent for her stories to be used in this chapter but asked that her name be withheld.

References

American Association of University Professors. (2015). *Background facts on contingent faculty*. Retrieved from http://www.aaup.org/issues/contingency/background-facts

Arum, R., & Roksa, J. (2011). *Academically adrift: Limited learning on college campuses*. Chicago, IL: University of Chicago Press.

Astin, A. W. (1993). *What matters in college? Four critical years revisited* (Jossey-Bass Higher and Adult Education Series). San Francisco, CA: Jossey-Bass.

Babcock, P., & Marks, M. (2011). The falling time cost of college: Evidence from half a century of time use data. *Review of Economics and Statistics, 93*(2), 468–478.

Berger, J. B., & Braxton, J. M. (1998). Revising Tinto's interactionist theory of student departure through theory elaboration: Examining the role of organizational attributes in the persistence process. *Research in Higher Education, 39*(2), 103–119.

Berk, R. A. (2005). Survey of 12 strategies to measure teaching effectiveness. *International Journal of Teaching and Learning in Higher Education, 17*(1), 48–62.

Berk, R. A. (2006). *Thirteen strategies to measure college teaching*. Sterling, VA: Stylus.

Biggs, J. B. (2003). *Teaching for quality learning at university: What the student does*. Buckingham, UK: Society for Research into Education & Open University Press.

Bok, D. (2003). *Universities in the marketplace: The commercialization of higher education*. Princeton, NJ: Princeton University Press.

Bok, D. (2006). *Our underachieving colleges: A candid look at how much students learn and why they should be learning more*. Princeton, NJ: Princeton University Press.

Bowen, W. G., & Bok, D. (1998). *The shape of the river: Long-term consequences of considering race in college and university admission.* Princeton, NJ: Princeton University Press.

Boyer, E. (1990). *Scholarship reconsidered. Priorities of the professoriate.* Stanford, CA: Carnegie Foundation for the Advancement of Teaching.

Braxton, J. M., Sullivan, A. S., & Johnson, R. (1997). Appraising Tinto's theory of college student departure. In J. Smart (Ed.), *Higher education: Handbook of theory and research* (Vol. 12, pp. 107–164). New York, NY: Agathon.

Brint, S. (2002). The rise of the practical arts. In S. Brint (Ed.), *The future of the city of intellect: The changing American university* (pp. 222–259). Stanford, CA: Stanford University Press.

California Faculty Association. (2015). *Race to the bottom: Salary, staffing priorities, and the CSU's 1%.* Retrieved from http://www.calfac.org/race-to-the-bottom

Champbliss, D. F., & Takacs, C. G. (2014). *How college works.* Cambridge, MA: Harvard University Press.

College Board. (2008). *Trends in college pricing.* New York, NY: Author.

Felder, R. M., & Brent, M. (1996). Navigating the bumpy road to student-centered instruction. *College Teaching, 44,* 43–47.

Ginsberg, B. (2011a, September/October). Administrators ate my tuition. *Washington Monthly.* Retrieved from http://www.washingtonmonthly.com/magazine/septemberoctober_2011/features/administrators_ate_my_tuition031641.php?page=all

Ginsberg, B. (2011b). *The fall of the faculty and the rise of the all-administrative university and why it matters.* New York, NY: Oxford University Press.

Grigsby, M. (2009). *College life through the eyes of students.* Albany, NY: State University of New York Press.

Institute for Higher Education Policy. (2011). *The role of mentoring in college access and success* (Research to Practice Brief). Retrieved from http://www.ihep.org/sites/default/files/uploads/docs/pubs/the_role_of_mentoring_in_access_and_success_final_spring_2011.pdf

Jencks, C., & Riesman, D. (1968). *The academic revolution.* New York, NY: Doubleday.

King, J. E. (2007). *The American college president 2007.* Washington, DC: American Council on Education.

Kuh, G. D. (2003). What we are learning about student engagement. *Change, 35*(2), 24–32.

Kuh, G. (2008). *High-impact educational practices: What they are, who has access to them, and why they matter.* Washington, DC: Association of American Colleges and Universities.

Lizzio, A., Wilson, K., & Simons, R. (2002). University students' perceptions of the learning environment and academic outcomes: Implications for theory and practice. *Studies in Higher Education, 27*(1), 27–52.

Mangan, K. (2016, January 20). A president's plan to steer out at-risk freshman incites a campus backlash. *Chronicle of Higher Education.* Retrieved from http://chronicle.com/article/A-President-s-Plan-to-Steer/234992

McFarland, D. A. (2001). Student resistance: How the formal and informal organization of classrooms facilitate everyday forms of student resistance. *American Journal of Sociology, 107*(3), 612–678.

Mitchell, M., & Leachman, M. (2015). *Years of cuts threaten to put college out of reach for more students.* Center on Budget and Policy Priorities. Retrieved from http://www.cbpp.org/research/state-budget-and-tax/years-of-cuts-threaten-to-put-college-out-of-reach-for-more-students

National Center for Education Statistics. (2003). *Remedial education at degree-granting postsecondary institutions in fall 2000.* Washington, DC: U.S. Department of Education.

Nugent, T. T. (2009). *The impact of student-teacher interaction on student motivation and achievement* (Unpublished doctoral dissertation). University of Central Florida, Orlando, FL.

Pascarella, E. T., & Terenzini, P. T. (1991). *How college affects students: Findings and insights from twenty years of research.* San Francisco, CA: Jossey-Bass.

Pascarella, E. T., & Terenzini, P. T. (2005). How college affects students, vol. 2: A third decade of research. *Review of Higher Education, 24*(3), 339–332.

Pfaff, E., & Huddleston, P. (2003). Does it matter if I hate teamwork? What impacts student attitudes toward teamwork. *Journal of Market Education, 25*, 37–45.

Price, J., & Cotton, S. R. (2006). Teaching, research, and service: Expectations of assistant professors. *American Sociologist, 37*(1), 5–21.

Quacquarelli, N. (2010). *Rating teaching quality: Rankings methodology.* Retrieved from http://www.topuniversities.com/university-rankings-articles/world-university-rankings/rating-teaching-quality-rankings-methodology

Reyes, P., & Rincon, R. (2008). The Texas experience with accountability and student learning assessment. *New Directions for Institutional Research* (Assessment Supplement 2007), 49–58. doi: 10.1002/ir.261

Seidel, S. B., & Tanner, K. D. (2013). "What if students revolt?"—Considering student resistance: Origins, options, and opportunities for investigation. *CBE Life Science Education, 12*(4), 586–595.

Tinto, V. (1975). Dropout from higher education: A theoretical synthesis of recent research. *Review of Educational Research, 45*, 89–125.

Toward top-tier teaching. (2007, March–April). *Harvard Magazine.* Retrieved from http://harvardmagazine.com/2007/03/toward-top-tier-teaching-html

U.S. Department of Education. (2006). *A test of leadership: Charting the future of U.S. higher education.* Washington, DC: Author.

Van Note Chism, N. (1999). *Peer review of teaching: A sourcebook.* Bolton, MA: Anker Publishing.

Weimer, M. (2008). Positioning scholarly work on teaching and learning. *International Journal of Scholarship and Teaching, 2*(1), Article 4.

Wilshire, B. (1989). *The moral collapse of the university: Professionalism, purity, and alienation* (SUNY Series in Philosophy of Education). Albany, NY: State University of New York Press.

Zemsky, R., Wegner, G. R., & Massy, W. F. (2005). *Remaking the American university: Market-smart and mission-centered.* New Brunswick, NJ: Rutgers University Press.

5

SOCIETAL AND ENVIRONMENTAL INFLUENCES THAT SHAPE STUDENT MOTIVATION

Christopher Lee and Amy Lindstrom

Five minutes into the lecture the door cracks open. The seated students habitually turn toward the interruption. Instead of quickly returning their gaze back to the instructor, eyes linger on the tardy classmate as she enters. Although the instructor continues speaking, eyes follow the student as she approaches the only empty desk at the front of the neatly arranged forward-facing rows. Some look quizzically, others with seeming aversion. Sensitive to the uncomfortable attention, she makes a concerted effort to calmly blend into class once seated, immediately turning her focus onto the notebook she hurriedly pulls from her bag. Face down, hunched over her desk, she nervously scribbles, knowing that several of her peers continue to stare. As the instructor attempts to engage students with questions throughout the remainder of the class, this student remains silent, despite her competence in course content.

The non-Caucasian student, attending a large public university with a mostly Caucasian student body and wearing clothing that does not conform to the dominant religious culture, has paradoxically become accustomed to both attention and invisibility. Avoiding any spotlight, often manifested

The authors would like to acknowledge the assistance and contributions of Averie Hamilton to this chapter.

by avoidance of classroom participation, is a victory, another class period checked off, even if it means being perceived as an academic underachiever by the instructor and peers. Although this particular student is academically mature and capable of success within the academy, her avoidance of participation, due to perceived cultural and ethnic marginalization from the dominant culture and perceived stereotypes held by peers and the instructor, can function as a form of resistance and an inhibitor to active learning.

This scenario exemplifies the experience of a diverse range of minority students in higher education. These academic and socially competent students often perceive instructors, peers, and the institutional culture as threats to cultural, political, or religious identity and often respond met with decreased motivation and resistance to cultural, ethnic, or socioeconomic perceived pressures to assimilate. Additionally, many minority students, aware of long-standing and false cultural stereotypes regarding intelligence and academic performance, choose to withdraw and passively resist in an effort to avoid even the possibility of potentially playing into these stereotypes, which can negatively affect motivation and performance.

This chapter explores how elements of student identity such as race, class, and gender—among a myriad of other complicated, overlapping identities including first-generation college and nontraditional student status—can adversely influence motivation, resulting in active and passive resistance in the classroom. Through the lenses of oppositional culture theory (Fordham & Ogbu, 1986), including consideration of campus culture and stereotype threat (Steele, 1997), we explore how students of various minority statuses can participate, even subconsciously, in resistant behaviors, particularly in reaction to a hidden curriculum—that is, the unofficial and perhaps unintended lessons and values students learn in university. We conclude with practical suggestions that faculty can employ for preventing and mitigating resistant attitudes and behaviors caused by social forces. Although the impact of race, class, and gender in relation to student learning has been studied, particularly in regard to academic achievement and educational hegemony in general, little has been proposed regarding how these social forces can influence student resistance to learning in general and active learning pedagogies in particular.

Resisting Dominant Educational Norms

Hidden Curriculum

Similar to how children discern and mimic parental behavior and attitudes despite parents' overt teaching efforts (Goldberg, Gorn, Peracchio, &

Bamossy, 2003), schools transmit unintended messages to students. Considerable attention has focused on the implicit cultural and social norms that students ascertain, known as the hidden curriculum, particularly in elementary and secondary schools. Although not usually a deliberate effort by instructors or administrators to tacitly convey culturally normative messages to students, these cultural expectations and mores pervade all curricula on micro and macro levels. Understanding the hidden curriculum provides a frame through which minority student resistance—particularly in regard to race, class, and gender—can be better conceptualized. Specifically, if aspects of dominant hidden curricula conflict with cultural, racial, economic, and other identities, resistance can be a likely reaction.

While Jackson (1968) first used the term *hidden curriculum* in the context of elementary education, several other authors also contributed to the understanding of this concept (Apple, 2004; Dreeben, 1967; Durkheim, 1961; Willis, 1977), and recent scholarship has significantly influenced critical pedagogy. Giroux (2001) provided a comprehensive definition of *hidden curricula:* "unstated norms, values, and beliefs embedded in and transmitted to students through the underlying rules that structure the routines and social relationships in school and classroom" (p. 47). In the classroom, hidden curriculum manifests itself in unstated norms that govern schools, such as neatness and punctuality, on-time completion of work, rewards for exemplary work and behavior, the importance of consensus over conflict, and perhaps most significant, deference to the instructor. These expected behaviors are not systematically built into the curriculum but reflect dominant social values, such as obedience and loyalty to authority, and token reward systems prevalent in consumer culture (see chapter 6). Although not all are inherently problematic, some of these norms can result in implicit conditioning that can conflict with norms held by minority students. Class, gender, race, and sexual orientation are prime examples, as some scholars argue that upper/middle-class, patriarchal values are dominant in schools, and social inequality is, therefore, reinforced and embedded in school socialization practices through hidden curricula.

Oppositional Culture Theory

The ramifications of hidden curricula, in regard to student resistance, can be explored through oppositional culture theory (OCT), proposed by Fordham and Ogbu (1986). Originally offered to explain underperformance among black students, OCT posits that in order to avoid "acting white," black students resist the semblance of academic success because success is perceived as conforming to dominant white culture, thus acknowledging assimilation. Among other manifestations of acting white, Fordham and Ogbu (1986) found that "speaking standard English, working hard to get good grades in school, and listening to white music and radio" were considered to be a departure from black culture (p. 196).[1] Fordham and Ogbu's (1986) theory has been criticized (Foster 2004; Lundy, 2003) for oversimplifying minorities as static and, perhaps ironically, as operating under a Eurocentric frame in which white, male culture is the reference point from which "other" groups are measured. Still, Fordham and Ogbu's (1986) work has maintained its theoretical foothold and can be useful in exploring student resistance resulting from a conscious or unconscious decision to avoid acting white, male, middle/upper class, heterosexual, and so on, particularly if applied beyond the exclusivity of academic performance.

In Fordham and Ogbu's (1986) study of black students in predominantly black high schools, they claimed resistance to academic learning was common, partly because of cultural opposition. As much of the hidden curriculum reflects dominant white culture, academic achievement, defined and set by white culture, is interpreted as "becoming acculturated into the White American cultural frame of reference at the expense of [their] frame of reference and collective welfare" (p. 194). Fordham and Ogbu (1986) continued: "The perception of schooling as a subtractive process causes subordinate minorities to 'oppose' or 'resist' academic striving, both socially and psychologically" (p. 194). Fear of negative social consequences from peers in the minority group regarding assimilation contributes to collective opposition to the dominant culture, which manifests as classroom resistance to academic norms and practices.

Fordham and Ogbu (1986) studied secondary students who were arguably less motivated than black college students to learn; therefore, resistance would undoubtedly have been more apparent. Weis (1985), however, studied dominant and subordinate conflicting cultural values among black students in a college setting. Despite the desire to advance their education, students often resisted various practices. Among other examples, Weis specifically identified the concept of time as being problematic—a part of the hidden curriculum. Weis observed that students had problems arriving to class on time and concluded that time in black culture was more dynamic and fluid than the chronological, industrialized time under which the school—and the dominant culture—functioned. Because of this conflicting conception of time, or cultural assumptions about the value and significance of punctuality, and despite overall student motivation to succeed academically, students unconsciously resisted policies heavily predicated on dominant conceptions of time and punctuality. Weis studied black college students from working-class backgrounds, which may limit her conclusions to students from low-income inner cities, and her findings can't be generalized. Nonetheless, her observations serve as an example of oppositional culture leading to resistant attitudes and behaviors.

The work of Weis, Fordham, and Ogbu centered on black students opposing, to various degrees, dominant white culture in schools, partly because of perceived pressure to assimilate that posed a threat to minority identity. Huffman (2001) studied high attrition rates among American Indian college students and observed similar opposition. As the students in the study were in the minority among their peers and the institutional culture, opposition seemed exacerbated. Huffman cited a female student who expressed frustration over perceived efforts at assimilation from the university curriculum and culture:

> It is important to me to keep my Indian values and more or less put up with the non-Indian values because it is not for the non-Indian society that I am trying to get a degree. Do you understand? . . . It is hard to be an American Indian in a world that thinks that you should adjust to their type of a culture. It makes me angry at the closed minds of people who will not open their eyes to let the Indian people be who they were born to be. (p. 14)

The student isn't explicit about resisting specific institutional or classroom practices, and she seems to conceptualize identity as being inherent. However, it's clear that this oppositional mentality can lead to classroom resistance, especially given the psychological pressure of negotiating a bicultural identity in order to be academically successful.

Working-class students can also exhibit cultural opposition as explored by Willis (1977). Willis studied students transitioning into working-class jobs in the United Kingdom and proposed that these students viewed academic achievement as conformance to an upper-class, demasculinized culture and a negation of one's cultural identity (similar to "acting white"). Students perceived their transition into working-class jobs as a conscious rejection of upper-class values. Willis also proposed that schools subtly reproduce socioeconomic stratification through the hidden curriculum. In other words, the way schools functioned seemed to cater differently to upper/middle- and working-class students, perpetuating class hierarchy. Aynyon (1981) took this hypothesis further in U.S. studies finding that "while there were similarities in curriculum topics and materials, there were also subtle, as well as dramatic, differences in the curriculum and the curriculum-in-use among the schools" (p. 4). Aynyon, building off the work of Bowles and Gintes (1976), confirmed that certain kinds of knowledge are made available to upper-class students (managerial, legal, medical), whereas working-class students are taught vocational knowledge (clerical, manual skills). Furthermore, entire schools may serve one model or the other depending on the student socioeconomic demographic.

Many students from working-class backgrounds enroll in college to climb the socioeconomic ladder, but they may still reject conforming to upper/middle-class educational norms. Given the work of Willis and Aynyon (who also studied postsecondary students), it's reasonable to extrapolate that students from working-class backgrounds may view their courses, instructors, and peers as trying to "enlighten them" through prevailing dominant values of liberal, Western education. If these students are primarily motivated by the promise of a higher paying job through a degree, much of what is done in the classroom may seem irrelevant. They may accept the economic promises of higher education but reject any accompanying demands of liberal education, especially if there is pressure from home not to "sell out" their cultural identity. The situation may be more problematic if students come from working-class schools (as described by Aynyon) and transition into a postsecondary institution that is primarily centered on more classical and liberal theoretical knowledge. This may affect student expectations and motivation in a way that frustrates academic performance.

Potential opposition can also arise in reaction to institutional and classroom norms related to gender. Historically, education in the United States slowly shifted from exclusive male admission into a strong cultural discouragement of women seeking education. Harvard professor Edward Clarke (1873) advocated that women were physiologically and psychologically incapable of dealing with the stresses of college because they "lose health, strength, blood, and nerve, by a regimen that ignores the . . . reproductive apparatus of their organization" (p. 129). Academic performance, therefore, was a threat to the domestic and reproductive role of women. Thankfully, the treatment of women in higher education has progressed since Clarke, but part of the hidden curriculum still maintains patriarchal norms, manifesting as gender bias. Sadker and Sadker (1994) chronicled instances of gender bias in elementary schools, observing that teachers called on boys more frequently than girls and gave boys more precise and helpful feedback. They claimed that societal gender inequality in the workplace can be traced back to gender bias in the elementary classroom.

College admission practices and standardized tests have been shown to reinforce gender biases. Boys, for example, tend to score higher on the SAT, which originated as a military sorting mechanism and aptitude placement screen. Research from the 1980s and 1990s suggested that testing format, time limit, penalization for guessing, and content (among many other hypotheses) seem to unintentionally favor men. Furthermore, standardized tests—most notably the SAT—consistently underpredict female academic performance relative to men (Leonard & Jiang, 1999; Rosser, 1989; Wilder and Powell, 1989). Female students aware of the ongoing discussion of gender bias on college entrance exams have considerable reason to question instructional practices when the very gatekeepers to these institutions seem to perpetuate gender bias.

Enrolled female students may also experience gender bias. Recent studies suggest professors may express gender and ethnicity bias even when responding to student e-mails. Milkman, Akinola, and Chugh (2012) designed a study in which fictitious e-mails from potential doctoral students with obvious ethnic and gender identifiers were sent to over 6,000 professors, inquiring about individual meetings. When professors were asked for appointments a week in advance, "Caucasian males were granted access to faculty members 26% more often than were women and minorities. . . . Caucasian males received more and faster responses" (p. 710).[2]

Most discussion of gender bias in postsecondary education centers on traditionally male-dominated disciplines. McLoughlin (2013) discussed gender bias in engineering in the context of singling out females, which she called "spotlighting." She described three types of spotlighting: overt sexism, tacit sexism, and what could be termed *benevolent sexism* (singling out females with the intention to help them). Female survey respondents indicated that benevolent spotlighting was the most common, generating unease and discomfort; ironically, this type of behavior reinforces the inequalities it attempts to quell. One student reported, "Sometimes I feel people try to make things easier for me because I'm a girl, but I never try to take advantage of that; however, I feel that many girls . . . take advantage of their 'girl-ness,' both with their professors and with other students" (quoted in McLoughlin, 2013, p. 375). Benevolent sexism can negatively influence self-esteem (female students begin to question their ability) and lead to resistant behaviors in an effort to remain out of the spotlight; it can also snowball when male students in the classroom perceive an imbalance that seems to favor women over men. Thus, gender bias that takes the shape of spotlighting seems to have adverse consequences for both female and male students, even if intentions are positive. Female students who perceive male-dominated norms in programs or classes, implicit and explicit, may behave in passive and active opposition.

Whether centered on race, class, or gender, oppositional culture theory is one explanation that can aid in understanding why and how students of minority status may resist learning at the college level. Although macro in scope, conceptualizing OCT on a micro, classroom level may help instructors to become more aware of classroom practices and procedures that reflect dominant hidden curricular norms, which may function to generate resistance from some minority students.

Chris Lee

In teaching freshman composition courses, I often assign readings that present new and challenging ideas to unseasoned college students, which frequently— and ideally—result in engaging class discussions. One reading in particular often contests common student perspectives regarding gender and sexuality. Specifically, the author calls for a reexamination of dominant societal sexual mores, arguing that the promotion of virginity and chastity among young women in the United States is destructive and misplaces genuine self-worth. For many socially conservative students, the piece is often perceived as abrasive. Although the purpose of these discussions is ultimately directed toward argument analysis, initial class discussion regarding the topic of the reading can be both useful and thought-provoking, particularly when a diverse range of student perspectives are present.

In one course a few years ago, I was excited about the discussion of this reading as the students in that class had an unusual rapport with each other and me, which elevated discussion and inquiry. The conversation was indeed engaging. When one perspective seemed to dominate, a class member would provide a new or competing perspective to keep the discussion from turning stale. When disagreements arose, students were diplomatic. It was a snapshot of how discussion should function, and I try to replicate it (often unsuccessfully). Despite the model success of this particular discussion, I wondered how much better it could have been if one of the strongest and most critically reflective students hadn't missed that day.

I found it odd, and somewhat suspicious, that this particular student was absent that day, given an otherwise perfect attendance record. Despite my best efforts to avoid prodding, I e-mailed the student and indicated that we all missed out on his perspective and that I was sorry he didn't, or couldn't, attend the day of the reading discussion. He promptly replied, relating that he was sick and simply not up to it that day. He apologized and said he wished he could have made it. Before I had a chance to respond, he sent me another e-mail, this time acknowl-edging that he wasn't actually sick. To paraphrase, he expressed to me his concern about participating in a discussion about a relatively sensitive, if not controver-sial, issue on which he knew he would hold a minority opinion, especially given the local cultural geography. He feared that his opinion would reflect elements of his identity that he didn't want paraded in front of his peers and that, even just in the short term, it would negatively affect the class's cohesive community. In fact, this student read the article and was eager to discuss it but felt that the risks were greater than the rewards of attending class. He even offered to meet and discuss the article with me as assurance that he wasn't simply trying to duck out of the assigned reading.

The fact that his potential fear never registered on my radar was frustrating and somewhat embarrassing as I naively assumed that I had facilitated a diverse and inclusive class, eradicating any level of social discomfort. Although my first instinct was to classify his fear as unfounded and unfair to his peers, his concern was legitimate and, according to the student, based on previous experience in other classes. When he was outspoken about an issue he found himself in the minority on, the social consequences weren't worth it. He explicitly expressed that his minority status in regard to sexual orientation sometimes made for uncomfortable, borderline hostile, classroom interactions and that it was better to simply avoid them if possible.

Although not actively resistant, this student chose to avoid collaborative discussion in a more passive way. The dominant heteronormative culture provided instances of potential discomfort, and simply the threat of negative interactions was enough to discourage participation in classroom engagement.

A Disconnect in Discourse

Related to oppositional culture but more specific is the disconnect that many students face—again, exacerbated among minority students—when entering college unaware of institutional "rules" regarding discourse and literacy. Universities function around monolinguistic academic language and norms seemingly inaccessible to students who are never explicitly taught how to navigate academia; rather, *academic discourse*, defined by White and Lowenthal (2010) as "the specific yet tacit discursive style expected of participants in the academy" (p. 284), is further complicated by the variations among disciplines and can act as a barrier leading to resistance in the classroom. White and Lowenthal claimed that literacy is not simply an impartial, procedural skill but is imbued with ideological and cultural significance, "enmeshed in power relations and situated in specific cultural meanings and practices" (p. 288). In other words, literacy is highly contextual and fluid rather than objectively static.

White and Lowenthal (2010) posited that because language is inseparably connected to culture, minority students adhere to their own native and familiar language practices, which may prevent academic success.[3] Learning academic literacy is not only difficult but also often overtly resisted to avoid assimilating into the dominant culture at the expense of abandoning one's existing culture (similar to Fordham and Ogbu's [1986] observations). Even students who learn to code-switch in order to be academically successful feel they are selling out their true culture. White and Lowenthal cited a study in which a Native American student indicated his frustration with academic literacy: "I just don't want to participate [in class] because I don't want to be judged. I guess if I was more confident, like, in how I talked, if I felt safer, I would talk more" (quoted in White & Lowenthal, 2010, p. 298). This student's act of passive resistance resulted from the disconnect between his native literacy and the literacy necessary for academic inclusion and achievement.

Students like this, according to White and Ali-Kahn (2013), prefer large lecture classes because the expectation to verbally participate in class is significantly reduced. White (2011) studied minority students in the context of discussion-based classroom participation and found that participants demonstrated reluctance to speak because of a perceived sense of exclusion from academic discourse, despite awareness that their grades would be negatively affected. Adding to the burden was the sense that these students, aware that they were in the minority, were somehow responsible for speaking on behalf of their representative cultures. Minority students viewed participation as a punishment rather than an opportunity to voice opinions. One student reported, "I feel a lot of intimidation from them [his peers and professors] because of how different I am from them, how I talk and all. . . . *I came here* [to college] *not speaking the language of everyone else* [emphasis added]" (quoted in White, 2011, p. 257). Another student said, "It just doesn't feel right, like to have to talk that way. . . . I shouldn't have to change who I am, or the way I talk to make them happy" (quoted in White, 2011, p. 259). Whether students lack discursive confidence or are more acutely aware of cultural linguistic differences, the result, as found by White, can result in classroom resistance, such as avoidance of engaged classroom discussions as described previously.

The Effect of Campus Climate

Negative classroom experiences can contribute to student resistance (see chapter 7). When students feel marginalized from the campus community, whether perception or reality, they may socially withdraw, and in a class involving peer collaboration, this could take the form of resistance. Although this can be true for students of all backgrounds, minority students are affected more frequently and more severely. Student resistance in postsecondary education, particularly in regard to race, class, gender, or sexual orientation, can result from the general campus climate—as well as that of the classroom—which is often culturally at odds with minorities. Rankin (2005) defined *campus climate* as "the cumulative attitudes, behaviors and standards of employees and students concerning access for, inclusion of, and level of respect for individual and group needs, abilities and potential" (p. 17). Race is particularly prominent, although gender, class, and certainly sexual orientation can be situated alongside.

A significant body of scholarship has demonstrated a mismatch in perceived campus climate, in regard to race, between minority students and majority student populations, faculty, and administration. Rankin and Reason (2005), studying instances and perceptions of racial harassment on many college campuses, reported that significantly more students of color perceived the campus as "racist," "hostile," and "disrespectful" than their white counterparts did. Conversely, a higher proportion of white students viewed the campus climate as "nonracist," "friendly," and "respectful" (p. 52). The ratio was paralleled when students were asked about personal experiences involving harassment.[4] This disconnect in perceptions of racist attitudes on campus confirms what antiracism activist Tim Wise described when he spoke at a Minnesota university. Upon greeting the administrators, Wise was told, "Tim, we're very glad you're here for our diversity day. But we do think you should know, we don't have any racism at our school" (Wise, 2006). This postrace mentality continues to pervade universities, but how common is racism in higher education? Kent (1996) claimed that campuses tend to reflect the racial climate of society and that racist attitudes are very much a part of higher education. Kent noted:

> Since most campuses don't provide a supportive infrastructure, and have a generally unfavorable racial climate, African-Americans increasingly form their own campus enclaves. "It's a Black thing. You wouldn't understand," read the t-shirts worn by college students, who increasingly choose to segregate themselves from whites in dormitories. (p. 92)

Other racial minority students face similar campus climates. Marcus and colleagues (2003) found that college campuses are not immune to racism, which can occur "in all aspects of campus life including admissions, curriculum, sports, social interaction, and residence halls" (p. 611). Sydell and Nelson (2000) specifically discussed indirect racist beliefs on campuses. Even attempts to learn about other cultures (art, food, literature, etc.) can be perceived as shallow attempts that reinforce the falseness of postrace ideology on college campuses.

Sexual minority students face particular challenges with acceptance into campus culture. Rankin (2005) reported that "despite [LGBT] initiatives, LGBT people fear for their safety, keep their identities secret, experience harassment, and feel that their universities are unsupportive of LGBT people" (p. 20). Many of the universities studied self-identified as being proactive in generating a climate more accepting of LGBT students, yet perceptions and occurrences of discrimination were apparent. Tetreault, Fette, Meidlinger, and Hope (2013) reported that, in addition to struggling with campus climate, many LGBT students considered leaving campus due to perceived or experienced hostility. The combination of unfair treatment by instructors, anti-LGBT bias from peers, and the feeling that they had to hide their identity from others caused psychological stress and negatively influenced performance and psychosocial well-being.

Although institutional programs have worked to mitigate unfriendly climates and improve inclusion, females and others may still face unwelcoming campus and classroom climates, in subtle ways. Vaccaro (2010) reported that although female faculty, students, and staff indicated no overt hostility in their campus climate, all three groups expressed a desire for deeper dialogue regarding diversity, beyond just tolerance. One respondent said, "The University still has a long way to go in terms of developing a healthy campus climate" (quoted in Vaccaro, 2010, p. 206). Female subjects reported hearing disparaging remarks about parenting and pregnancy and often felt devalued, disrespected, and underpaid. Vaccaro also noted that students with conservative political and religious views felt marginalized by what they viewed as dominant liberal bias. "Their experiences were in stark contrast to men's perspectives" (p. 212). This could further harm campus climate if students view others as the privileged majority, negatively affecting active learning environments and collaborative classrooms.

If minority students feel marginalized, whether because of their perceptions or actual experiences, they may be less likely to engage in collaborative classrooms because they lack social confidence or are angry. Innovative pedagogies that are learner centered and provide students more autonomy and opportunities for proactive participation may be met with resistance from minority students who lack a sense of inclusion in class and the university at large.

Stereotype Threat

In the 1960s, Jane Elliot demonstrated how expectations influence student behavior and resistance by dividing her classroom into blue- and brown-eyed students (Peters, Cobb, & Peters, 1985). On the first day, she told the children that blue-eyed students outperform brown-eyed students in school achievement, IQ, and behavior at home; they were the superior students. She also told them that brown-eyed students struggle and do worse in the classroom and in behavior. Throughout the day, blue-eyed students embraced their superiority though volunteering answers, participating, engaging in discussion, and putting down the brown-eyed students. The brown-eyed students became withdrawn, and their scores fell below their baseline scores. The next day, Elliot told the students she had been mistaken and that brown-eyed students were superior. As expected, the effects of previous day reversed. The students' performance and resistance were heavily influenced by the classroom cultural expectations and stereotypes, though they were completely fabricated.

The fear of potential academic and social exclusion underpins motivational problems that can result in resistance to active pedagogies. A useful theory to enhance understanding of the dynamics of motivation and resistance in conjunction with social and environmental factors is what Steele (1997) coined as *stereotype threat*. Alongside Aronson (Steele & Aronson, 1995), Steele defined this as "being at risk of confirming, as self-characteristic, a negative stereotype about one's group" (p. 797). Farr (2003) described it as "the pressure individuals may feel when at risk of confirming, or being seen by others as confirming," the negative stereotypes associated with one's group (p. 179). Simple awareness of a group's negative stereotype is believed to be threatening enough to disrupt performance and is exacerbated by the sense that one's individual confirmation is seen as representative of everyone in their group (Steele & Aronson, 1995).

Steele (2010) described an example of stereotype threat experienced by a white student in an African American political science class, in which he and one other were the only nonblack students out of 45. The student immediately felt out of place, despite his desire to broaden his knowledge, and questioned his decision to enroll in the class. His anxiety rose as students discussed African American history in the South and instances of oppression. In particular, the student noted the collective use of *we* among most students, a pronoun than made him feel further out of place. In an interview with Steele, the student explained that some in the class claimed that "White people try to avoid this part of history" and "White people don't want to take responsibility for these transgressions" (p. 85). Subsequently, he felt pressure to prove himself a nonracist, adding to the pressure of academic success. Steele (2010) explained:

> In class, he felt he was multitasking. He was involved . . . but he also worried that perhaps his statements, even his thoughts, would confirm the suspicion over his head. He kept his comments at the "tip of the iceberg" level, trying to be inoffensive—for example, saying out loud in class that he really liked the civil rights leader Bayard Rustin, while keeping to himself his ignorance about exactly what Rustin's role in the civil rights movement was. He noticed the same thing in the other whites. (p. 85)

Steele's observations of this student's experience is one example of how stereotype threat contributes to student resistance, particularly the self-protective type (chapter 1). The student admitted to Steele in an interview that he felt that the tension he experienced was interfering with his learning and feared his lack of understanding was born of his own bias. He was concerned that his "thinking was unknowingly contaminated by prejudice, stereotypes, or just naïveté" (Steele, 2010, p. 87). Even alone in his dorm room the threat pervaded his mind and caused him to deeply question himself.

Ted's experience in this class—his lack of participation, his self-consciousness, his hesitancy in thinking about the material, his lower-than-usual performance—would seem to reflect a threat similar to that experienced by women taking a difficult math test, or by blacks taking a difficult academic test of any sort. (p. 88)

Stereotype threat has been shown to affect the intellectual performance of different groups, but the phenomenon can affect anyone from a group with negative stereotypes.

Testing Stereotype Threat

Steele and Aronson (1995) performed four studies that tested the stereotype of black intellectual ability. In the first, they divided black and white college students into three groups. Each group took a 30-minute test with items from the verbal Graduate Record Examination (GRE). The questions were difficult enough to be at the limit of most participants' skill level. In the stereotype threat group, the test was described as diagnostic of intellectual ability, activating the racial stereotype about blacks demonstrating lower intellectual abilities and establishing the threat of fulfilling it. In the non–stereotype threat group, the test was described as a laboratory problem-solving task that was unrelated to ability. This was aimed at removing the threat of confirming the negative stereotype. The third group was also advised that this was a test that would not diagnose ability, but they were strongly encouraged to see the test as a challenge.

As predicted, black students showed lower scores in the group told they were taking a diagnostic test due to the stress of confirming the negative stereotype about their intelligence. Black students in the nondiagnostic groups had scores consistent with the white students. This confirmed that stereotype threat had influenced the test results of black students in the first group. Steele and Aronson completed three more studies addressing concerns or assumptions made during the first study. In the end, the conclusion remained: Black students who had been told the test would measure their intelligence consistently showed lower test results than the white students, whereas the black students in the other two groups who were told that the test was not diagnostic tested at the same level as the white students in their groups.

This study is one of many evaluating how stereotype threat causes anxiety and lowers academic performance. For example, Fogliati and Bussey (2013) showed how stereotype threat impaired performance and reduced motivation and self-esteem in female math students in comparison to male test takers when they activated the stereotype that women are not good at math; stereotype threat plays a role in academia and beyond.

Results of Stereotype Threat in the Classroom

In education environments, the anxiety of inadvertently substantiating a stereotype can lower test performance in particular ways (Steel, 1992, 1997; Steele & Aronson, 1998; Steele, Spencer, & Aronson, 2002). For instance, studies have indicated that the stress caused by stereotype threat reduces working memory capacity (Schmader, 2010; Schmader & Johns, 2003; Schmader, Johns, & Forbes, 2008), the ability to focus one's attention on a task while ignoring task-irrelevant thoughts (Engle, 2002). Johns, Inzlicht, and Schmader (2008) conducted a study revealing that individuals who experience anxiety or stress as a result of stereotype threat often try to regulate or suppress the emotion, which taxes the memory used to study or to take an exam.

Student retention is also affected by stereotype threat. Johnson-Ahorlu (2013), quoting the U.S. Department of Education, stated, "African Americans have one of the lowest retention and degree completion rates nationwide with only 42% earning their bachelor's degree within six years. The national average is 57%" (p. 382). The University of California, Los Angeles Higher Education Research Institute conducted a project involving seven two- and four-year institutions. The goal was to collect data via student surveys and focus groups in order to comprehend how multiple factors, such as campus climate, campus policies, or curricular and cocurricular environments, interact with and affect student outcomes (Hurtado, Alvarez, Guillermo-Wann, Cuellar, & Arellano, 2012). African American students reported explicitly that stereotypes and stereotype threat are the biggest barrier to their academic success.

Resistance, or lack of engagement, resulting from stereotype threat among minority students can emerge in many different ways. Students may resist engagement in group activities, afraid they will not fit in, or, more commonly, fear that by linking themselves to the group, they will lose part of their own identity or be seen as "selling out." Students may also self-handicap, a defense mechanism in which individuals erect barriers to performance to provide explanations for failure. If these barriers undermine student performance, they may point to the barriers rather than deficiencies in ability in order to protect themselves from proving that a stereotype is correct. For example, Keller (2002) showed that girls who performed poorly on a math test under stereotype threat were more likely to claim that they were experiencing stress before taking the test. Steele and Aronson (1995) found African American students under stereotype threat also produced excuses for possible failure. When asked to indicate race on a demographics questionnaire, 75% of black participants did not do so following the test.

Perhaps revisiting the story of the white student in the African American political science class serves best in demonstrating how stereotype threat plays a role in class resistance. The student was a self-motivated, bright student; however, in his African American political science class, he struggled to understand concepts, kept his questions to himself, and didn't participate in discussion. He was the minority in this classroom. In his other classes, the African American students were the minority and engaged less, generally keeping to themselves; however, in this classroom, where they held the majority, they were fully engaged. It is vital that instructors understand these patterns to avoid labeling and to determine how best to help students learn.

Methods of Reducing Resistance

Underrepresented Students

As illustrated by Chris's story, instructors need to be aware of students who are in the minority in a class or who may even perceive themselves to be of minority status in some way. Instructors also need to become aware of their own implicit biases that shape expectations and classroom practices and that require critical reflection in order to avoid what King (1991) termed *dysconscious racism*, which is "an uncritical habit of mind (including perceptions, assumptions, behaviors, and beliefs) that justifies inequality and exploitation by accepting the existing order of things as given" (p. 135).

Awareness and sensitivity to institutional and classroom norms that may be at odds with the cultural backgrounds of students need to be embedded into curriculum and pedagogy, and particular effort is needed in not diluting diversity down to rather shallow discussion points like ethnic cuisine and dress. Additionally, the spotlighting of minority students ("Alicia, you're Latina; can you share with us how Latinos would respond . . . ?") in the name of inclusion can be counterproductive. This mentality often exacerbates the very stereotypes that faculty are trying to dispel and places an unreasonable burden on students already struggling with inclusion. In 2008, before his election, candidate Obama was asked about his relationship to the black community. He responded that he was "rooted in the black community, but not limited to it" (Coates, 2012). Instructors need to be aware that identity is complex and that reducing students to simplistic labels and unconsciously prioritizing certain forms of identity over others without student acknowledgment can be harmful and even enhance resistance.

The multicultural education literature may serve as a starting point when institutional initiatives or programs fall short. The *International Journal of Multicultural Education* includes promising research in the field as well as specific practices. Drawing from a range of pedagogies aimed at uncovering and challenging dominant cultural norms and utilizing meaningfully inclusive instructional practices (beyond counterproductive notions of "color blindness") can also aid in potentially preventing resistance or intervening when resistance occurs. Mun Wah (2012) warned that, for minorities, common and simplistic notions of multiculturalism often translate into the dominant culture making all decisions about programs, procedures, and content. True multiculturalism, he explained, means "having a relationship based on a willingness to not only stay in the room when a conflict occurs, but to hear and value what is not working and to see that as an opportunity and not a threat" (p. 1). Critical, feminist, queer, and critical literacy pedagogies, among others, are based on theories that seek to remedy cultural and institutional hegemony and provide a truly multicultural classroom.

Equity pedagogy may be particularly relevant and was defined by Banks and Banks (1995) as "teaching strategies and classroom environments that help students from diverse racial, ethnic, and cultural groups attain the knowledge, skills, and attitudes needed to function effectively within . . . a democratic society" (p. 152). Equity pedagogy, which includes complex contextual factors and maintenance of an inclusive environment, offers an alternative to what many faculty seem to dilute into equality of outcome, wherein all are assigned equal outcomes without consideration of individual and cultural differences. Equity, in contrast, focuses on *quality* of outcome.

Equity pedagogy aligns particularly well with active learning and engaged practices because it seeks to empower students of all backgrounds to be active participants in knowledge creation rather than passive observers and regurgitators, creating "an environment in which students can acquire, interrogate, and produce knowledge and envision new possibilities for use of that knowledge for social change" (Banks & Banks, 1995, p. 153). Students are taught to examine and question the pervasive existing power structures, what Paulo Freire referred to as "problematization" (Freire, 1968). For example, in a literature course, rather than having students simply read classic literature and memorize the instructor's "correct" interpretation, students could be asked, "What qualifies as 'classic' literature? Who decides on the canon that is compiled and taught in schools? What is excluded, and how do these exclusions reflect current implicit sociocultural norms?" Hidden curriculum is exposed and examined, providing opportunities for underrepresented and majority students alike to reflect on their role in dominant power structures and discuss methods of balancing power. This level of inclusion can open students up to critical discussions about systemic inequality rather than passively or actively resisting classroom practices they perceive as perpetuating inequality.

Implementation of equity pedagogy (and others with similar goals) can't be reduced to a set of prescribed strategies; rather, it's a pedagogical orientation that involves constant self-reflection on the instructor's own position and an understanding of implicit dominant institutional norms that often marginalize students of different ethnicity, gender, and class, including choice of text and reading materials, assignments, and other course elements.[5] This requires the competency to "make an informed decision about when to use culturally sensitive pedagogy, and decide when to focus on the individual characteristics of students" (Banks & Banks, 1995, p. 157), without calling on students to act as single spokespersons for their groups. Even so, specific practices can assist in implementing pedagogies to empower students and mitigate resistance. For example, even discussing the standard seating arrangement of straight rows facing the instructor can be a way into uncovering hidden assumptions about power and the implicit roles of students and instructors. Instructors can also openly ask students for other examples of hidden assumptions manifested in specific educational practices or procedures in order to assist students in problematizing and taking ownership over their education.

As described in other chapters, resistance is a communicative act, an outcome of interacting internal and external elements. Some exhibitions of resistant behavior may result from students seeking autonomy or individuation. It is possible that not all resistant attitudes should necessarily be repressed or controlled but perhaps channeled to meaningful and productive conversations about the nature of power, learning, and identity. Various pedagogies provide useful frames through which this may happen. These pedagogies can also help raise student metacognitive awareness regarding their own resistant attitudes, what causes them, and whether or not they inhibit, or in some cases assist, genuine learning.

Improving Classroom Climate

Strategies for mitigating resistance at the campus level are explored in chapter 10; however, instructors can build on and contribute to positive inclusion efforts in how they handle the microcosm of the campus climate in the classroom. For instance, faculty can create a community of learners from the start of the semester rather than maintain a status quo of passive learners. Facilitating an active learning environment opens the door for more instances of prejudice and bias from students; however, open discussion at the beginning of the semester to augment explicit syllabus expectations about civility and respect can help mitigate problems. In order for an inclusive classroom climate to be established and maintained, instructors need to be culturally literate and acknowledge that forms of discrimination are prevalent both institutionally and at the classroom level. Instructors need to be equipped to facilitate discussions about racism and other forms of discrimination, particularly when racist or offensive speech surfaces. A lengthy discussion of how instructors can effectively broach these challenging topics is beyond this chapter's scope; however, there are a wealth of research-based resources to aid instructors in negotiating difficult dialogues in class, which is an important skill for instructors in all disciplines.

Kite and colleagues (2013) provided over 60 pages of classroom activities, worksheets, and discussion points to help students understand and negotiate prejudice and discrimination as well as examine existing biases that may contribute to problems in the class, even (perhaps especially) in classrooms that may be lacking in diversity. These activities are accompanied by references providing theoretical support and assisting students to deeply reflect on potential hidden biases and assumptions. For example, one such activity calls on students to think of an instance in which they would identify themselves as being in the minority in some capacity, allowing students to empathetically think about marginalization and how subtle forms of discrimination can further disenfranchise underrepresented students. Many faculty development centers in universities and colleges provide resources for creating an inclusive classroom environment. A common thread throughout these resources is openly discussing these issues in a nonthreatening but assertive way. Starting the semester by allowing students to interact beyond a superficial level can ease these potentially uncomfortable conversations about prejudice and discrimination.

Reducing Stereotype Threat

Since it was first conceptualized, researchers have examined methods to alleviate the effects of stereotype threat. Much of this research has focused on variables that may influence the individual's perceptions. For example, Marx and Roman (2002) found that exposure to, interaction with, or knowledge about competent female role models mediated poor test performance and perceptions of weaker math ability for women. Aronson, Fried, and Good (2002) found that when they persuaded students to view intelligence as malleable, both black and white students were able to achieve higher grade point averages and reported greater engagement in and enjoyment of the academic process. Martens, Johns, Greenberg, and Schimel (2006) discovered that when stereotype-threatened women used self-affirmations before taking a math test, they achieved scores similar to nonthreatened women and men. Making a concerted effort to discuss and remedy common misconceptions of ability and intelligence may help students to question the validity of cultural stereotypes and feel empowered to rise above them.

In all disciplines, early and open discussions about the nature of intelligence and ability can provide a foundation to empower students to view ability as contingent on effort rather than as innate. This relates to the work of Carol Dweck, discussed in more detail in chapter 9. Another practical approach is for instructors to model their own growth, over time, beginning with initial failures and subsequent setbacks, perhaps in teaching and research. An English instructor could demonstrate the process of revision by showing students their flawed written work (or perhaps an early syllabus) and demonstrating the process of improving the quality of their thinking and writing in the face of obstacles, possibly including negative stereotypes about a specific part of their identities. This kind of modeling can be invaluable to students who lack confidence in their abilities and can be an effective catalyst for discussions about intelligence.

Additionally, instructors can alleviate potential stereotype threat with equitable, consistent, and clear expectations by communicating the reality that all students regardless of background have the capabilities to succeed academically. Unfortunately, some instructors exacerbate stereotype threat when negative expectations are implicitly or explicitly communicated to students, particularly those who are underrepresented. Drakeford (2015) argued, "Racial stereotypes have a profound impact on the schooling experiences of students of color. These stereotypes not only influence teachers' appraisal and response to the behavior of students of different races but also alter the climate in the classroom by establishing a basis for differential expectations and stereotype threat" (p. 173).

Good (1987) found that low expectations, most often attributed to minorities (or "low-achievers"), were manifested by instructors calling on minority students less, giving them less time to respond, praising them less frequently, seating them further from the instructor, and generally expecting less from them. To combat the effects of unequal treatment based on teachers' negative expectations, Good suggested classroom practices that align well with active learning approaches, including allowing students to more actively engage in their own assessment of learning objectives; providing opportunities for more active participation in their own learning; and pushing students beyond factual content knowledge into analysis, synthesis, and evaluation.

Conclusion

Most causes of resistance described in this chapter are evident in traditional lecture-based classes as well as active learning classes. Instructors teaching a lecture class may not notice student resistance, however, because students are not expected to actively participate. When instructors use high-impact practices like collaborative, service, problem-based, or inquiry-based learning, resistant behaviors are more visible due to oppositional culture, hostile or unaccommodating campus climate, and stereotype threat. Resistance could be exacerbated because these practices require students to take an active role in their own education and create interaction rather than simply receiving content. Collaborative teaching practices provide opportunities for exposure to different beliefs and background, which can be productive if designed and coordinated intentionally (versus having students loosely group up). Additionally, many engaged learning practices involve peer collaboration, which can increase student fears or frustrations with feeling in the spotlight. Examining how external social forces connect to perceptions of identity and how they interact with motivation and resistance can help instructors in preventing and mitigating (or channeling, as the case may be) resistance in the classroom.

Notes

1. To explain why some minorities succeed academically, Ogbu, as referenced by Foster (2004), differentiated between voluntary and involuntary minorities. African Americans are an involuntary minority; they never chose to immigrate to the United States (enslavement). Asian Americans are voluntary minorities because they, generally, chose to immigrate. Voluntary minorities perform better because they more readily accept dominant norms of academic achievement; a primary motive for migration was the chance of economic upward mobility.

2. It should be noted that instances of bias decreased when students (female and ethnic) inquired about a same-day meeting. The authors attribute this to the psychological concept of temporal discrimination effect, in which objects and events at a distance become conceptualized more abstractly (see "construal level theory").

3. White and Lowenthal acknowledged the narrowness of the current state of academic discourse in higher education (which they claimed is part of the hidden curriculum) and called for a more inclusive discourse (new literacy studies) that allows multicultural participation without coercion into the dominant model.

4. White female responses aligned more with students of color (rather than white males) on perceptions and experiences with harassment. Additionally, of respondents who indicated that they were subjected to harassment in the form of physical violence, 82% were female.

5. Although this section has focused on humanities and social sciences, instructors in fields such as the sciences, business, and others can consider common stereotypes and dominant norms in their fields, recognize the contributions of minorities to the discipline, and acknowledge the hidden curriculum as well as identify other useful ways to implement equity pedagogies.

References

Apple, M. W. (2004). *Ideology and curriculum.* London, UK: Routledge & Kegan Paul.

Aronson, J., Fried, C. B., & Good, C. (2002). Reducing the effects of stereotype threat on African American college students by shaping theories of intelligence. *Journal of Experimental Social Psychology, 38,* 113–125.

Aynyon, J. (1981). Social class and school knowledge. *Curriculum Inquiry, 11*(1), 3–42.

Banks, C. A., & Banks, J. A. (1995). Equity pedagogy: An essential component of multicultural education. *Theory Into Practice, 34*(3), 152–158.

Bowles, S., & Gintes, H. (1976). *Schooling in capitalist America: Educational reform and the contradictions of economic life.* New York, NY: Basic Books.

Clarke, E. H. (1873). *Sex in education, or, A fair chance for the girls.* Boston, MA: J. Osgood.

Coates, T. (2012, October 18). The burden of a black president. *The Atlantic.* Retrieved from http://www.theatlantic.com/politics/archive/2012/10/the-burden-of-a-black-president/263775/

Drakeford, L. D. (2015). *The race controversy in American education* (Vol. 1). Santa Barbara, CA: Preager.

Dreeben, R. (1967). *On what is learned in school.* London, UK: Addison-Wesley.

Durkheim, E. (1961). *Moral education.* New York, NY: Free Press.

Engle, R. W. (2002). Working memory capacity as executive attention. *Current Directions in Psychological Science, 11,* 19–23.

Farr, J. L. (2003). Introduction to the special issue: Stereotype threat effects in employment settings. *Human Performance, 16*(3), 179–180.

Fogliati, V. J., & Bussey, K. (2013). Stereotype threat reduces motivation to improve: Effects of stereotype threat and feedback on women's intentions to improve mathematical ability. *Psychology of Women Quarterly, 37*(3), 310–324.

Fordham, F., & Ogbu, J. (1986). Black students' school success: Coping with the burden of "acting white." *Urban Review, 18*(3), 189–207.

Foster, K. M. (2004). Coming to terms: A discussion of John Ogbu's cultural-ecological theory of minority academic achievement. *Intercultural Education, 15*(4), 369–384.

Freire, P. (1968). *Pedagogy of the oppressed.* New York, NY: Seabury Press.

Giroux, H. A. (2001). *Theory and resistance in education.* London, UK: Bergin & Garvey.

Goldberg, M. E., Gorn, G. J., Peracchio, L. A., & Bamossy, G. (2003). Understanding materialism among youth. *Journal of Consumer Psychology, 13*(3), 278–288.

Good, T. L. (1987). Two decades of research on teacher expectations: Findings and future directions. *Journal of Teacher Education, 38*(32), 32–47.

Huffman, T. (2001). Resistance theory and the transculturation hypothesis as explanations of college attrition and persistence among American Indian students. *Journal of American Indian Education, 40*(1), 1–39.

Hurtado, S., Alvarez, C., Guillermo-Wann, C., Cuellar, M., & Arellano, L. (2012). A model for diverse learning environments: Creating and accessing conditions for student success. In J. Smart & M. Paulsen (Eds.), *Higher education: Handbook of theory and research* (Vol. 27). New York, NY: Springer.

Jackson, P. W. (1968). *Life in classrooms.* New York, NY: Holt, Reinhart & Winston.

Johns, M., Inzlicht, M., & Schmader, T. (2008). Stereotype threat and executive resource depletion: Examining the influence of emotion regulation. *Journal of Experimental Psychology: General, 137,* 691–705.

Johnson-Ahorlu, R. (2013). "Our biggest challenge is stereotypes": Understanding stereotype threat and the academic experiences of African American undergraduates. *Journal of Negro Education, 82*(4), 382–392.

Keller, J. (2002). Blatant stereotype threat and women's main performance: Self-handicapping as a strategic means to cope with obtrusive negative performance expectations. *Sex Roles, 47*(3/4), 193–198.

Kent, N. J. (1996). The new campus racism: What's going on? *NEA Higher Education Journal.* Retrieved from http://www.nea.org/assets/img/PubThoughtAndAction/TAA_00Fal_10.pdf.

King, J. E. (1991). Dysconscious racism: Ideology, identity, and the miseducation of teachers. *Journal of Negro Education, 60*(2), 133–146.

Kite, M. E., Gabourel, S. A., Ballas, H. E., Chance, K. L., Ellison, S. M., Johnson, S. B., . . . Stringer, D. (2013). *Activities for teaching about prejudice and discrimination.* Retrieved from http://teachpsych.org/page-1599567/1413148

Leonard, D., & Jiang, J. (1999). Gender bias and the college predictions of the SAT: A cry of despair. *Research in Higher Education, 40*(4), 375–407.

Lundy, G. F. (2003). The myths of oppositional culture. *Journal of Black Studies, 33*(4), 450–467.

Marcus, A. M., Mullins, L. C., Brackett, K. P., Tang, Z., Allen, A. M., & Pruett, D. W. (2003). Perceptions of racism on campus. *College Student Journal, 37*(4), 611–626.

Martens, A., Johns, M., Greenberg, J., & Schimel, J. (2006). Combating stereotype threat: The effect of self-affirmation on women's intellectual performance. *Journal of Experimental Social Psychology, 42*(2), 236–243.

Marx, D. M., & Roman, S. (2002). Female role models: Protecting women's math test performance. *Personality and Social Psychology Bulletin, 28*(9), 1183–1193.

McLoughlin, L. A. (2013). Spotlighting: Emerging gender bias in undergraduate engineering education. *Journal of Engineering Education, 94*(4), 373–381.

Milkman, K. L., Akinola, M., & Chugh, D. (2012). Temporal distance and discrimination: An audit study in academia. *Psychological Science, 23*(7), 710–717.

Mun Wah, L. (2012). Will the *real* multiculturalism please stand up? [Newsletter]. *StirFry Seminars and Consulting: Innovative Tools for Diversity Training.* Retrieved from https://nursebuddha.org/2012/06/14/will-the-real-multiculturalism-please-stand-up/

Peters, W., Cobb, C. (Writers), & Peters, W. (Director). (1985). A class divided [Television series episode]. In R. Aronson-Rath (Executive Producer), *Frontline.*

Boston, MA: WGBH. Retrieved from http://www.pbs.org/wgbh/frontline/film/class-divided/

Rankin, S. R. (2005). Campus climates for sexual minorities. *New Directions for Student Services, 111*, 17–23.

Rankin, S. R., & Reason, R. D. (2005). Differing perceptions: How students of color and white students perceive campus climate for underrepresented groups. *Journal of College Student Development, 46*(1), 43–61.

Rosser, P. (1989). *The SAT gender gap: Identifying the causes*. Washington, DC: Center for Women Policy Studies.

Sadker, M., & Sadker, D. (1994). *Failing at fairness: How our schools cheat girls*. New York, NY: Touchstone.

Schmader, T. (2010). Stereotype threat deconstructed. *Current Directions in Psychological Science, 19*, 14–18.

Schmader, T., & Johns, M. (2003). Convergent evidence that stereotype threat reduces working memory capacity. *Journal of Personality and Social Psychology, 85*, 440–452.

Schmader, T., Johns, M., & Forbes, C. E. (2008). An integrated process model of stereotype threat effects on performance. *Psychological Review, 115*, 336–356.

Steele, C. (1992). Race and schooling of black Americans. *The Atlantic, 269*, 68–78.

Steele, C. (1997). A threat in the air: How stereotypes shape intellectual identity and performance. *American Psychologist, 52*, 613–629.

Steele, C. M. (2010). *Whistling Vivaldi: How stereotypes affect us and what we can do*. New York, NY: W. W. Norton.

Steele, C. M., & Aronson, J. (1995). Stereotype threat and the intellectual test performance of African Americans. *Journal of Personality and Social Psychology, 69*(5), 797–811.

Steele, C., & Aronson, J. (1998). Stereotype threat and the test performance of academically successful African Americans. In C. Jencks & M. Phillips (Eds.), *The black-white test score gap* (pp. 401–427). Washington, DC: Brookings.

Steele, C. M., Spencer, S. J., & Aronson, J. (2002). Contending with group image: The psychology of stereotype and social identity threat. In M. P. Zanna (Ed.), *Advances in experimental social psychology* (Vol. 34, pp. 379–440). New York, NY: Academic Press.

Sydell, E. J., & Nelson, E. S. (2000). Modern racism on campus: A survey of attitudes and perceptions. *Social Science Journal, 37*(4), 627–635.

Tetreault, P. A., Fette, R., Meidlinger, P. C., & Hope, D. (2013). Perceptions of campus climate by sexual minorities. *Journal of Homosexuality, 60*(7), 947–964.

Vaccaro, A. (2010). What lies beneath seemingly positive campus climate results: Institutional sexism, racism, and male hostility toward equity initiatives and liberal bias. *Equity and Excellence in Education, 43*(2), 202–215.

Weis, L. (1985). *Between two worlds: Black students in an urban community college*. Boston, MA: Routledge & Kegan Paul.

White, J. W. (2011). Resistance to classroom participation: Minority students, academic discourse, cultural conflicts, and issues of representation in whole class discussions. *Journal of Language, Identity, and Education, 10*, 250–265.

White, J. W., & Ali-Kahn, C. (2013). The role of academic discourse in minority students' academic assimilation. *American Secondary Education, 42*(1), 24–42.

White, J. W., & Lowenthal, P. R. (2010). Minority college students and tacit "codes of power": Developing academic discourses and identities. *Review of Higher Education, 34*(2), 283–318.

Wilder, G. Z., & Powell, K. (1989). *Sex difference in test performance: A survey of the literature.* New York, NY: College Entrance Examination Board.

Willis, P. (1977). *Learning to labor: How working class kids get working class jobs.* New York, NY: Colombia University Press.

Wise, T. (2006). *Beyond diversity: The hidden curriculum of privilege* [Video file]. Retrieved from http://www.youtube.com/watch?v=D30GOWsnVuA

6

THROUGH THE STUDENTS' EYES

Internalized Forces That Shape Student Motivation

Christopher Lee, Andy Sechler, and Shea Smart

The instructor moves around the room, occasionally interjecting comments and questions as students collaboratively discuss the prompt. Most groups are engaged, with students contributing ideas and expanding the discussion in insightful directions in a tapestry of different perspectives. A few groups appear unengaged. Rather than participating in discussion, some students isolate and occupy themselves with smartphones and laptops or simply do nothing to abide until the instructor resumes lecturing. Even efforts from peers to include them prove ineffective. Observing these passive forms of resistance, the instructor approaches the unengaged students to jump-start participation. Some become engaged with nudging; others begrudgingly feign involvement. One student questions the validity of using class time for collaborative work, claiming, "You're the expert, right? What's the point of talking to other students who don't know anything?" The instructor has heard this before yet isn't quite sure where the attitude, which is quite common, comes from and how to remedy it.

Despite the convincing scholarly literature demonstrating the potential benefits of collaborative work on learning (Johnson, Johnson, & Stanne, 2000; Slavin, 1990), instructors commonly face resistance to active learning methods that often manifests in the context of collaborative work. Indeed, even the term *group work* is often met with skepticism and frustration among students. Even instructors can be doubtful of collaborative work, partly because of experiences with unwilling students who find little to no value in the perspectives and contributions of peers. Although much of this stems from negative classroom experiences (see chapter 7) and poorly designed classroom activities, there are more complex societal factors that intersect with internal forces to contribute to student resistance.

This chapter furthers the discussion of how societal factors, beyond those linked to race, class, and gender, influence student motivation (see chapter 5) and specifically examines how these influences are internalized and can negatively affect student motivation. Student expectations about higher education are explored as significant factors leading to resistance. Of particular interest are expectations influenced by academic entitlement and consumerist attitudes as well as internal expectations of college rigor and self-efficacy, specifically among underrepresented college students. Understanding how these attitudes and expectations affect students can help instructors mitigate resistance to active pedagogies such as collaborative work.

Internalized Expectations of Higher Education

Academic Entitlement

Students' minds are not tabulae rasae; students bring with them ingrained expectations and attitudes that promote or harm active learning. One source of these resistant behaviors is academic entitlement, the tendency of an individual to expect academic success without a sense of personal responsibility for achieving that success (Chowning & Campbell, 2009). What many faculty may interpret as laziness or uncivil behavior can be a manifestation of academic entitlement, which has been shown to negatively correlate with metacognitive development and deep learning (Ciani, Summers, & Easter, 2008). Conversely, academic entitlement has been positively correlated with surface learning (Andrey et al., 2012). Although students of varying backgrounds exhibit academic entitlement, research suggests that males perceive themselves as more entitled, possibly due to cultural gender norms about the nature of success in academia and the workplace (Boswell, 2012). Sparks (2012) suggested that students who score higher on scales of academic entitlement believe they have less control over their learning and often blame external factors, such as instructor biases, social pressures, work, and family, as explanations for poor academic performance. Thus, entitlement provides a defensive bulwark against poor academic performance and anxiety.

Goodboy and Frisby (2014) found that when academically entitled students' expectations were not met, they engaged in resistant behaviors.

They categorized observed resistance as expressive, vengeful, and rhetorical dissent. Some students, for example, went as far as publicly insulting their instructors when low grades defied entitled expectations. Lippman, Bulanda, and Wagenaar (2009) provided an example of entitlement in the form of an e-mail:

> After getting my grade . . . I keep going over and over what exactly you expected out of your SOC 152 students. I'm questioning who/what sets the standards for your class. . . . To me, if a student does/hands in all assignments, misses class no more than two times, participates during lecture, takes notes, attentively watches videos, and obviously observes/notes sociology in his/her life, it would make sense for that student to receive a respectable grade—an A. It seems like the work and time that I (and I'm assuming other students) put into this class didn't create the results that I (or you) wanted. Personally, I can't comprehend how my performance in your class equated to an 87 percent. (p. 197)

In the classroom, entitlement is often manifested when students passively or actively challenge instructors' authority and instructional decisions. One of the most prominent manifestations is so-called grade grubbing, the tendency of students to negotiate—or even demand—a higher grade (even a point or two) for minimal effort, despite legitimate reasons for the initial grade. Students may try to avoid classes that are known as difficult or that require a significant amount of time and effort, although it should be noted that demanding financial aid and scholarship GPA requirements are also prominent factors in students' decisions to engage in grade grubbing, a form of self-preservation resistance. Delucchi and Korgen (2002) surveyed 195 undergraduate sociology majors and found that when students received a grade below their expectations, they resorted to active resistance through arguments with their instructors, essentially demanding a higher grade. Overall, nearly half of respondents in their study claimed they were entitled to a degree, in part because of costly tuition. This attitude can lead students to object to grades they deem as denying them what they are entitled to. Additionally, entitled attitudes can develop into behaviors like cheating and plagiarism.

One of the most prominent theories of academic entitlement suggests that it can be fueled by parental expectations of their children, both academically and socially. Greenberger and colleagues systematically measured academic entitlement among college students and found that "students who reported more academically entitled attitudes perceived their parents as exerting achievement pressure marked by social comparison with other youth" (Greenberger, Lessard, Chen, & Farruggia, 2008, p. 1193). Furthermore, academically entitled students reported parents who relied on extrinsic motivators. Continuing into college, grades offer a form of competitive extrinsic motivation, particularly when scholarships and financial aid demand high grades. Extrinsically motivated students are driven by performance goals rather than learning goals, and the pressure to achieve high grades can exacerbate entitled attitudes. Instructors enable academic entitlement by reneging on established course policies like assignment requirements and due dates, as well as offering excessive extra credit for missed deadlines or poor performance on assignments or tests.

In these instructional environments, a student who fails to submit an essay on time will simply take advantage of inflated extra credit work to compensate, setting up a problematic expectation that is bound to end when another class fails to institute such safety nets. Additionally, instructors who exhibit entitled attitudes themselves, such as expecting or demanding respect by virtue of their positions as professors, rather than earning respect through their actions, can set a negative precedent for students (Oberlin, 2009).

Academic entitlement is also heavily informed by how students perceive their role in higher education, specifically as consumers of knowledge. Rising tuition and the associated pressures of working while attending college can give students the sense that they are entitled to receive education in a customized, quickly deliverable manner, which can result in instances of resistance, such as the one described in the following section, to courses that undermine these expectations.

Students as Consumers

Chris Lee

"Tuition is expensive. Why should I have to pay to listen to students who don't know anything?" This is a question—although there are certainly many iterations of it—I've become accustomed to hearing when I attempt to engage students in collaborative work. The first time a student explicitly expressed her reasoning for what I observed to be detached and passive participation in peer review— students' providing and receiving feedback on essays—I was unprepared with a convincing counterargument.

While students provided feedback, I walked around, observing, contributing input when questions arose. One student summoned me over and subtly pulled away from her peers. Clearly frustrated, she indicated she wasn't "paying for this" and wondered why I didn't just do my job and "teach," indicating that her other classes consisted of lecture and note-taking. Because she viewed education as simply a pathway to a degree, and an expensive one at that, she viewed collaborative work (or its more sinister term, group work) as useless. In fact, it was an obstacle to memorizing content, in this case the rules and requirements for the upcoming essay.

An honest response at the time might have led to a philosophical discussion on the purpose of liberal education and conflicting expectations between students and instructors. I conceded that instructors and universities carried some blame for this perception, especially considering how some institutions market their campus almost explicitly as a pathway to a degree and a high-paying job. Ultimately, I tried to explain that given my understanding of effective means of facilitating genuine learning, based on research, I tried to structure my classes accordingly. Notwithstanding, I doubt I succeeded in inspiring this student to embrace collaborative work; this actually led me to implement much more front-loading of engaged learning principles on the first day of classes so as to better align student expectations.

Consumer culture has increasingly become a part of higher education in the United States and abroad, and the student-as-consumer metaphor abounds. Students are often viewed as consumers of education by university administrators, instructors, and by students themselves, a pattern reinforced by external pressures to meet social needs and the demands of the marketplace. This perspective conflicts with students viewing themselves as learners, responsible for their own learning and skill development. McMillan and Cheney (1996) found that instructors in higher education began to embrace the student-as-consumer metaphor as a way to increase accountability for student and societal needs. In part, faculty felt it was important to make sure that the highest standards were met to keep up with the increasing cost of attending college (McMillan & Cheney, 1996). In spite of genuine and important efforts toward accountability, students perceiving themselves as consumers can be a damaging proposition for higher education, especially because it increases student resistance to active learning classes while decreasing student responsibility.

Education as a Commodity
Arguably, the central element of consumerism is the perception of education as a commodity, meant to be fun, entertaining, and easily digestible, rather than intellectually challenging, thought provoking, transformational, or involving stress or pressure to grow (Edmundson, 1997). This perception may promote a serious lack of effort by students, which is problematic in itself and inhibits the development of the skills necessary for participating in engaged learning, scholarship, or a career. Naidoo and Jamieson (2005) emphasized that learning requires taking risks and trusting instructors as guides on the path of learning. As students focus on their desire to be entertained, the instructor is not expected to be of assistance in the challenging process of transformation but rather is expected to minimize any risk of effort or challenge to the students' current level of development.

In fact, Titus (2008) suggested that in the consumer model of education, instructors are customer service representatives and are expected to act accordingly: meet or exceed expectations, never insinuate that the customer might be wrong, and perform well while wearing a smile. Titus (2008) proposed that students not only want their educational experience to be comfortable but also want the instructor, as an authority figure, to reinforce rather than to challenge their beliefs or worldview. In light of this expectation, it is not surprising that students may believe that their instructors and the educational system are actually failing them when they do not live up to the expectations inherent in the consumer mindset (Molesworth, Nixon, & Scullion, 2009). Student resistance is likely to increase when students are dissatisfied with their experience and think that their instructors are not assisting them in achieving the goals that they see as paramount, no matter how far these goals may miss the actual mark.

Problematic student expectations can result in what Robinson, Kraatz, and Rousseau (1994) described as a psychological contract breach. If students approach their college courses with consumer-informed expectations, they may feel psychologically betrayed by instructors who use active learning methods, especially if students view instructors as customer service representatives who are not living up to their expected role and duties.

Edmundson (1997) indicated that consumer culture is reinforced in students when the university allows a "shopping period" at the beginning of the semester in which students can attend a course and determine whether or not they like the professor or believe that it will be too challenging before they commit to take the course. This example, again, highlights the trend in higher education to appeal to consumer desires in order to retain as many students as possible. One could argue that the two-week shopping period allows students to openly resist any course, for any reason, in an institutionally sanctioned form. Arguably, aside from outright withdrawing, this allows students a safe zone to test the boundaries of any given professor with few consequences. The shopping period can increase resistance because it gives students the idea they are in control of their education and its standards and have the right to reject anything they find objectionable. Starting off the semester under these premises shifts the power and expectations in a manner that creates negativity toward and conflicts with the goals of active learning methods.

Student Evaluations

One contributor to the persistence of consumerist notions in education is students' evaluation of instructors. The influence of departmental and institutional policies that contribute to faculty reluctance to engage in behaviors that might threaten positive student ratings is described in chapter 4.

However, it is important to recognize that some of the institutional assumptions regarding the value or utility of student ratings may be flawed. Titus (2008) pointed out the false assumption that students take the evaluations seriously and strive to offer thoughtful commentary for the instructor and administration. Instead, many students may hurriedly fill out the forms as the last task at the end of the semester. Alternatively, because of the extra, usually uncredited work involved, those students most interested and motivated to actually complete the ratings may be those who hold the most extreme positions regarding the instructor and the class; this form of bias can have a large effect, especially if the overall response rate is low. Freng and Webber (2009) have suggested that instructor attractiveness can factor into students' views on the course and instructor, and Titus (2008) noted that students may rate instructors on the basis of first impressions or personality, which has very little to do with the process of learning.

Charismatic instructors who do little to challenge students are often rated highly despite failing to provide students with genuine, transformative learning experiences. Naftulin, Ware, and Donnelly (1973) designed a now-infamous study referred to as the Dr. Fox Lecture in which an actor was instructed to teach in an entertaining fashion, utilizing shallow appeals to authority and incorporating humor into a lecture that lacked substance in content. The actor was specifically instructed to provide "irrelevant, conflicting, and meaningless" content to his audience (p. 630). Student evaluations of Dr. Fox were, overall, consistently high, and students, according to the authors, were seduced into thinking they had learned.

However, this study has been criticized for methodological flaws. Specifically, critics have discussed the lack of control groups, the raters' lack of prior knowledge about the content, and flaws in the questionnaire leading to positive responses, among other problems. More recently, Peer and Babad (2014) replicated the original study using the same video and procedures and found that students were not "seduced" into the perception of learning, per the original claim. Although Peer and Babad refuted the original study's conclusion on student learning, they conceded that students were entertained and rated the instructor highly in this area and that anecdotal cases of charismatic instructors who do little to instill genuine learning are a reality on college campuses.

The overall conclusion is that the reality of high student ratings based on what students have found to be entertaining is supported by the literature. Evaluation scores can drop in challenging classes, engaging and effective teaching notwithstanding. In a survey of their students, Delucchi and Korgen (2002) found that, informed by a consumer mentality, students expect to be entertained and unchallenged, and they "demand a level of 'entertainment' from faculty commensurate with the price of tuition" (p. 104). Students also share their perceptions and seek online avenues to evaluate potential instructors according to consumer-driven expectations. For instance, Rate-MyProfessors.com, as described by Davison and Price (2009), "establishes an anti-intellectual tone that manifests itself in comments about instructors' personality, easiness of workload and entertainment value rather than knowledge attained" (p. 51). In their sample, one student comment read, "Really fun class. He gets a little off the subject sometimes, but his stories are always entertaining. I couldn't wait to go to class" (p. 59). Clearly, this student valued entertainment over learning, because nothing about learning was mentioned. These kinds of reinforced expectations carry over into institutional rating scales, especially when they look like customer satisfaction surveys. Delucchi and Korgen (2002) pointedly ask, "How can college educators expect students to respect both learning and their professors when they are asked to rate their instructors in the same manner as they would the staff of a resort complex?" (p. 105).

"Cool" Consumers

Edmundson (1997) explained that an important implication of the consumer culture that students are mired in is that they often take on the persona of the "cool consumer." The "cool consumer" is informed at a distance, does not express enthusiasm, and avoids conflict with the status quo or greater culture (Edmundson, 1997).[1] This persona creates conflict with engaged teaching at almost every turn. Students do not want to stand out, so they are not likely to embrace collaborative work or engage in class discussion. Because students do not explore the topics that interest them most with enthusiasm, the hope for creating lifelong learners is diminished. The cool consumer does not want to engage in the risk taking, temporary failures, and anxiety that are required in a deep approach to learning, the construction of knowledge, and the long journey toward a well-informed perspective and a professional identity. Students with the "cool consumer" mentality may participate verbally in class, but comments and motivations are focused primarily on pleasing their peers. Challenging anyone or engaging critically is a sin in the world of the "cool consumer."

Naidoo and Jamieson (2005) noted that universities have shifted from working with mostly an elite group to becoming a more integrated aspect of American culture. As increasing numbers of student consumers, especially first-generation and nontraditional students, engage in transactions with commercialized universities, they tend to view themselves as outsiders to academia rather than as scholars in training (Naidoo & Jamieson, 2005), particularly if the ultimate goal is a higher-paying job in the marketplace. Students who feel separate from the learning process and construction of knowledge are not likely to be fully invested and are more likely to embrace a passive model of education. Inherent to this perspective is a lack of responsibility for making the most of education and becoming a lifelong learner.

Students are also more likely to view instructors in traditional ways rather than as collaborators, colleagues, or facilitators in the process of learning, and unfortunately, traditional models of instruction only reinforce these expectations. Gibbs (2009) emphasized that the consumerist model of education may cause instructors and students to be unsure of their specific identities and roles within higher education, interfering with effective instructor-student relationships. For example, a student may wish that an instructor would simply give a correct answer to a question rather than directing a discussion meant to illustrate the point that there might be many correct answers to a given quandary. In this way, the student may become frustrated that the instructor is behaving mysteriously and making learning difficult, whereas the instructor grows tired of nudging students who do not want to cooperate. If both reach the conclusion that change is needed, they each may choose the easier path to completing the course, engendering additional resistance to deep learning or developing skills as an engaged learner.

Pathway to a Degree

Molesworth, Nixon, and Scullion (2009) suggest that when students do not view their education in terms of learning, it becomes simply about doing what it takes to live a life of higher consumption. This increases resistance in many ways. For example, students might disengage completely or openly rebel against course material that is reflective and critical about the values of society, including consumer culture. Furthermore, active learning classrooms and lifelong learning hinge on students becoming passionate about learning and participating in their chosen disciplines. When passion is directed at, and derived from, consumption, it becomes difficult to shift a student's values in the classroom. This principle of education as a stepping-stone to higher consumption complements the idea that students are not likely to perceive themselves as a part of an academic community. As students view themselves as outsiders and consumers, crucial relationships are impaired.

McMillan and Cheney (1996) have argued that students who perceive themselves as consumers expect to participate in education in a passive way. When students believe they are purchasing a product, they often feel content to sit back and receive what they have ordered. This is obviously problematic in the classroom, where students expect to have neat packages of information given to them through the instructor's lively and entertaining performance, which is commonly referred to as a lecture. Students not only find little value in hearing from their classmates but also are likely to resist working in collaborative groups, rejecting the premise that knowledge is socially constructed with others. Furthermore, McMillan and Cheney (1996) have noted that consumer culture is intertwined with self-centeredness and competition. Students wish to autonomously receive what they have purchased without having to engage with persons other than the customer service representative. Specifically, they do not want their grades tied to other students in any way. In some respects, students view themselves as in competition with their peers, both with those in their classes and in universities across the globe. Graduate schools often have stringent requirements, and the competition for admittance can be fierce. This reinforces the importance of grades while also running counter to goals of collaborative seminars and group projects.

Social/Cultural Identity and Avoiding Assumptions

The relationship between academic entitlement and consumer expectations is worth considering in context with student resistance arising from social and cultural identity elements (see chapter 5); however, instructors should be careful to avoid making assumptions on the basis of resistant behaviors and misdiagnosing the causes, generating more resistance. Different from entitlement motivated by consumer culture, academic entitlement may manifest more often in white middle-class students who have greater access and privilege in the market economy and more familial support for college attendance. Although the literature doesn't specifically report a higher frequency among such students, it's clear that entitlement is not representative of all students. Lippman and colleagues (2009) asserted that "growing levels of affluence along *some* [emphasis added] segments of the population coupled with shifts in labor market institutions" (p. 198) are contributing causes of increased entitlement. Lippman and colleagues (2009) further suggested that entitlement may not be increasing in a broad, uniform way; rather, it may be growing in a limited proportion of students, disproportionately taking up more time and energy from instructors. Thus, an argument can be made that white middle-class students are more prone to entitled attitudes and behaviors; however, more research is needed for clarification.

Additionally, common stereotypes about traditional college students can distort identification of the causes of resistance; instructors should take care not to use entitlement and consumer expectations as an excuse to avoid accountability for their teaching practices. Arnett (2007) identified pervading myths among instructors about emerging adults that include the perception that they are unhappy and anxious, self-centered, and unwilling to "grow up." He refuted these myths by claiming that emerging adults are developmentally self-focused at a time in their lives when they are learning to live on their own, hold part-time or full-time jobs, develop meaningful relationships, and explore educational opportunities. Arnett pointed out that today's emerging adults are more likely to participate in volunteer work and that, by age 30, "three-fourths have entered marriage and parenthood, nearly all have entered stable employment, nearly all have become financially independent, and hardly any live with their parents" (p. 28). Instructors need to examine their expectations of students and identify common stereotypes that may be leading to a false diagnosis of entitlement. A further distinction should be made between entitled students, motivated by consumerism, and those who may be underprepared for college.

Underprepared Students and Self-Efficacy

Although entitlement and consumerism are factors that enable forms of student resistance, many students are simply unprepared for the rigors of college demands and expectations, even though they may think they are prepared. Instructors need to be aware of this and be prepared to aid students and intervene in appropriate and effective ways. Recent research on *college readiness*, commonly defined as the knowledge and skills students need to avoid remedial classes and persist to graduation, can further explain more passive forms of resistance due to a lack of preparedness, confidence, and positive self-efficacy, which affects students of all backgrounds; however, underrepresented students are more likely to be at risk.

Although the definition and methods of measurement for college readiness vary and are debated,[2] Duncheon (2015) delineated three categories: cognitive academic factors, noncognitive academic factors, and campus integration factors. The categories are useful because they extend beyond basic content knowledge (math, reading, etc.) into "attitudes, beliefs, and emotions students have about themselves and schooling" (p. 9) as well as procedural skills like applying for financial aid. Among the attitudes that shape student expectations and motivation is self-efficacy. Students' perceptions of their abilities, both socially and academically, contribute to classroom behaviors, which can be negative, particularly in a collaborative social context involving peers and instructors who hold considerable amounts of power.

A useful frame to examine internal expectations and resistance is the relationship between cognitive task appraisals and self-efficacy. Because students are relatively competent members of a broader social and economic consumer culture (potentially resulting in academic entitlement as discussed), their knowledge of, and participation in, the marketplace intrudes into educational contexts. This is relevant to the rising cost of tuition, the marketing of universities, and review websites like RateMyProfessors.com that reinforce consumerist attitudes and behaviors. As in the marketplace, students base academic decisions on cost-benefit appraisals such as how stressful and difficult a given task will be and, by extension, how capable they perceive they are at achieving academic goals. As a result, students gravitate toward courses that ensure the highest grade for the least amount of effort, which are often courses with shallower approaches to learning, mostly involving retention of content and a safe, structured environment that allows for little critical and independent thinking. Essentially, students want to increase the benefit (good grades) while keeping costs low (cognitive effort), and this model works, providing little incentive for students to change attitudes and behaviors. Some research suggests that self-efficacy can influence these cognitive appraisals.

Bandura (1977) specifically connected self-efficacy (a set of beliefs about one's capability to succeed at a task or set of tasks) with cost appraisal, claiming, "Efficacy expectations determine how much effort people will expend and how long they will persist in the face of obstacles and aversive experiences" (p. 194). Students try to minimize effort and maximize positive outcomes before even registering for classes by seeking professors and courses that peers describe as easy, a form of market research before purchasing a product or service. "Easy A" seems to have become a buzzword among many students, an appraisal that usually functions as a positive endorsement of a professor or course.

Karademas and Kalantzi-Azizi (2003) studied student self-efficacy expectations in the context of test taking and studying and found that "self-efficacy expectations play a significant role in shaping threat, challenge, and stakes" and that "self-efficacy expectations . . . are negatively [related] to psychological symptoms and self-isolation and denial/passive acceptance strategies" (pp. 1033–1041). Thus, students will often avoid tasks or learning environments not only because they perceive them as challenging but also because low self-efficacy can skew cost-benefit appraisals, particularly if students have a history of punishment in the form of poor grades or if students have heard or read about challenging professors and courses. Courses that have opportunities, or even requirements, for active engagement can strengthen negative self-efficacy, resulting in passive avoidance behaviors (resistance). Karademas and Kalantzi-Azizi (2003) further reported, "Self-efficacy plays a *major* [emphasis added] role in determining behavior and functioning, as it moderates perceived stressfulness of the situation, and . . . experienced emotions (i.e., threat, challenge), coping efforts, and psychological functioning and well-being" (p. 1041). Consistent and constant doubting of academic abilities can lead students to resist active learning methods that they appraise as functioning as barriers to their perceived level of cognitive abilities.

Underrepresented students are particularly at risk for negative self-efficacy. A significant body of literature has shown that first-generation college students from underrepresented groups face more challenges than traditional college students face. Some of these include less family support due to parental or sibling inexperience navigating the college environment, deficits due to coming from underrepresented ethnic groups and lower socio-economic strata, and often language barriers. These factors have been studied individually and linked with academic performance, but Ramos-Sanchez and Nichols (2007) synthesized them to explore the resulting cognitive processes and help explain lower academic performance. Although they reported that self-efficacy was not solely responsible for lower academic performance, they found that a "powerful relationship" exists between self-efficacy and college adjustment: "Given that first-generation college students had lower self-efficacy levels, the effort to persist in achieving the goal of graduation could be less vigorous than the effort of non-first generation college students" (p. 14).

Underrepresented students such as adult learners (older or returning students) have been found to have lower levels of self-efficacy than traditional students, even though they often perform better academically (Carlan, 2001). Nontraditional students may face additional stressors such as parenting duties, busy work schedules, and frequent feelings of inadequacy due to prolonged absence from academic life as well as from being older than student peers. Lundberg, McIntire, and Creasman (2008) reported that "adult learners' self-doubts about their non-traditional status and their fit within the academic environment may lead to decreased confidence and lower levels of academic self-efficacy" (p. 59). Nontraditional students often feel socially disconnected from the university culture at large and in the classroom.

Underrepresented students have been shown to lack awareness of the tacit cultural norms that pervade the college landscape (e.g., syllabi, office hours, online assignment submission), which can further increase anxiety, negative self-efficacy, and passive resistance. Rodriguez (2015) discussed how university policy changes emphasizing completion have favored overall graduation rates (upon which institutional funding is becoming more and more contingent) over access, increasing the hurdles for underprepared students, those he called "the least ready," who are often underrepresented (p. 181). Because many of these students are enrolling in non-credit-bearing remedial courses and relying on financial aid, graduation is pushed back, meaning further reliance on financial aid for an extended period. These economic stresses that disproportionately affect low-income students further exacerbate the problem of readiness and shape cognitive task appraisals, as students may potentially drop out of school altogether in order to avoid amassing debt.

If underrepresented students often have lower levels of self-efficacy than their traditional college student counterparts, they may be at particular risk of appraising academic challenges in unrealistic ways (both over- and under-estimating). This may motivate these students to resist potentially threatening academic situations, particularly if engaged learning practices call for increased socialization with peers as well as the instructor. This form of resistance isn't necessarily, or even likely, going to result from a conscious rejection of active pedagogy; rather, it is a form of self-protection, as discussed in chapter 1. Sub-sequently, instructors need to consider *why* students may be exhibiting resistant attitudes and behaviors in order to implement appropriate reduction strategies.

Methods of Reducing Resistance

Academic Entitlement and Consumerism

A useful starting point for quelling academic entitlement can be to explicitly challenge the notion that instructors are responsible for student learning. As John Tagg noted in the foreword, even the best efforts by gifted teachers come to naught if the students do not decide to learn. Helping students understand that they are ultimately responsible for learning and that the instructor's role is to facilitate is critical. The one who does the work does the learning (Doyle, 2008), which increases the rationale for high-impact teaching practices. True achievement requires skill or effort, which is ulti-mately manifested in performance or outcome (Singleton-Jackson, Jackson, & Reinhardt, 2010).

Academically entitled students view the responsibility for learning as dependent on the instructor. They see it as the instructor's job to learn for the student, whereupon the student regurgitates information back to the instruc-tor, a pattern established early in the academic careers of many. For exam-ple, K–12 assessment instruments have stayed relatively consistent over time; however, grades have risen. This suggests that students are being rewarded with higher grades for equivalent or even decreasing performance (Twenge & Campbell, 2009). "A is for effort" becomes the mantra for many class-rooms and can lead students to resist change once actively engaged learning is expected and implemented in higher education. Students who receive grades below expectations may become angry with the professor because expectations have not been clearly defined and students' expectations weren't met.

Thus, delineating clear expectations that students are responsible for learning can reorient those conditioned to view instructors as exclusively accountable for learning. Establishing the instructor's role as the facilitator of learning, early in the semester, can mitigate resistance to more academically challenging and learner-centered collaborative coursework. Additionally, providing formative feedback on low-stakes assignments early in the semester may help students adjust to the reality of difficult coursework, providing time for improvement before the stakes are raised. McGuire and McGuire (2015) described engaging students with questions such as "What is the difference between studying and learning?" to help them self-evaluate whether they have been functioning primarily in study mode (surface learning) or learn mode (deep learning), a strategy that emphasizes the students' own responsibility for learning outcomes.

This type of work and discussions with students early in the semester can help students shift expectations and come to view education as experiential and transformative rather than, or at least in addition to, a product or service to be purchased and reduce resistance to engaged learning due to a consumer mentality. Fox (2014) suggested that inviting students on the first day of the semester to explore the relationship between the consumer market and higher education can help in teasing out problematic assumptions. In essence, Fox twisted the metaphor rather than fighting it. She specifically tried to guide students to view the "capital" of higher education to be time and attention, rather than money, because any positive yield can only be directly traced back to time and attention. If students are paying a high price for a good or service, then they should be more invested in the quality of that good or service, which can be a window to discussing what genuine learning is and the best methods of instruction to reach that goal.

Furthermore, a survey published in the *Chronicle of Higher Education* revealed that many employers are dissatisfied with college graduate employees. Overall, employers claimed that graduates had the technical skills for the job but that "colleges weren't adequately preparing students in written and oral communication, decision-making, and analytical and research skills" (Fischer, 2013, para. 7). One employer stated that "it's not a matter of technical skill but of knowing how to think" (para. 6). If students are aware that employers prefer graduates capable of deep learning, they may be more open to methods of instruction that help students achieve higher levels of thinking, enabling them to potentially be more marketable in the workplace.

Similarly, reorienting students to view education, at the very least, as a service (rather than a manufactured product) can be a step to reduce resistance. In health care, for example, the doctor-patient relationship goes beyond prescriptive lecture. Patients are typically expected to take responsibility for behaviors to ensure the likelihood of a return to full physical or mental health. This metaphor, or others like it, may help students complicate the simplified consumer mentality and enable them to take a more active role in their learning.

Instilling a longer term view of education beyond a degree can also reduce resistance, particularly if students come to realize the value of learning on their own, with the guidance of instructors. A useful strategy to achieve this, described in chapter 3, is Smith's (2008) "first-day questions" asking students to vote on the most important learning outcome for the course. He reported that students almost always select either application of the material to new contexts or development of lifelong learning skills. This suggests that student perceptions about the purpose of higher education may actually align with instructors' perceptions; the mismatch lies in the method of reaching those goals. Coming to an understanding of common goals can be an effective step toward persuading students that engaged learning practices are more likely to meet long-term goals centered on developing lifelong learning, as opposed to acquiring short-term content knowledge in an effort to obtain a degree.

Additionally, institutions should proactively develop end-of-semester evaluation instruments, or select from existing instruments, that focus on learning outcomes, avoiding questions that mimic satisfaction surveys and reinforce expectations of entertainment and ease. The literature on effective and valid student evaluations of teaching (SETs) is abundant (e.g., Clayson, 2009; Wright & Jenkins-Guarnieri, 2012). Faculty can also develop or adopt their own measurements that focus on learning in their courses, both at midterm and at the end of the semester. Maintaining evidence of effective teaching with valid student evaluations of learning can provide additional support in tenure and promotion decisions as opposed to institutional SETs that function more to enable academic entitlement and consumer expectations of education.

Underprepared Students

Unfortunately, some instructors write off students who are not prepared for college, perhaps justifying that they're doing students a favor by "weeding them out" and saving them money. This "weeding out" mentality is counterproductive if the goal of instructors (and institutions) is to facilitate inclusive environments where students can succeed. It is also, at least, patronizing if not arrogant, and as this attitude gets communicated to students in ways both obvious and subtle, it can only increase student resistance. Instructors have an ethical obligation to teach, and this obligation requires consideration of ways to support students who struggle.

To assist underprepared students, the Association of American Colleges and Universities (2015) has recommended that instructors develop a clear understanding of the demographic trends and shifts that characterize student populations and, subsequently, an understanding of the expected classroom cultural landscape. They proposed helpful reflective questions to use in evaluating whether institution and classroom practices are in alignment with inclusive goals:

> How are your institution's practices and policies designed to accommodate differences in students' contexts for their learning? How do you ensure that underserved students receive the appropriate amount of challenge and support to ensure their success, without marginalizing these students? What can you learn from your own successes and failures and from other institutions working to increase underserved student success? Who else needs to be included in the conversation about culturally competent practices? Are all faculty at your institution engaged in supporting underserved students? (p. 5)

Clearly, campuswide discussions of inclusivity need to be inclusive in and of themselves to ensure effective implementations of programs and practices. The goal of greater inclusion within the academy rests largely on the institution (supporting student clubs, assisting underrepresented students with financial aid and support, providing career support and time-management services, etc.); however, there are actions instructors can take within their classrooms to both provide an inclusive environment and potentially reduce passive resistance.

Faculty teaching freshman courses are in a prime position to assist underprepared students by identifying gaps in readiness and intervening. An attempt to help students increase perceived abilities and self-efficacy is critical if instructors want students to embrace the intellectual challenges that engaged learning provides, perhaps even demands. Social support systems, which can be a benefit of collaborative classrooms, have been found to potentially increase levels of student self-efficacy, although initial anxiety may occur (Ramos-Sanchez & Nichols, 2007). Adult learners, particularly, have been shown to benefit from social support systems. If students can accept that higher education is more collaborative and cooperative rather than competitive, they can realize the potential benefits of working with peers who may share similar fears in perceived academic ability. The instructor, of course, can also be part of the social support system, rather than solely an authoritative figurehead.

Teacher immediacy—the perceived psychological closeness that students feel to instructors through verbal and nonverbal behaviors—can improve motivation and mitigate negative self-efficacy. Simple behaviors such as smiling, making eye contact, walking around the room, telling relevant stories, and calling students by name have enhanced motivation and, indirectly, academic performance. Allen, Witt, and Wheeless (2006) reported that "high levels of teacher immediacy function as a means of increasing the motivation of a student to learn, and that such motivation increases the cognitive mastery of material" (p. 21). Additionally, the practice of more deliberately walking students through assumed procedures, such as the process for submitting assignments and standard formatting, on the first day of class (or for a few minutes after for those who need it) can greatly aid students unfamiliar with tacit knowledge.

Although providing or pointing to resources for students is useful, Stephens, Hamedani, and Destin (2014) have argued that explicit classroom interventions are needed to effectively assist students who are both underprepared and underrepresented, particularly first-generation students. They have suggested that providing opportunities for students to reflect on, and discuss with others, how their cultural backgrounds shape their college experiences can increase students' sense of belonging within the institution and classroom. They show that "helping students understand how their different backgrounds matter is a powerful insight that has the potential to not only increase students' sense of comfort and ability to operate in diverse settings, but also equip them to better navigate their own college experience" (p. 944). In another study, Stephens, Townsend, Hamedani, Destin, and Manzo (2015) claimed that brief classroom interventions involving reflective writing and discussion can also benefit first-generation students in the long term as the process of reflection becomes recursive and habitual, increasing the likelihood of resilience when students encounter various setbacks. McGuire and McGuire (2015) have described how early discussions focusing on helping students accept responsibility for their own learning and explicit teaching of what they call the *study cycle,* incorporating validated and effective deep-learning methods, can produce significant gains in student learning and mastery of course material. These methods would be particularly effective for first-generation and underrepresented students who often have not been exposed to effective learning strategies from parents or family.

Furthermore, Dweck's (1999) work on entity and incremental self-theories (explored in more detail in chapter 9) can enhance self-efficacy in underprepared and underrepresented students, particularly if discussed at the beginning of the course. Although the student challenges are not uniform, an ongoing discussion of the nature of intelligence and ability throughout the duration of a course can serve to change student attitudes for the better. For example, many students enter composition courses with the self-perception that they "aren't writers." Demystifying this flawed assumption early in the term by modeling how struggling students have overcome challenges with content or skills sets the stage for more positive and productive attitudes regarding the learning process and nature of intelligence as being dynamic rather than static. Additionally, by providing students with opportunities to self-assess and improve, with accompanying instructor formative feedback, students are more likely to view their limitations as temporary setbacks that function as benchmarks in a larger learning process rather than as permanent markers of ability and intelligence.

Conclusion

The internalized expectations that students carry about the nature and purpose of higher education as well as their own academic abilities can intersect with engaged classrooms, and the university experience at large, in problematic ways. As experienced consumers in a market economy, students may approach education with similar assumptions that dramatically conflict with the aims of active learning pedagogies and the general values and objectives of a liberal education. Consumer attitudes and academic entitlement can result in student resistance when internalized expectations are misaligned or when performance is below student expectations. Engaged learning practices can further exacerbate tensions because the learning environment is distinctly different from traditional passive learning environments. As in the marketplace, students often seek classes that are easy and entertaining because of cost-benefit appraisals. Although students may be confident consumers in the marketplace, they often lack confidence in academic ability. Lower levels of self-efficacy, more common among first-generation and nontraditional students, can negatively influence appraisals of risk and threat.

Many students are underprepared for college and lack the knowledge and skills necessary to navigate higher education, which can have a deleterious impact on student expectations and motivation. An awareness of these internalized expectations can aid instructors in identifying and mitigating resistance in the classroom. As resistance is multifaceted and complex, identifying contributing factors and then evaluating how they intersect in the classroom can lead to a more targeted approach at solving problems that arise from student resistance and to preventative steps to proactively address issues before they arise.

Notes

1. In describing Edmunson's (1997) position and description of the *cool consumer*, we want to acknowledge that the definition of what is culturally *cool* is subjective and the phrase may appear condescending to many students. We do not

believe that the term is a general description of students in our classes, but instructor experience suggests that it may be useful in understanding the passive resistance of some students.

2. Scholars disagree on whether the definition of *readiness* should focus on the necessity of remedial courses or success within credit-bearing courses. Also, disagreements arise concerning how social skills and other nonacademic factors should be included (Duncheon, 2015).

References

Allen, M., Witt, P. A., & Wheeless, L. R. (2006). The role of teacher immediacy as a motivational factor in student learning: Using meta-analysis to test a causal model. *Communication Education, 55*(1), 21–31.

Andrey, J., Joakim, E., Schoner, V., Hambly, D., Silver, A., Jayasundera, R., & Nelson, A. (2012). Academic entitlement in the context of learning styles. *Canadian Journal of Education, 35*(4), 3–30.

Arnett, J. J. (2007). Suffering, selfish, slackers? Myths and reality about emerging adults. *Journal of Youth Adolescence, 36*, 23–29.

Association of American Colleges and Universities. (2015). *Committing to equity and inclusive excellence: A campus guide for self-study and planning.* Washington, DC: Author.

Bandura, A. (1977). Self-efficacy: Toward a unifying theory of behavioral change. *Psychological Review, 34*(2), 191–215.

Boswell, S. S. (2012). "I *deserve* success": Academic entitlement attitudes and their relationship with course self-efficacy, social networking, and demographic variables. *Social Psychology of Education: An International Journal, 15*(3), 353–365.

Carlan, P. (2001). Adult students and community college beginnings: Examining the efficacy of performance stereotypes on a university campus. *College Student Journal, 35*, 169–182.

Chowning, K., & Campbell, N. (2009). Development and validation of a measure of academic entitlement: Individual differences in students' externalized responsibility and entitled expectations. *Journal of Educational Psychology, 101*(4), 982–997.

Ciani, K. D., Summers, J. J., & Easter, M. A. (2008). Gender differences in academic entitlement among college students. *Journal of Genetic Psychology, 169*(4), 332–344.

Clayson, D. E. (2009). Student evaluations of teaching: Are they related to what students learn? A meta-analysis and review of the literature. *Journal of Marketing Education, 31*(1), 16–30.

Davison, E., & Price, J. (2009). How do we rate? An evaluation of online student evaluations. *Assessment and Evaluation in Higher Education, 34*(1), 51–64.

Delucchi, M., & Korgen, K. (2002). "We're the customer—We pay the tuition": Student consumerism among undergraduate sociology majors. *Teaching Sociology, 30*(1), 100–107.

Doyle, T. (2008). *Helping students learn in a leaner centered environment: A guide to teaching in higher education.* Sterling, VA: Stylus.

Duncheon, J. C. (2015). The problem of college readiness. In W. G. Tierney & J. C. Duncheon (Eds.), *The problem of college readiness* (pp. 3–44). Albany, NY: State University of New York Press.

Dweck, C. S. (1999). *Self-theories: Their role in motivation, personality and development.* Philadelphia, PA: Taylor and Francis/Psychology Press.

Edmundson, M. (1997). On the uses of a liberal education: I. As lite entertainment for bored college students. *Harper's Magazine, 295*(1768), 39–49.

Fischer, K. (2013, March 4). The employment mismatch: A college degree sorts job applicants, but employers wish it meant more. *Chronicle of Higher Education.* Retrieved from http://chronicle.com/article/The-Employment-Mismatch/137625

Fox, D. M. (2014, May 19). Education and consumerism: Using students' assumptions to challenge their thinking. *Faculty Focus.* Retrieved from http://www.facultyfocus.com/articles/effective-teaching-strategies/education-consumerism-using-students-assumptions-challenge-thinking/

Freng, S., & Webber, D. (2009). Turning up the heat on online teaching evaluations: Does "hotness" matter? *Teaching of Psychology, 36,* 189–193.

Gibbs, P. (2009). Adopting consumer time: Potential issues for higher education. *London Review of Education, 7*(2), 113–124.

Goodboy, A. K., & Frisby, B. N. (2014). Instructional dissent as an expression of students' academic orientations and beliefs about education. *Communication Studies, 65*(1), 96–111.

Greenberger, E., Lessard, J., Chen, C., & Farruggia, S. P. (2008). Self-entitled college students: Contributions of personality, parenting, and motivational factors. *Journal of Youth and Adolescence, 37*(10), 1193–1204.

Johnson, D. W., Johnson, R. T., & Stanne, M. B. (2000). *Cooperative learning methods: A meta-analysis.* Unpublished manuscript, Cooperative Learning Center, University of Minnesota, Minneapolis, MN.

Karademas, E. C., & Kalantzi-Azizi, A. (2003). The stress process, self-efficacy expectations, and psychological health. *Personality and Individual Differences, 37,* 1033–1043.

Lippman, S., Bulanda, R., & Wagenaar, T. C. (2009). Student entitlement: Strategies for confronting entitlement in the classroom and beyond. *College Teaching, 57*(4), 197–204.

Lundberg, C. A., McIntire, D. D., & Creasman, C. T. (2008). Sources of social support and self-efficacy for adult learners. *Journal of College Counseling, 11,* 58–72.

McGuire, S. Y., & McGuire, S. (2015). *Teach students how to learn: Strategies you can incorporate into any course to improve student metacognition, study skills, and motivation.* Sterling, VA: Stylus.

McMillan, J. J., & Cheney, G. (1996). The student as consumer: The implications and limitations of a metaphor. *Communication Education, 45*(1), 1–15.

Molesworth, M., Nixon, E., & Scullion, R. (2009). Having, being and higher education: The marketisation of the university and the transformation of the student into consumer. *Teaching in Higher Education, 14*(3), 277–287.

Naftulin, D. H., Ware, J. E., & Donnelly, F. A. (1973). The Doctor Fox Lecture: A paradigm of educational seduction. *Journal of Medical Education, 48*, 630–635.

Naidoo, R., & Jamieson, I. (2005). Empowering participants or corroding learning? Towards a research agenda on the impact of student consumerism in higher education. *Journal of Education Policy, 20*(3), 267–281.

Oberlin, K. (2009, February 5). *The teacher-student entitlement gap.* Retrieved from http://profpost.uc.edu/2009/02/the-teacherstudent-entitlement-gap/

Peer, E., & Babad, E. (2014). The Doctor Fox research rerevisited: "Educational seduction" ruled out. *Journal of Educational Psychology, 106*(1), 36–45.

Ramos-Sanchez, L., & Nichols, L. (2007). Self-efficacy of first-generation and non-first-generation college students: The relationship with academic performance and college adjustment. *Journal of College Counseling, 10*(1), 6–18.

Robinson, S. L., Kraatz, M. S., & Rousseau, D. M. (1994). Changing obligations and the psychological contract: A longitudinal study. *Academy of Management Journal, 37*(4), 137–152.

Rodriguez, B. A. (2015). On the path to completion: Exploring how higher education policy influences the least ready college students. In W. G. Tierney & J. C. Duncheon (Eds.), *The problem of college readiness* (pp. 179–197). Albany, NY: State University of New York Press.

Singleton-Jackson, J., Jackson, D., & Reinhardt, J. (2010). Students as consumers of knowledge: Are they buying what we're selling? *Innovative Higher Education, 35*(5), 343–358.

Slavin, R. E. (1990). *Cooperative learning: Theory, research, and practice.* Boston, MA: Allyn & Bacon.

Smith, G. A. (2008). First-day questions for the learner-centered classroom. *National Teaching and Learning Forum, 17*(5), 1–4.

Sparks, S. D. (2012). "Academic entitlement" leads to reduced student effort. *Education Week, 31*(33), 15.

Stephens, N. M., Hamedani, M. G., & Destin, M. (2014). Closing the social-class achievement gap: A difference-education intervention improves first-generation students' academic performance and all students' college transition. *Psychological Science, 25*(4), 943–953.

Stephens, N. M., Townsend, S. S. M., Hamedani, M. G., Destin, M., & Manzo, V. (2015). A difference-education intervention equips first-generation college students to thrive in the face of stressful college situations. *Psychological Science, 26*(10), 1556–1566.

Titus, J. J. (2008). Student ratings in a consumerist academy: Leveraging pedagogical control and authority. *Sociological Perspectives, 51*(2), 397–422.

Twenge, J. M., & Campbell, W. K. (2009). *The narcissism epidemic: Living in the age of entitlement.* New York, NY: Free Press.

Wright, S. L., & Jenkins-Guarnieri, M. A. (2012). Student evaluations of teaching: Combining the meta-analyses and demonstrating further evidence for effective use. *Assessment and Evaluation in Higher Education, 37*(6), 683–699.

7

NEGATIVE CLASSROOM EXPERIENCES

Janine Kremling, Colt Rothlisberger, and Shea Smart

Quite simply, it's not my job to motivate these kids. If they come to my class and sit quietly and learn history, I will gladly give them the facts, information, and concepts that they need. If they are not motivated to learn, they can sit in the back of the class and sleep if they wish. It's their choice. It's their loss. I communicate information . . . and I do that very well. But, if a kid doesn't care to learn it, that is not my problem. I'm a teacher, not a cheerleader.

—quoted in R. Lavoie (2008), *The Motivation Breakthrough*

This statement demonstrates what many faculty may think about educating students. They are very willing to work with students who are intrinsically motivated to learn, and they may resist or abandon students who lack such intrinsic motivation, assuming that motivating students is not part of their job. Yet learning and motivation are interrelated concepts that can hardly be separated (Lavoie, 2008). All learning theories since Maslow include motivation as a prerequisite of learning (Nugent, 2009). Motivation to learn can be present or it can be created, but it can also be destroyed.

Motivation and learning require interaction between students and instructor. Positive interactions can reduce resistance and motivate students to learn, and successful student learning can motivate instructors to continue their efforts to build relationships and encourage them. On the other hand, poor student-teacher interaction can decrease or destroy motivation to learn, increase student resistance and misbehavior, and intensify faculty frustration, continuing a negative cycle. But poor student-teacher interaction and lack of instructor motivation can also be the result of past negative experiences for both students and instructor. This chapter builds on chapters 5 and 6. It aims to disentangle the relationships among learning, motivation, interaction, and student resistance and suggests solutions for improving student-teacher interactions, enhancing motivation to learn, and reducing student resistance.

Student-Teacher Interaction and the Classroom Experience

Student-teacher interaction is at the core of students' classroom experience, even in online courses. Students who report positive experiences and intrinsic motivation to learn often talk about positive interactions with their instructor and encouragement, advice, or mentoring they have received. Students who report negative classroom experiences and a lack of motivation may have experienced little interaction or negative interactions with the instructor, including personal issues or teaching-related issues (Skinner, 2002; Stipek, 2002). Whereas positive experiences enhance learning, negative experiences affect students in a way that hinders learning and graduation. In some ways negative interactions create a "toxic" classroom environment in which both students and instructors suffer.

The negative consequences of a toxic class environment are manifold.

Colt Rothlisberger

When I was taking Sociology 101, the professor was discussing racial profiling and prejudice. As she was discussing racial profiling, she would point to a student and sarcastically mention what strangers might assume about him or her. She would point to one student and say, "Oh, she's blonde, you can't trust her to do anything right" and "Oh, she's Asian, so you know she must be great at math." The student that the professor thought was Asian turned out to actually be Hispanic. The student became offended and exclaimed her frustration with people assuming she was Asian. This student was not one that contributed verbally very often. However, after this incident I never saw her back in class. Not even on the day of finals.

The consequences of this minor lapse of judgment on the part of the professor are apparent in the behavior of the girl of mistaken ethnicity. This was not an example of teacher misbehavior per se. The professor was trying to teach a principle by engaging students and made an honest mistake. Unfortunately, this mistake created a negative classroom experience for the students and led to one student dropping out of the class. Honest mistakes can be difficult to avoid when instructors try to engage students, especially in controversial topics such as racism or discrimination, but instructors should be prepared to recognize and act to correct these mistakes when possible. More problematic are negative classroom experiences created by teacher misbehavior and teacher nonimmediacy. The following section will explore how such misbehaviors and nonimmediacy manifest themselves and how they affect student-teacher interaction and student resistance.

Student Resistance as a Result of Teacher Nonimmediacy and Misbehavior

To date, much research on student resistance to active learning has focused on resistance to the actual teaching method, assuming that it is the teaching method that leads to resistance (Prince & Felder, 2007). Some researchers, however, have looked at the instructor's behavior as the potential cause of student resistance (Kearney, Plax, Hays, & Ivey, 1991; Seidel & Tanner, 2013). These studies suggest that students may have valid reasons for their resistance, grounded in negative interactions with the instructor (Nugent, 2009; Seidel & Tanner, 2013). Just as instructors react to student resistance with frustration, anxiety, and even anger, students react to instructor behaviors with similar emotions.

Two terms—*instructor nonimmediacy* and *instructor misbehavior*—have been used repeatedly in the literature to describe behavior by instructors that can create a negative classroom environment and hinder learning. Research suggests not only that teacher nonimmediacy and misbehavior are correlated but also that nonimmediacy may be interpreted as misbehavior by students, even if no actual misbehavior occurred (Thweatt & McCroskey, 1996). *Teacher nonimmediacy* can be defined as communication behavior that fails to reduce perceived psychological distance between students and the teacher, the authority figure. For instance, teachers who appear absentminded, don't smile or make eye contact, don't move around the classroom, don't attend to students' questions, or blow off student requests without explanation would likely fit into the category of nonimmediate teachers. *Teacher misbehavior* has been defined as "those teacher behaviors that interfere with student learning" (Kearney et al., 1991). It is possible that perceived teacher nonimmediacy and misbehavior have a close relationship because nonimmediate behaviors inhibit student learning (Dolin, 1995).

The following behaviors are examples illustrating perceived teacher misbehavior related to nonimmediacy: (a) being unprepared, (b) not understanding material or being disorganized, (c) offending one or more students, or (d) arriving late for a class period (Goodboy & Bolkan, 2009). According to Kearney and colleagues (1991), teacher misbehavior can be placed into three main categories: offensiveness, incompetence, and indolence.

Offensiveness mostly consists of verbal abuse directed toward students, such as humiliating, embarrassing, or insulting remarks (Kearney et al., 1991). It can also manifest through other behaviors, such as loud negative commentary about students to other faculty. The coffee shop story from chapter 1 in which faculty members voiced negative opinions about students represents an example of offensive behavior that outraged the students and had long-lasting effects on the students' perceptions of these particular professors and possibly faculty in general. When students perceive their professor as offensive, they are less likely to communicate with the professor, even for educational purposes (Goodboy, Myers, & Bolkan, 2010). However, offensiveness, like beauty, is in the eye of the beholder. The ambiguity of what is considered offensive makes this category more difficult to define. You can know it when you see it. Here, Colt shares two stories from his own experiences.

Colt Rothlisberger

#1: *I once had a professor who taught Introduction to Psychology. This professor was very opinionated and often criticized viewpoints she did not share. One student, we'll call her Marlena, asked a question about methods of psychotherapy. Her concern was whether a therapist should be sensitive to a patient's religion when prescribing treatment. This professor proceeded to vehemently criticize certain religions. One of those she criticized, and deemed unimportant in administering a treatment, was the very religion Marlena confessed to being a part of in an earlier lecture. The room was full of discomfort as many of the students either felt sorry for Marlena or were uncomfortable having religion discussed in this way. Marlena did not participate in class again, though she continued to attend classes to take notes and tests. To some, this will seem like an extreme example of offensiveness, but it has happened, and similar incidents will probably continue to occur.*

#2: *I have observed verbal abuse (I may be using this term a bit loosely) in an organic chemistry class. While lecturing, the professor asked if there were questions regarding the material. One student, we'll call him Jeremy, raised his hand and asked a simple and relevant question about bonding in organic compounds. On hearing the question, the professor, visibly annoyed, quickly gave a basic answer and shouted, "Do not ask questions like that again!" Most in attendance looked surprised at the professor's outburst. After class, some classmates teased Jeremy, to make the professor's outburst seem like less of a big deal. Those in the conversation all agreed that the question Jeremy had asked was a good one and one many of them had been wondering about themselves. I do not know how everyone else felt, but I never felt like I could safely ask a question in that class again.*

For teachers it is imperative to be aware of potential biases and prejudices to which students may take offense, particularly in regard to discussions involving race, sexuality, ethnicity, and gender. This is important because lacking this awareness, instructors may speak out, as they did in the previous examples, in ways that act to shut down student participation or create anger and resentment. Having different life experiences and expectations and working through those with students is one thing. Offensive attacks, whether subtle or overt, against student characteristics and explicit commentary or insinuations of student lack of intelligence or competence is another.

The category of incompetence includes lecturing in a monotonous voice, providing instructions that are confusing, and holding unreasonable expectations. The three misbehaviors scoring highest in the incompetence category were "unclear or confusing lectures," "boring lectures," and "unfair testing." All can be associated with a decline in student motivation. Here is an example:

Colt Rothlisberger

I had a chemistry teacher that many students struggled to learn from. Often he would rework a problem because of a mistake he had made. Not long after, he would claim, "Actually, I had it right the first time." Each time he made a mistake, he would tell the students they should make sure to "keep an eye out for this when working these types of problems." Eventually many of the students stopped attending class because they had a difficult time understanding what he was teaching and were unsure about how to find the right answer for the example problems. As a result, many of the students felt frustrated. Attendance was not required for the class, which caused students to attend even less. To the students it was obvious that the professor spent little time, if any, preparing his lectures.

Faculty unpreparedness is also an example of indolence, the third type of misbehavior.

Indolence includes behaviors that show disregard for students, such as being absent or tardy, returning work late, deviating from the syllabus, and being unprepared or disorganized. Colt had such an experience in one of his classes.

Colt Rothlisberger

I had a statistics professor who was often tardy to class, which was held in a computer lab. He would not try to provide enough working computers for every student in the classroom. This was problematic because all of the homework and study material was to be worked out using software on the computers. This showed indolence to the students; we thought the professor was apathetic and lazy. We all assumed he did not care about our education or the subject he was teaching. When we asked questions, he would simply tell us to work it out on the software program. He would not answer questions about how the math worked out. Many of us wanted background knowledge and felt frustrated and lost.

Instructor nonimmediacy and misbehaviors negatively affect student motivation to learn, increase student resistance, and can result in cognitive consequences such as temporizing and retreating. *Temporizing* is defined as impeding cognitive progression—that is, keeping a student from progressing to the next step in cognitive development. Likewise, retreating occurs when a student reverts to a more primitive cognitive stage in which they feel more comfort and security (Love & Guthrie, 1999). Cognitive development is affected by how students view their professors. As students begin to understand the status and experience of their professor, they begin to trust the professor. This stimulates growth in cognition for the students (Baxter Magolda, 1992). In the absence of trust and a healthy student-teacher interaction, cognitive development is impaired and, as the previous examples demonstrated, students become increasingly resistant, which inhibits learning. In a toxic learning environment, active learning pedagogies may not be successful but rather create a negative learning experience, because these pedagogies require trust and positive student-teacher interactions. These negative experiences can carry over to other classes, and if such a negative experience occurs in an active learning class, students may equate the negative experiences with this particular teaching approach and resist other instructors who are using active learning pedagogies.

Negative experiences in class also carry forward in the shape of instructor attitudes or behaviors that can negatively affect future courses and students and may lead some instructors to reduce their emotional investment in teaching, faculty development, and mentoring (Alsharif & Yongyue Qi,

2014). Institutional culture can also contribute to these negative classroom experiences; the issue of faculty priorities was discussed in detail in chapter 4. Faculty, especially junior faculty at research-oriented universities, may choose to prioritize research and grant activities because they understand the decision-making processes in regard to tenure and promotion. This is a problem that needs to be addressed at the institutional level by changing the way teaching is evaluated and valued in the tenure and promotion process.

Negative Experiences due to Instructor Attitudes Toward Students and Teaching

Instructors are role models for students in a variety of ways. Students look to the instructor for guidance and motivation and as an example of the profession. Research has shown that instructor beliefs and attitudes can create either a positive or negative learning environment (Alsharif & Yongyue Qi, 2014). Faculty have certain beliefs and attitudes toward teaching in general and certain teaching strategies in particular. Salem and Jones (2010) found that instructor attitudes that were important in writing-intensive courses included (a) enthusiasm about teaching, (b) confidence in teaching ability, (c) belief in the fairness of the workplace, (d) belief that grammar instruction belongs to the writing center, and (e) preference for teaching underprepared students.

Salem and Jones (2010) elaborated on these attitudes and beliefs:

1. Instructors who agreed or strongly agreed that writing-intensive courses were worthwhile also felt professionally fulfilled teaching these courses. Instructors who disagreed that writing-intensive courses were worthwhile stated that they were frustrated teaching these courses. Instructor enthusiasm has been associated with the strength of students' intrinsic motivation.

2. Instructors who were satisfied or very satisfied with the writing assignments they created also felt confident in their own performance.

3. Faculty teaching writing-intensive courses believed they worked more than other faculty, were not compensated fairly for teaching higher workload courses, and did not receive adequate support from the university. The instructors believed that their other duties suffered because of increased workload. These experiences may result in frustration and possibly discontinuation of teaching writing-intensive courses or other best practices that increase workload.

4. Faculty who agreed that grammar instruction belongs to the writing center thought that such tasks are not part of the faculty's job. For these

faculty, correcting grammatical errors may become frustrating and may result in lower grades because these faculty may perceive certain papers as inferior to their expectations.

5. Faculty who believed their students were underprepared for writing-intensive courses showed higher satisfaction with teaching the courses compared to faculty who believed their students were well prepared. Possibly, faculty who believed students were well prepared had a greater chance of being disappointed with student work. Faculty who thought that their students were underprepared may have had lower expectations and less room for disappointment.

Other research has found that use of humor by the instructor is linked to a positive classroom atmosphere and learning environment (Will & Wheeless, 2001). An encouraging attitude by the instructor, regardless of whether student answers are correct or not, helps to establish trust and motivates students to participate and engage in the class discussions (Monteiro, Almeida, & Vasconcelos, 2012). Monteiro and colleagues (2012) also found that patience, openness, and availability of the instructor improved the learning experience of students.

These attitudes and characteristics of effective instructors are well documented. However, in the daily routine of academia instructors may not consistently exhibit these positive attitudes and characteristics. Instructors may not feel enthusiastic about a topic or class, especially if the topic is not within their research area or if the class has a large number of students or requires writing assignments and extra work in general. As noted in chapter 4, institutional expectations for faculty can add to stress and conflict with expectations of students, who demand time, advice, and mentoring. Each instructor must consider whether spending a lot of time on developing an active learning class is worth the effort, especially if it may result in low student ratings and threaten the instructor's position. At the same time, faculty understand the importance of active learning and the development of key skills among students. This struggle is captured in the words of one instructor and may be reflected in class behaviors, intentional or not:

> My writing intensive course is taught in the upper senior semester. It is completely asinine to attempt to teach competent writing in the last semester of a student's career. As someone who has been compelled to teach this course, and this course only for the last decade, I have substantial experience with [my department's] undergraduates. . . . It is clear to me that whatever efforts are made to enhance the writing skills of our students are either not sufficient or not effective. (Salem & Jones, 2010, p. 71)

Faculty who invest much time and effort to implement high-impact practices may get frustrated if students resist, give low teaching evaluations, or complain to a supervisor. These experiences can cause instructors to change their attitudes toward teaching and switch back to a "content delivery" class. If instructors then receive good or even great evaluations, they may never attempt active learning again because not only did they "waste" their time on students who don't want to learn but also they could have potentially hurt their own career by implementing student-centered practices. Some faculty may even develop a sarcastic attitude toward teaching and become resistant to the effort it takes to provide a high-quality learning experience, especially if they feel that students are capable but are not putting forth enough effort. This can also result from adhering to the types of human biases described in chapter 3.

Like students, instructors may hold cultural biases that can be complex. Lindsey and Crusan (2011) described bias against nonnative English speakers if assignments were graded analytically but conducted a study showing that instructors perceived native speakers as less intelligent than nonnative speakers if their writing had a similar amount of errors. The reason may be that nonnative speakers are expected to have more problems with writing in general and grammar in particular. For native English speakers writing expectations are higher and a "disappointment" of these expectations may have been interpreted as lower intelligence.

Helping faculty understand the student population and their level of college preparedness could prove a useful strategy in avoiding frustrations due to unrealistic expectations. For instance, universities could implement teaching workshops for new faculty to address these issues and provide guidance and help if faculty experience problems in their classes or with students outside classes during advising sessions. Faculty too often are left alone if problems occur or are simply punished by having a class taken away or receiving negative evaluations. The mindset of department chairs and universities in general is often not to solve the problem but to make the problem disappear by simply reassigning classes or other methods. It requires a change in the institution's attitude toward faculty and teaching to positively address these types of issues.

Teacher Misbehavior as a Consequence of Student Resistance

The relationship between teacher misbehaviors (see chapters 1 and 3) and student resistance is not a one-way street. Student biases and resistance can also play a significant role in the dynamics of the classroom; they may manifest through subtle cues of disrespect toward an instructor. Several researchers have found student biases based on race and gender (Alexander-Snow, 2004; Alkandari, 2011; Basow, Codos, & Martin, 2013; Feldmann, 2001). For instance, students have shown more resistance to instructors who are part of a racial minority. Alkandari (2011) reported that students tend to respect minority instructors less, resulting in more incivility. Alexander-Snow (2004) found that women and faculty of color had the hardest time creating an environment of mutual respect and therefore had higher levels of classroom incivility than their white male counterparts. Students' ingrained biases can make it challenging for these instructors to overcome such discrimination.

Many students subconsciously respect most those who are perceived as having power in society—namely, white males. These biases are mainly due to gender and racial stereotypes and adversely affect student expectations for instructors who are cultural minorities. When an instructor violates or does not meet cultural expectations, students may respond with resistance and incivility, especially in their student ratings of the instructor. Sinclair and Kunda (2000) found that students' reactions to critical feedback differed by instructor gender. Female instructors who gave negative feedback on a class assignment were rated as less competent compared to male instructors who gave negative feedback. This may be due to the expectation that females should be more nurturing and caring, which may be perceived as at odds with giving critical feedback. Students may be less resistant and show less uncivil behavior with male instructors because males are respected due to perceptions and expectations of dominance (Basow et al., 2013). Finally, students may pay attention and learn differently depending on the race and gender of the instructor. Basow and colleagues (2013) used an experimental design to test the impact of race and gender on student learning as represented by their quiz scores. Students received higher quiz scores when the instructor was white compared to black and when the instructor was male compared to female (Basow et al., 2013). This study does not indicate that an instructor's race or gender makes for an inherently better instructor, but it suggests that students may be primed to give more respect to culturally authoritative figures, which influences their behaviors, such as being more attentive or coming to class on time, and thus their performance.

Student gender also influences teacher ratings. Male students rated female instructors lower than they rated male instructors (Basow, Phelan, & Capotosto, 2006). Male faculty generally receive higher ratings for knowledge/scholarship and enthusiasm/dynamism, whereas female instructors receive higher ratings for student-instructor interaction (Basow & Montgomery, 2005). Because the student is usually unaware of these biases, it can be difficult to mitigate them. Furthermore, these ingrained biases can trigger nonimmediate behaviors and misbehaviors by instructors as tensions develop and the instructor feels the need to defend against student bias and resistance and establish authority.

Unfortunately, faculty often try to assert authority through coercive measures, including grades, negative feedback, pop quizzes, and so on. They may also punish students by limiting the amount of time they make available to students. This may be especially true of instructors who use very time-consuming teaching methods, such as scaffolded writing assignments, portfolios, or other high-impact practices. They may feel resentful and decide that students are not worth the time involved. Other faculty may react to student misbehaviors by embarrassing or scolding the student in front of the class. These strategies by instructors may only make the problems between instructor and students worse, creating a toxic class environment in which learning is compromised. This experience can have long-lasting effects not only for students but also for the instructor, who may carry the fear that this may happen again into subsequent classes.

Biases against instructors can be exacerbated by biases against certain teaching methods—namely, active learning pedagogies. There are several biases against active learning, as discussed in previous chapters, including pushback against responsibility or workload, concern about bad grades, and fear of the unknown. One of the most salient negative experiences for instructors and students in active learning environments can be collaborative work or group work. In fact, group work or collaborative work may be one of the strongest demotivators for students in the context of active learning classes.

Student Biases and Negative Experiences with Collaborative Work

Collaborative work generally refers to a learning strategy in which students work together to learn, solve problems, apply knowledge, or create a product (Smith & McGregor, 1992). The increased focus on active learning methods and high-impact practices (see Kuh, 2008) has also lead to more group work in the classroom (Gamson, 1994). This shift has been bolstered by increases in the number of returning and older students who already work full-time and who appreciate interactive learning experiences (Watkins, 1990). Some accrediting agencies, like the Accreditation Board for Engineering and Technology (ABET), require all engineering majors to work effectively in teams and have good communication skills (ABET, 2014). Research also supports the notion that collaborative work can result in greater learning and greater interpersonal skills, which can better prepare students for their careers (Slavin, 1991).

Collaborative student work also has advantages for instructors. Instructors may find group work useful in establishing better student-instructor interaction and mentoring students (Gillies, 2010). In large classrooms, instructors may find it too time-consuming to meet with each student individually; however, meeting with small groups of students can give instructors more time to mentor students (Gillies, 2010).

Finally, students can benefit from group work in several ways. Students may feel less anxiety about participating in a discussion with a smaller group than in front of the class (Meseke, Nafziger, & Meseke, 2010). Students may feel more obligated to attend class and participate when their group grade is partially dependent on their performance. Students will discover resources they can use to complete tasks with their group, be it a textbook, instructor, or other group members. In a traditional lecture class the student may become dependent on the instructor for knowledge, whereas collaborative work allows students to use resources around them, making them more independent learners (Meseke et al., 2010).

Unfortunately, these advantages of collaborative learning are often not accomplished, and students may have negative experiences with lasting effects that can lead to resistance when another instructor implements group work (Fiechtner & Davis, 1984/1985). Despite the proven positive effects of collaborative work, students often resent group work because of these prior negative experiences. The reasons for negative experiences are manifold and embedded in institutional structure and goals. There is often little to no training for instructors on collaborative work, and as a result, group work is often implemented without the proper guidance and support for students (Johnson & Johnson, 1993). The consequences of poor implementation of group work include problems within the groups and resulting negative attitudes toward group work. One such problem is that work assigned as a whole to students in collaborative groups is often split up among the students themselves. This can lead to fractured learning, in which each student only learns about the area assigned (McCorkle et al., 1999). The student may not see the subject as a whole, the big picture, leading to the learning blockades of unconnected facts and perceived lack of relevance.

Perhaps the most common negative experience students may have with collaborative work is when workload is unequally distributed among members of the group. Students don't hold each other accountable; rather, some students will do a majority of the work in a group, and they expect that in future group work assignments they will also have to do a majority of the work (Johnson & Johnson, 1993). The dominant students feel used and the other students are less involved in the project. Though some dominant students may report positive experiences because they have power, have greater self-confidence, and achieve significant learning outcomes (Pescosolido, 2001), other research suggests that the opposite is also possible. For instance, Pfaff and Huddleston (2003) found that leaders typically felt more used and had a negative outlook on future group work. Other members of the group, especially those who contributed very little, also had a negative outlook on group work. Those students who do little to no work benefit little from collaborative work (Pescosolido, 2001). Students' negative experiences with group work are reinforced when students who contributed a lot and students who contributed very little earn the same grade. The hardworking student feels cheated, and the student who did little work doesn't have any reason for increased effort because there is no punishment for not participating.

Unfair grading is also a significant negative factor in group work (Fiechtner & Davis, 1984/1985). For instructors, especially if they have little experience with group work, it can be very difficult to assign fair grades to the students in one group. In the absence of individual work it may be a guessing game which students contributed how much, and grades can't be assigned by guessing—thus, everybody gets the same grade.

Another important factor for student experiences is who grades the group work. Students typically have more negative thoughts about work that is only graded by the instructor. In surveys collected by Fiechtner and Davis (1984/1985) students expressed anger and regret when they were unable to give feedback and evaluation on their own group members. Reasons for this may be that students feel more responsible when they know they will be evaluated by their own group members. Students may feel that there is more fairness within the group as a result. Therefore both students and instructors should give evaluations to collaborative work.

Peer evaluations are not without problems. It is important that instructors monitor how students evaluate each other because some research shows that students' biases may affect how they evaluate each other. For example, one student may be ganged up on by the others in a group, being forced to do more work or receiving a poor grade from their peers. O'Neil (1985) found that gender bias may also play a role in student grading within a group. He found that students often devalued work contributed by members of the same sex, but Eagly and Carli (1981) reported the exact opposite. They found that students favored members of the same sex and gave them higher grades than opposite gender students in the same group. Naturally, students who receive higher grades on collaborative work typically have more positive expectations for future collaborative work than those receiving low grades. Many of the problems in grading and peer evaluation of teams can be effectively managed through careful designs with strategies like using rubrics or requiring students to differentiate the scores (can't give everyone the same score). Sibley and Ostafichuk (2014), for instance, described at least five different ways (including an online method) that peer evaluation can be used more effectively with collaborative teams: evaluation of teammate performance with real impact on a fixed percentage of the final grade; evaluation of teammate performance using a ratio (individual student's average team rating divided by the overall team average) multiplied by the team's performance grade for a final score; student evaluation of teammates on several dimensions, including cooperation, self-directed learning, and interpersonal skills, combined with instructor evaluation of the quality of students' feedback to each other; qualitative peer assessment asking students to provide feedback on what they appreciated in each teammate and what they would request of the teammate; and use of SPARK or iPeer software to facilitate student online peer evaluations based on instructor-created dimensions and grading impact.

Student attitudes toward collaborative work can be affected by the size of the groups. Typically smaller groups have performed better and have a more positive outcome than larger groups. In larger groups, students can opt out of work more easily, especially when not enough work is given for the size of the group (Cosse, Ashworth, & Weisenberger, 1999). The opposite has also been true for groups given too much work. Therefore, the amount of work given should be fine-tuned to match the size of the groups.

Others have found the most important factor for the success of group work is not size of group (Pfaff & Huddleston, 2003) but rather the ability of the instructor to provide guidance in regard to interpersonal and communication skills, encouraging positive interdependence and making the attainment of good grades dependent on students' individual contributions as well as the accomplishment of the group goal (Johnson & Johnson, 1993). In addition, to create a more symbiotic relationship between student and faculty, Cole (2007) stated that faculty should enthusiastically engage students in the learning process, value students and their comments, create racially and ethnically diverse student groups, and allow students the opportunity to be challenged by professors. These factors have been shown to be helpful for success.

To make group work a positive and productive learning experience, certain requirements are foundational: (a) clear intention, (b) good group formation, (c) structure, (d) scaffolding, and (e) individual accountability (Miller, 2014). First, the instructor must clearly communicate the intent of the group work as well as the purpose, rationale, and benefits of working in a group. Students must understand the expectations of the instructor and what they need to do to accomplish these expectations. Second, group formation should be established by the instructor using criteria such as balancing course-relevant strengths and weaknesses and student diversity to increase learning and exposure to new ideas (Sibley & Ostafichuk, 2014). Sibley and Ostafichuk also emphasized that in team-based learning, teams should be large (5–7 students) and permanent across the semester; these factors may also be useful in other collaborative approaches. Third, structure is critical to make group work a productive learning experience. Instructors should provide guidelines for students. For instance, instructors could provide example protocols that students follow or have all teams working on the same problem so that they can compare thinking and solutions. Fourth, assignments should be scaffolded, providing students with feedback and opportunities to revise their work and increasing in complexity over time as students master course material. Students also need to learn to effectively communicate with their group members, build consensus, and critique each other. Fifth, students must be held accountable as individuals and as a group for their performance. Each group member should have a clear and authentic role within the group. The group members must understand that they can only accomplish the task if each member contributes substantially. This can increase the willingness to help each other and build a sense of community. Instructors should include formative and summative assessments that help students understand what they are doing well and what they need to work on. It also helps instructors understand what students still need to learn to ensure individual and comprehensive learning (Miller, 2014).

Conclusion

The interactions that occur among the instructor and their students and among student peers in the classroom are at the core of motivation, learning, and skill development. Though these interactions are fraught with potential biases and stereotypes, recognized or not, capable instructors are aware of them and should have a plan for how to address them when they arise. At the least, it is helpful to have a colleague mentor or faculty development center to turn to for assistance should negative patterns emerge. It is very important that instructors strive to proactively design their courses and assignments to minimize negative experiences and boost positive interactions and to take steps to ameliorate emergent negative situations and avoid instructor biases and misbehaviors. Not doing so can lead to student memories and expectations of these experiences that increase resistance to future learning, poison the attitudes and expectations of other students, and negatively affect instructors as well. By creating positive, flexible, and respectful classroom experiences, instructors lay the foundation for reduced resistance and enhance the effectiveness of active learning environments.

References

Accreditation Board for Engineering and Technology. (2014). *Criteria for accrediting engineering programs*. Baltimore, MD: Author. Retrieved from http://www.abet.org/accreditation/accreditation-criteria/criteria-for-accrediting-engineering-programs-2015-2016/

Alexander-Snow, M. (2004). Dynamics of gender, ethnicity, and race in understanding classroom incivility. In J. M. Braxton & A. E. Bayer (Eds.), *Addressing faculty and student classroom improprieties* (New Directions for Teaching and Learning No. 99; pp. 21–31). San Francisco, CA: Jossey-Bass.

Alkandari, N. (2011). The level of student incivility: The need of a policy to regulate college student civility. *College Student Journal, 45*(2), 257.

Alsharif, N. Z., & Yongyue Qi, M. S. (2014). A three-year study of the impact of instructor attitude, enthusiasm, and teaching style on student learning in a medicinal chemistry course. *American Journal of Pharmaceutical Education, 78*(7), Article 132.

Basow, S. A., Codos, S., & Martin, J. L. (2013). The effects of professors' race and gender on student evaluations and performance. *College Student Journal, 47*(2), 352–363.

Basow, S. A., & Montgomery, S. (2005). Student evaluations of professors and professor self-ratings: Gender and divisional patterns. *Journal of Personnel Evaluation in Education, 18*, 91–106.

Basow, S. A., Phelan, J. E., & Capotosto, L. (2006). Gender patterns in college students' choices of their best and worst professors. *Psychology of Women Quarterly, 30*(1), 25–35.

Baxter Magolda, M. B. (1992). *Knowing and reasoning in college: Gender-related patterns in students' intellectual development*. San Francisco, CA: Jossey-Bass.

Cole, D. (2007). Do interracial interactions matter? An examination of student-faculty contact and intellectual self-concept. *Journal of Higher Education, 78*(3), 249–281.

Cosse, T. J., Ashworth, D. N., & Weisenberger, T. M. (1999). The effects of team size in a marketing simulation. *Journal of Marketing Theory and Practice, 7*(3), 98–106.

Dolin, D. J. (1995). *Ain't misbehavin': A study of teacher misbehaviors, related to communication misbehaviors, and student resistance* (Unpublished doctoral dissertation). West Virginia University, Morgantown, WV.

Eagly, A. H., & Carli, L. L. (1981). Sex of researchers and sex-typed communications as determinants of sex differences in influenceability: A meta-analysis of social influence studies. *Psychological Bulletin, 90*, 1–20.

Feldmann, L. J. (2001). Classroom civility is another of our instructor responsibilities. *College Teaching, 49*(4), 137–140.

Fiechtner, S. B., & Davis, E. A. (1984/1985). Why some groups fail: A survey of students' experiences with learning groups. *Organizational Behavior Teaching Review, 9*, 58–71.

Gamson, Z. F. (1994). Collaborative learning comes of age. In S. Kadel & J. A. Keehner (Eds.), *Collaborative learning: A sourcebook for higher education* (Vol. 2, pp. 5–17). University Park, PA: National Center on Postsecondary Teaching, Learning and Assessment.

Gillies, R. M. (2010). Teachers' and students' verbal behaviours during cooperative and small-group learning. *British Journal of Instructional Psychology, 76*(2), 271–287.

Goodboy, A. K., & Bolkan, S. (2009). College teacher misbehaviors: Direct and indirect effects on student communication behavior and traditional learning outcomes. *Western Journal of Communication, 73*(2), 204–219.

Goodboy, A. K., Myers, S. A., & Bolkan, S. (2010). Student motives for communicating with instructors as a function of perceived instructor misbehaviors. *Communication Research Reports, 27*(1), 11–19.

Johnson, D. W., & Johnson, R. T. (1993). Implementing cooperative learning. *Education Digest, 58*(8), 62–66.

Kearney, P., Plax, T. G., Hays, E. R., & Ivey, M. J. (1991). College teacher misbehaviors: What students don't like about what teachers say and do. *Communication Quarterly, 39*(4), 309–324.

Kuh, G. (2008). *High-impact educational practices: What they are, who has access to them, and why they matter.* Washington, DC: Association of American Colleges and Universities.

Lavoie, R. (2008). *The motivation breakthrough: 6 secrets to turning on a tuned out child.* New York, NY: Touchstone.

Lindsey, P., & Crusan, D. (2011). How faculty attitudes and expectations toward student nationality affect writing assessment. *Across the Disciplines, 8*(4). Retrieved from http://wac.colostate.edu/atd/ell/lindsey-crusan.cfm

Love, P. G., & Guthrie, V. L. (1999). Perry's intellectual scheme. *New Directions for Student Services, 99*(88), 5–15.

McCorkle, D. E., Reardon, J., Alexander, J. F., Kling, N. D., Harris, R. C., & Iyer, R. V. (1999). Undergraduate marketing students, group projects, and teamwork: The good, the bad, and the ugly? *Journal of Marketing Education, 21*(2), 106–117.

Meseke, C. A., Nafziger, R., & Meseke, J. K. (2010). Student attitudes, satisfaction, and learning in a collaborative testing environment. *Journal of Chiropractor Education, 24*(1), 19–29

Miller, A. (2014). *Not just group work—Productive group work* (Edutopia report for George Lucas Educational Foundation). Retrieved from http://www.edutopia.org/blog/productive-group-work-andrew-miller

Monteiro, S., Almeida, L. S., & Vasconcelos, R. M. (2012). The role of teachers at university: What do high achiever students look for? *Journal of Scholarship of Teaching and Learning, 12*(2), 65–77.

Nugent, T. T. (2009). *The impact of student-teacher interaction on student motivation and achievement* (Doctoral dissertation, University of Central Florida). Retrieved from http://etd.fcla.edu/CF/CFE0002884/Nugent_Tisome_T_200912_EdD.pdf

O'Neill, C. (1985). Imagined worlds in theatre and drama. *Theory Into Practice, 24*(3), 158–165.

Pescosolido, A. T. (2001). Informal leaders and the development of group efficacy. *Small Group Research, 30*, 309–329.

Pfaff, E., & Huddleston, P. (2003). Does it matter if I hate teamwork? What impacts student attitudes toward teamwork? *Journal of Marketing Education, 25*, 37–45.

Prince, M., & Felder, R. (2007). The many faces of inductive teaching and learning. *Journal of College Science Technology, 36*, 14–20.

Salem, L., & Jones, P. (2010). Undaunted, self-critical, and resentful: Investigating faculty attitudes toward teaching writing in a large university writing-intensive course program. *WPA Writing Program Administration, 34*(1), 60–83.

Seidel, S. B., & Tanner, K. D. (2013). "What if students revolt?"—Considering student resistance: Opinions, options, and opportunities for investigation. *CBE Life Science Education, 12*(4), 586–595.

Sibley, J., & Ostafichuk, P. (2014). *Getting started with team-based learning.* Sterling, VA: Stylus.

Sinclair, L., & Kunda, Z. (2000). Motivated stereotyping of women: She's fine if she praised me but incompetent if she criticized me. *Personality and Social Psychology Bulletin, 26*, 1329–1342.

Skinner, C. H. (2002). An empirical analysis of interpersonal research: Evidence, implications, and applications of the discrete task completion hypothesis. *Journal of School Psychology, 40*, 347–368.

Slavin, R. E. (1991). *Student team learning: A practical guide to cooperative learning.* Washington, DC: National Education Association.

Smith, B., & McGregor, J. T. (1992). What is collaborative learning? In A. Goodsell, M. Maher, V. Tinto, B. L. Smith, & J. T. McGregor (Eds.), *Collaborative learning: A sourcebook for higher education.* University Park, PA: National Center on Postsecondary Teaching, Learning and Assessment.

Stipek, D. (2002). *Motivation to learn: Integrating theory and practice.* Boston, MA: Allyn and Bacon. (Original work published 1988)

Thweatt, K. T., & McCroskey, J. C. (1996). Teacher non-immediacy and misbehavior: Unintentional negative communication. *Communication Research Report, 13*, 198–204.

Watkins, B. T. (1990, August 1). Growing number of older students stirs professors to alter teaching styles. *Chronicle of Higher Education,* pp. A1, A12.

Will, P. L., & Wheeless, L. R. (2001). An experimental study of teachers' verbal and nonverbal immediacy and students' affective and cognitive learning. *Communication Education, 50*(4), 327–342.

8

SEEING THE INVISIBLE

How Cognitive and Developmental Influences Shape Student Resistance

Trevor Morris, Rob Blair, and Colt Rothlisberger

A student in an introductory history class takes her seat near the front of the room to get a good view of the day's PowerPoint lecture. The instructor approaches the class, but instead of lecturing he announces there will be a class discussion on today's topic. The student is confused and put off by the deviation from what she expected; didn't she pay tuition to learn from the professor, not to hear the opinions of her classmates? She sits quietly during the discussion, refusing to participate while her classmates share their views on the subject. The student wants to learn the facts from her instructor; after all, he is a world-renowned history expert.

This example illustrates an "invisible" aspect of student development that affects engagement with learning environments: cognitive development. As students progress through college, they develop cognitively through encounters with complex material and situations that challenge their assumptions about the certainty, absoluteness, and even validity of information from authority figures or the way knowledge is constructed. Research has shown that students' thinking changes, incrementally and developmentally, from a simple absolute viewpoint into a multifaceted and more complex approach during college (Thomas, 2008; West, 2004). As this shift occurs, student resistance to instruction may take many different forms. Furthermore, the maturation of the brain is a relevant factor to consider in relation to cognitive development of college students. Instructors need a framework for understanding the invisible aspects of brain maturation and cognitive development to assist students in developing as learners.

Cognitive Development

The cognitive development models discussed in this chapter share a number of epistemological assumptions that further illustrate the invisible aspect of cognitive development. Hofer and Pintrich (1997) argued that students shift in their views on the nature of knowledge and nature of knowing. The nature of knowledge has the following corollary dimensions: (a) the certainty of knowledge, whether it is fixed or malleable, and (b) the simplicity of knowledge, from simple absolute facts to complex constructs that are highly contextual. The nature of knowing also has corollary dimensions: (a) source of knowledge, in which knowledge is transferred from an external authority to knowledge that is constructed internally, and (b) justification of knowing, which is how individuals evaluate authority figures' claims or use evidence and reasoning in decision-making. The models of cognitive development discussed here reflect these dimensions.

In this chapter, we discuss Perry's (1970) model, King and Kitchener's (1994) reflective judgment model, and Baxter Magolda's (1992) epistemological reflection model. Other models of cognitive development exist, but for brevity, we focus on these three models because each highlights different aspects of cognitive development. Each model either uses the term *stage* or *position*. The term *stage* can have different meanings (see King & Kitchener, 1994, pp. 24–27) and involves several important assumptions: (a) the model is organized, (b) the stages are qualitatively different, and (c) there is an invariant sequence. Perry's model rejected the invariant sequence of stages in favor of positions, which allows for regression back to an earlier position (see Perry, 1970, pp. 53–54, 204). King and Kitchener (2004) used stages to describe their model, with the caveat that categories can overlap and transitions between stages are not abrupt. Examining these three models will help instructors consider ways cognitive development contributes to student resistance.

William Perry's Nine Positions

Perry (1970) studied male Harvard students during their four years as undergraduates to document changes in students' intellectual and moral relativism.

His model included nine positions used to illustrate the intellectual change in students. In this model, change is any alteration from a previous position or condition; however, development is a qualitative difference in which an individual's view of the world becomes increasingly complex and allows the individual to integrate a wide range of experiences, viewpoints, and influences (Touchton, Wertheimer, Cornfeld, & Harrison, 1977). The truncation of positions in Perry's model to a fixed-stage model is common with practitioners. These stages are dualism, multiplicity, relativism, and commitment (Kloss, 1994; Love & Guthrie, 1999; Thompson, 1999).

The simplest structure is basic duality or dualism and is the starting point for most college freshmen. Dewey (1997) described the basic duality structure when he wrote, "Mankind likes to think in terms of extreme opposites. It is given to formulating its beliefs in terms of *Either-Ors,* between which it recognizes no intermediate possibilities" (p. 17). Knowledge is received from an authority with absolute certainty (Kloss, 1994; Perry, 1970). In college, the instructor is the authority from whom students receive absolute, certain knowledge. This is a common place for students, and sometimes faculty, to operate from. For example, an instructor strives to initiate critical thinking skills in an astronomy class by posing a question: "What kind of evidence did Cavendish need to support his theory on the size of the Earth's mass?" He waits in silence, not offering a quick answer. Students suggest "extraordinary evidence" and "ordinary evidence" as answers, both of which the professor explains are incorrect. After another period of silence, an annoyed student exclaims, "Why don't you just tell us the right answer?"

Apart from the issue of how the instructor might have handled this situation better to prepare and guide students in their thinking, this example illustrates the positioning of the instructor as an authority figure and student views of knowledge as absolute, right or wrong. In this stage, discussion on a topic such as debating the morality of the death penalty or a professor asking for students' thoughts on a subject without giving the correct answers right away can be difficult and often leaves dualistic students feeling uncomfortable, giving rise to resistant behaviors, even complaints.

The next developmental position is multiplicity. In this position, knowledge is subjective, opinion rather than facts, and instructors are not authorities with certain knowledge, but people with an opinion (Kloss, 1994; Perry, 1970). When authorities disagree or information is inconsistent, the view that knowledge is transferred whole from an authority figure to the student erodes. At this level, a student can accept multiple answers to a question and consider them equally valid. Such students may be baffled or frustrated when receiving poor grades on essays they think were graded according to personal opinion (Kloss, 1994); how can an assignment receive poor marks if there is no correct answer? A common attitude of students in this stage is to infer what the instructor wants or to perform a certain way so they will receive a good grade. For instance, a student may write an essay not because she believes it but because she believes this is what the professor wants to hear, a form of passive resistance.

Relativism follows the multiplicity position. In relativism, students begin to weigh evidence and begin to understand that knowledge is contextual. Not all opinions are equally valid (Kloss, 1994; Perry, 1970); some conclusions or opinions are better substantiated, and different disciplines and experts use their own disciplinary standards to judge and evaluate information. In the final stage of commitment, students make intentional choices and commitments to a discipline or worldview while still understanding and accepting relativism. According to Perry (1970) commitments are "ongoing activity relating a person as agent and chooser to aspects of his life in which he invests his energies, his care, and his identity" (pp. 150–151). Furthermore, there are implications for making those commitments. These students affirm beliefs and values in the context of relativism and develop their own personal and professional worldviews.

The underlying foundation for cognitive development is changes to cognitive structures. Widick (1977) described cognitive structures as "essentially a set of assumptions which act as a filter dictating how the individual will perceive, organize and evaluate events in the environment and, though less directly, how he/she will behave in response to those events" (p. 35). Perry drew on Piaget's concepts of how assimilation and accommodation produce cognitive change. Assimilation is the incorporation of environmental inputs into an existing cognitive structure; accommodation refers to a change in the cognitive structure to deal more effectively with stimuli from the environment (Piaget, 1980). Students' cognitive structures adapt through accommodation to deal with the challenges from the environment that facilitate student growth (Thompson, 1999). As a student changes positions, cognitive structures adapt to the new viewpoint. Cognitive structures for the nature and source of knowledge, the role of the learner, the role of the instructor, and the role of peers are potential sources of resistance as students organize and respond to the learning environment.

To facilitate genuine growth, the learning environment needs to be both challenging *and* supportive. Instructors can create a rigorous course, but in a cold, authoritarian classroom climate, the conditions for growth might be stymied (Pavelich, 1996; see also chapter 7). Humans organize and reorganize their cognitive structures according to their experiences, and to experience growth, they need experiences that are incongruent with their existing structures, such as a required diversity course (Bowman, 2009; King & Baxter

Magolda, 1996) or instructional activities designed to challenge assumptions about themselves or the world.

Blair had an experience in high school during a mock trial that illustrates how incongruence forced an existing structure to change. The idea of a mock trial is relatively simple: Two competing teams receive the same "court case materials," with one team assigned to defend and the other to prosecute the defendant. At the beginning of this process, each team is given a packet with case materials, including legal summaries, witness statements, official police reports, and so forth. Blair's team was tasked with prosecuting a man accused of eco-terrorism, and the team members thought the man was obviously guilty. They successfully achieved the guilty verdict and moved on to the next round of the competition. This time, however, Blair's team would have to defend the man they had just successfully prosecuted. Blair started reexamining the case files and noticed details he had missed. Put in a position to take an opposing stance, Blair experienced cognitive dissonance, and he had to reconsider the nature and certainty of the knowledge he had constructed.

Blair found that knowledge can be contextual and constructed according to one's perspective. For him, the lesson was twofold:

> First, by adopting a perspective, even one I initially disagreed with, I could better understand the strengths, weaknesses, and arguments of the position; and second, however strong my beliefs and assumptions on a topic were, there was always room to learn more if I could leave my perspective flexible.

This example demonstrates how Blair changed his cognitive structures to accommodate new information when he took a different perspective. Authority and absoluteness of knowledge are two internal structures that must be reconciled with the complex environment students encounter, leading to growth. Perry used the term *growth* to describe the movement from dualism toward commitment as cognitive structures accommodate new information or a new perspective. In Perry's model, growth is not guaranteed; students may stagnate in a position, which Perry called *temporizing*, or regress to a previous position, called *retreat*.

When students experience growth, other variables in the students' lives are subject to change. Those can include worldview, the ability to see more than one perspective, openness to alternative perspectives, the ability to assume responsibility, interpersonal view, and assessment of self (Touchton et al., 1977). Students who participate in diversity experiences or service-learning projects show positive cognitive development changes such as in the way they view poverty or social justice (Bowman, 2010). As students move through college, a pattern of moving from one position to another becomes more apparent as students change their internal structure to accommodate complex stimuli.

Although Perry has received criticism for only including men in his study (e.g., Baxter Magolda, 1992; Love & Guthrie, 1999; Schommer, 1990), his model has, nonetheless, been highly influential and useful for describing how students develop cognitively. A given teaching method will affect each student differently; what works for committed knowers may create resistance in dualistic students. This creates difficulty for instructors trying to anticipate potential sources of resistance. However, instructors who understand Perry's positions can use that understanding to better design their courses and assignments to reduce resistance while promoting growth.

King and Kitchener: Reflective Judgments

The key feature of the King and Kitchener (1994) model is reflective judgments. Dewey (1960) noted that reflective judgments have the following qualities important to thinking: (a) doubt and difficulty and (b) search or inquiry to resolve the uncertainty. Ongoing assessment of knowledge is needed to evaluate assumptions and beliefs against existing data or other plausible interpretations of the situation. Reflective judgments help students develop better, more valid conclusions than thinking solely from emotional or authority-based sources.

The Seven Stages of Reflective Judgment

The original seven stages (King & Kitchener, 2004) are often condensed into three areas. Stages 1 through 3 constitute prereflective thinking. The student views knowledge as certain, and authority figures are important sources of knowledge (King & Kitchener, 2004). Students don't use evidence to justify their position, and they often view personal experience as absolute knowledge. Students in stage 3 begin to recognize that authority figures might not have absolute or certain knowledge.

Stages 4 and 5 are quasi-reflective thinking. Students begin to realize that some problems are ill-structured and may involve ambiguity and uncertainty (King & Kitchener, 1994). They begin to use abstract thinking such as giving evidence for beliefs rather than justification based on experiences. However, students' knowledge is filtered through current perceptions, limiting their ability to interpret outside their own situation. A major advance in stage 5 is the ability to examine how knowledge may be justified in one context and not justified in another context. This allows students the ability to recognize alternative theories and the possibility that some evidence might not support an argument in a specific context. A potential source of resistance arises when hot-button issues, such as sexism, racism, and diversity issues, are discussed in the classroom.

In a *New York Times* op-ed, Judith Shulevitz (2015) related the experience of Wendy Kaminer, who received backlash for arguing that use of the "n-word" was appropriate when students study American history or read literature like the *Adventures of Huckleberry Finn* (Twain, 1885). Kaminer argued that in the context of studying history, using a euphemism would be inappropriate for "the n-word." Ms. Kaminer said, "It's amazing to me that they [students] can't distinguish between racist speech and speech about racist speech, between racism and discussions of racism" (Shulevitz, 2015). This quote deftly illustrates how students in this stage evaluate information according to current perception rather than the context from which the information came and the way it is used.

Constructing knowledge, using evidence to come to conclusions, and reconsidering positions are key characteristics of students in reflective stages 6 and 7 (King & Kitchener, 1994). Ill-structured problems that are complex require thinking before one can commit to a solution. Students can begin to compare and contrast evidence for or against a solution for an ill-structured problem and decrease use of the terms *right* or *wrong*. As King and Kitchener put it, "Conclusions are defended as representing the most complete, plausible, or compelling understanding of an issue on the basis of the available evidence" (p. 72). This is different from Perry's commitment position. In Perry's commitment position, a student develops an identity, "who he is," that guides his behaviors, and he assumes responsibilities for his decisions. This suggests commitment is a form of developing identity rather than appraising the nature of one's thinking that is argued in stage 7 of the reflective judgment model.

Research on the Model

Longitudinal and cross-sectional analyses have evaluated the reflective judgment model and suggested that graduate students score higher than college students, and college students score higher than high school students (King & Kitchener, 2004) on the use of reflective judgment. However, King and Kitchener (1994) offered a word of caution:

> Age alone would not be expected to lead to higher scores; there is no reason to believe that the passage of time alone should influence the development of reflective thinking unless it corresponds to some other intervening event (such as neurological maturation or age-related involvement in an intellectually stimulating environment). (p. 125)

It's not clear whether age or maturation, life experience, or education attainment causes the shift in reflective thinking, although the results suggest a steady progression through young adulthood. Interestingly, progress of students through the model shows some fuzziness; that is, a student predominantly in stage 3 might show some characteristics of stage 2 and stage 4. The boundaries between stages appear to be porous rather than clearly demarcated.

The time of progression through the stages is important to consider. College semesters typically last about four months. Results suggest that over longer periods (i.e., years), students' progress to higher levels. Major shifts in reflective thinking might not be evident in a semester class. However, smaller shifts can occur. For instance, "Barry Kroll (1992b) has described this type of development; students are abandoning 'ignorant certainty' (characteristics of earlier stage reasoning) in favor of 'intelligent confusions'" (King & Kitchener, 1994, p. 166). Intelligent confusion is an advancement over ignorant certainty and is evidence of development in the reflective judgment model. This small shift in reflective thinking may or may not be evident to the instructor; it is nonetheless an advancement to a higher level of reflective thinking.

Linvill and Mazer (2011) studied the role of reflective judgments in students' perceptions of faculty ideological bias. Sometimes the professoriate is perceived as having a liberal bias. The researchers concluded that students in prereflective thinking stages were more likely to perceive an ideological bias in faculty than students in higher stages; this seems likely to increase the probability of resistant behaviors. King (2000) advocated the use of controversial, ill-structured issues to help students develop beyond the prereflective stages. For example, a faculty member might use the topic of climate change to illustrate converging evidence and then explore different types of evidence used to reach a conclusion. To some students in the prereflective stage, this may appear as an attempt at liberal indoctrination rather than an exercise in reasoning; students in a higher reflective stage might view the faculty member as challenging their thinking.

To promote reflective thinking in students, King (2000) offered several suggestions. Instructors should be respectful of students and understand that students' assumptions are how they create meaning. Instructors who are disrespectful or lack warmth toward students (nonimmediate; see chapter 7) may provoke them to withdraw or actively resist. It is important for students to engage with controversial or ill-structured problems and to see how different lines of evidence or reasoning could be used. Students need opportunities to examine their viewpoints and others' viewpoints. They need to be shown how to gather information and interpret it. Students also need to be shown how to judge relevancy of the information. Instructors should give students feedback and emotional support when dealing with issues of uncertainty so that they can tolerate it without withdrawing or resisting for lack of concrete certainty.

Baxter Magolda: The Epistemological Reflection Model

Baxter Magolda's work is similar to Perry's, but she included women in her longitudinal study, correcting one of the main criticisms of Perry's work. Baxter Magolda's (1992) model contains the following salient assumptions: (a) Developmental patterns are related to gender but are not exclusive to one gender or the other, and (b) patterns are socially constructed. This aligns with constructivists who "emphasize that knowledge and understanding are highly social. We do not construct them individually; we co-construct them in dialogue with others" (Perkins, 1999, p. 7). Student interactions with peers and instructors assist or hinder cognitive development. For example, if the student views disciplinary knowledge as absolute whereas the instructor views it as relative, the student can respond in two ways. If he views the instructor as an adversary, then the chance of progress is slim. However, if he trusts the instructor and is willing to entertain the possibility of new information, then development is more likely to happen.

Baxter Magolda's (1992) epistemological reflection model contains four stages: absolute knowing, transitional knowing, independent knowing, and contextual knowing. Each stage interacts with the roles of the learner, peers, and instructor; the purpose of evaluation; and the nature of knowledge (see Baxter Magolda, 1992, p. 30). For example, in the absolute knowing stage, instructors are to communicate to students what they need to know, and students receive that knowledge. Students regurgitate what was learned as part of evaluation. Peers share materials and what they learned from authorities with each other. In the transitional knowing stage, the learner seeks to understand knowledge and shifts to the view that some knowledge may be uncertain. Peers provide a forum to exchange knowledge. Independent knowing learners begin to think for themselves and create their own perspectives. But because they view knowledge as uncertain, they conclude everyone has their own beliefs. Peers are a source of knowledge and opinions. Instructors promote exchanges of opinion and independent thinking. The last stage is contextual knowing. Knowledge is contextual, based on relevant evidence. The instructor encourages application of knowledge in specific contexts, and peers are a useful source of knowledge exchange. Evaluation measures competence, and both student and teacher work toward learning goals.

Students in Baxter Magolda's (1992) research articulated examples of each stage. For instance, one student illustrated the absolute knowledge stage, saying, "The factual information is cut and dried. It is either right or wrong. If you know the information, you can do well. It is because you just read or listen to a lecture about the ideas. Then you present it back to the teacher" (Baxter Magolda, 1992, p. 77). The student exemplifies both the certainty of knowledge and the belief that the role of evaluation is to show the instructor what was learned. Both of these are characteristics of the absolute knowledge stage. On the other end of the spectrum, a student in contextual knowing explained, "As you hear other people's opinions, you piece together what you really think. Who has the valid point? Whose point is not valid in your opinion? And come to some other new understanding" (Baxter Magolda, 1992, p. 173).

In this model, one stage tends to be predominant at a time. Absolute knowing is prominent during freshman year and declines throughout college. Transitional knowing is dominant in junior and senior years but declines after year five as independent knowing becomes stronger. Cognitive development progresses slowly according to this model. By the end of the fourth year, many students have only transitioned from the absolute knowing stage to the transitional knowing stage, although some may have progressed further. Instructors probably won't see significant shifts in students' cognitive development over a typical semester according to the reflective judgment model.

Baxter Magolda's model built on these four stages by adding the dimension of gender to each stage of cognitive development, except for the contextual knowing stage, in which no gender differences were found. For example, Baxter Magolda named the two patterns in the absolute knowing stage *receiving* and *mastering*. Her research shows that more women showed the receiving pattern and more men displayed the mastering pattern (Baxter Magolda, 1992). The receiving pattern was characterized by an internal approach, creation of comfortable learning environments and relationships with peers, plenty of opportunities to display knowledge, and minimal interaction with the instructor. Interaction with peers and instructor that facilitates mastery, is critical of instructor, and shows preference for verbal learning characterized the mastery pattern.

Likewise, Baxter Magolda (1992) described the patterns in the transitional knowing stage as *interpersonal* and *impersonal*. Women were more likely to display the interpersonal pattern, whereas men were more likely to display the impersonal pattern. Students with an interpersonal pattern focus on the uncertainty of knowledge and learning that is practical. They interact with peers to share ideas. The instructor allows students to explore self-expression and creates a positive interaction with students. Students with the impersonal pattern view knowledge as a balance between certainty and uncertainty to be resolved with logic and reasoning. The role of peers is to express opinions and debate ideas with each other. The learners' role is to engage in debates. Students shift from a focus on mastery of the content to mastery of the process.

In the independent knowing stage, women are more likely to manifest an interindividual pattern, while men tend to show an individual pattern in their development (Baxter Magolda, 1992). In this stage, knowledge shifts from certain truths learned from an authority to an understanding that knowledge is less certain. Students themselves become central to knowledge formation as they learn, relate new ideas to their own experiences, and begin to think for themselves. This generative process of knowledge formation changes how students interact with peers and authorities.

Students with the interindividual pattern acknowledge that others are also generating knowledge from their own perspective, which can include their own interpretations and biases. Even with the potential for bias in others' opinions, interindividual students value listening to what others think. These students view their peers and instructors as equals with opinions that can influence the still malleable knowledge perspective the student is generating. In this way, social interactions with others have an apparent influence on interindividual students' generative knowledge formation.

In contrast, students with an individual pattern recognize that others are generating their own perspective, but they tend to emphasize their own ideas and perspective. They are less likely to listen to or incorporate the perspective of others. Individual pattern students appreciate instructors who give students space to make meaning for themselves or allow them opportunities to pursue their own learning goals. Both of these independent knowing patterns move the instructor from being the sole source of knowledge and place more power in students to construct their own knowledge and perspectives.

Parallels can be drawn between Perry's model and Baxter Magolda's model: the changing nature of knowledge from absolute to contextual, from receiving knowledge to generating knowledge; the changing nature in the authority figure or instructor; and the changing role of the student from passively receiving knowledge to actively constructing knowledge. Additionally, resistance in the Baxter Magolda model can take on gender-related patterns. Receiving-pattern students see instructors as *holders of the truth*. It is, in the student's mind, the instructor's responsibility to provide adequate information for the student's advancement in his or her academic or professional career. In the perceived relationship, receiving-pattern students do not relate well to the instructor. The instructor is seen as a being on a higher plane of absolute knowledge who should transmit knowledge to the student. Interaction should take place only for the purpose of clarification and problem-solving.

How can instructors help students to develop cognitively? Baxter Magolda suggested the following:

- *Validating students as knowers is essential to promoting student voices.* Until students feel that what they think has some validity, it is impossible for them to view themselves as capable of constructing knowledge.
- *Situating learning in the students' own experience legitimizes their knowledge as a foundation for constructing new knowledge.*
- *Defining learning as jointly constructing meaning empowers students to see themselves as constructing knowledge.* The goal of validating students and situating learning in experience cannot be complete without defining learning as jointly constructing meaning. . . . Entertaining students' ideas does not necessarily mean acceptance of them, as both Shor and Freire (1987) and Noddings (1984) make clear. It does, however, require teachers to respect these perspectives, engage in dialogue about them, and be willing to alter their own as needed.
- *The relational component evident in all of these three findings is essential to empower students to construct knowledge.* Validation via relational approaches confirms students as people and knowers. (Baxter Magolda, 1992, pp. 376, 378, 380–381, 382; italics in original)

The relationships between instructors and students are highlighted in these suggestions. As students move from a view of knowledge as certain, received from authority, they can begin to contribute to the construction of knowledge. Instructors can facilitate this through dialogue with students. Resistance may rise to the surface from time to time, but the benefit to the student's cognitive development is invaluable. Students are on a journey of self-authorship and need faculty to convey respect and guidance as they move from the safety of having others define their identity to taking responsibility for their own identity and beliefs (Baxter Magolda, 2000).

Conclusions From the Three Models

Student resistance looks slightly different when viewed through the lens of each developmental model. Perry's model emphasizes how knowledge is construed; King and Kitchener's model emphasizes metacognitive, self-reflective development; and Baxter Magolda's takes into consideration gender and social interaction. Resistance to instructional methods is likely to occur throughout the cognitive development of the student. Instructors should view this as a natural progression of cognitive development rather than as an affront to instructor authority and should consider course level and ways to nudge students into higher levels of development (Kloss, 1994) through active engagement and an emphasis on relevance.

Troublesome Knowledge and Threshold Concepts

A social constructivist, Perkins (1999) defined four types of *troublesome knowledge*: inert, ritual, conceptually difficult, and foreign. Inert knowledge is held by a person but is not regularly used, mostly due to lack of connection or relevance to the person's life. Ritual knowledge lacks personal meaning; it is used when knowledge is part of a social ritual or "how we answer when asked such-and-such, the routine that we execute to get a particular result" (Perkins, 1999, pp. 8–9). A disruption to an expected routine may cause distress and could result in grade grubbing and academic entitlement. Students in the early stages of Perry's (1970) or Baxter Magolda's (1992) models are prone to relying on ritual knowledge. The instructor and students are part of an established routine: The instructor presents information, and students demonstrate what they know. Any disruption of this ritual causes uncertainty and anxiety in some students.

Conceptually difficult knowledge is more complex; it involves concepts that may be multifaceted or that may be counterintuitive to students' current understandings. In struggling with conceptually difficult knowledge, some students fall back on personal experience, which can lead to misunderstandings; they may use ritual knowledge to respond to certain questions (such as quantitative questions) and their personal beliefs or experiences to respond to others (like qualitative or reflective questions or concepts) (Hill, 2010). As a result, students may be able to define terms as is common in ritual knowledge but struggle when the knowledge is applied to another context. Students early in the developmental models often show these patterns.

Foreign knowledge comes from perspectives and values different from the student's own because of culture, religion, historical era, ethnicity, and other factors; foreign knowledge can be useful in provoking reflection in student reasoning because it challenges students to think in new ways, to see things from a different point of view. The key to helping students make progress developmentally is to help them see the relevance of course content to their lives and to understanding the world, and then actively engage them in making use of conceptually difficult and foreign knowledge with a variety of methods (Hill, 2010).

Another type of troublesome knowledge arises through a process akin to a paradigm shift called *threshold concepts*. The "basic idea [is] that in certain disciplines there are 'conceptual gateways' or 'portals' that lead to a previously inaccessible, and initially perhaps 'troublesome,' way of thinking" (Meyer &

Land, 2005, p. 373). Blair experienced threshold concepts in his mock trial example from high school. In his case, how evidence and how arguments are made in a law scenario were transformed in his thinking by looking at the case from the other side. In another example, idiosyncratic thinking that characterizes stage 4 of the reflective judgment model may result from students not grasping disciplinary threshold concepts. This may lead students to rely heavily on prior assumptions and conceptually difficult knowledge. The process of learning threshold concepts may make students feel uncomfortable because of the ambiguous learning process, and they may resist learning until threshold concepts are fully understood. Once threshold concepts are learned, students' thinking is transformed in new ways.

Brain Maturation

King and Kitchener (1994) noted that physical maturation of the brain contributes to cognitive development. It is commonly thought that cognitive development is the result of brain growth, specifically increases in brain volume. However, Fuster (2002) explained that anatomy and connectivity are both important. This nuanced account of brain maturation better explains cognitive development than looking at brain volume alone. Understanding brain development can help faculty think through course design elements and better explain to students why specific pedagogies are being used in class.

The cortex is the outer layer of the brain, the last part to mature. It is divided into four lobes: occipital, parietal, temporal, and frontal. Frontal cortex development continues well into the late teens and early 20s (Fuster, 2002). The prefrontal cortex consists of three regions related to problem-solving and decision-making and is of particular interest when considering cognitive development. Furthermore, these three regions are associated with attention, memory, motivation, reward, and inhibitory control of impulses (Fuster, 2002; Segalowitz & Davies, 2004; Shad et al., 2011), all of which play important roles in cognitive activity.

College students need to be able to sustain their attention and direct their behavior toward a goal. As the capacity to sustain attention and inhibit impulses increases, students are better able to direct their behaviors toward a learning goal. For instance, this may help students ignore distractions like Facebook or a text to work on a research paper for class. The ability to sustain attention increases with age. Furthermore, rewards have an "age-dependent impact on sustained attention networks. . . . In adolescence top-down executive attention control and reward processing systems are less mature and may consequently be less able to inhibit hyper-responsive paralimbic systems that respond to motivationally salient events" (Smith,

Halari, Giampetro, Brammer, & Rubia, 2011, p. 1702), such as Instagram updates.

Furthermore, positive feedback is more effective than negative feedback in improving student performance; late teens and young adults handle negative feedback better and make appropriate adjustments. This difference is associated with the development of the frontal cortex as it matures to the adult brain (van Duijvenvoorde, Zanolie, Rombouts, Raijmakers, & Crone, 2008). With increased access to communication technology, some students, especially younger ones, may struggle to ignore texts or Facebook postings. This may contribute to student resistance, especially if the instructor attempts to limit social media intrusions into the learning environment.

Memory development is also important. Maturation of the prefrontal cortex is related to increases in both working memory and prospective memory (Ward, Shum, McKinlay, Baker-Tweney, & Wallace, 2005). Prospective memory is the ability to remember to do something in the future at a specific time and is a key aspect of planning. Working memory is a limited space where information for the current task is held and manipulated (Bayliss, Jarrold, Baddeley, & Gunn, 2005). Attention is a key component of working memory; however, there is only a finite amount of attention and resources in working memory. Working memory is important for many cognitive abilities, like problem-solving, reading, and math, and is predictive of academic accomplishment (Crone, Wendelken, Donohue, van Leijenhorst, & Bunge, 2006).

Although prefrontal cortex maturation increases the specialization and capacity of working memory, instructors need to recognize that working memory is a limited resource. Instructors, as disciplinary experts, have the ability to "chunk" or condense related concepts and examples into working memory and then to manipulate them. For example, an instructor may pose a situation or problem to the class; she can quickly identify multiple concepts or relationships present in the problem and then analyze them to produce a solution. However, to novice learners, each concept is relatively new and takes up its own space in working memory; in addition, the student then has to work out the relationships and nuances in the data, which may overwhelm his or her capacity to maintain all of the information in memory, much less manipulate it. This cognitive "overload" can lead to student frustration, feelings of being overwhelmed, or even resentment if students believe the instructor is being patronizing or mocking their lack of understanding. This situation exemplifies the curse of knowledge described in chapter 3, but instructors who are aware of working memory can better scaffold such a discussion or assignment in ways that allow and encourage students to develop and gradually test new knowledge and cognitive networks to produce results with less resistance.

From a developmental approach, the brain develops into the late teens or early adulthood. However, even when the gross anatomy or architecture of the adult brain has matured in early adulthood, the brain is not static. Segalowitz and Davies (2004) cautioned that brain size alone may be insufficient to explain the differences among child, teen, and adult results. By age 7, 90% of the adult brain size is reached. The adult-sized brain is reached by age 11. Changes in the brain occur not in the gross anatomy of the brain but in the connections between neurons and the strengths of neuronal networks; in essence, neuronal networks are malleable, creating the conditions that enable cognitive structures to change and adapt to the environment.

In adolescence and adulthood, the neural networks developed at individual synapses become a more salient component of brain maturation that is affected by the environment (Geidd et al., 1999). This is referred to as *plasticity* and plays a crucial role in cognitive development. This is why engaging students with conceptually difficult knowledge, foreign knowledge, and threshold concepts can promote cognitive development as students' brains adapt to new information and revise or prune earlier networks and reduce the strength of preexisting beliefs and cognitive structures. This process encourages students to shift from perceiving their intelligence and abilities as fixed or static to realizing that they can continue learning and gaining intelligence throughout their lives; this will be described in more detail in chapter 9 during the discussion of the work of Carol Dweck.

Conclusion

Understanding the multifaceted nature of cognitive development and brain maturation can give instructors a view of the invisible forces that influence students' development. Humans are the only animals sophisticated enough to reflect on abstractions such as the nature and origins of knowledge. Perry (1970), King and Kitchener (1994), and Baxter Magolda (1992) have each presented a model that highlights different dimensions of cognitive development and the way humans systematically change along those dimensions. Resistance to learning may occur naturally and can be expected when instructors challenge students' underlying assumptions about themselves or the world or encourage students to move past views of knowledge as concrete and certain. With careful course design and scaffolding of challenges, a student may progress in cognitive development, although this may not be immediately apparent because of the time it takes for cognitive development to consolidate. Late adolescents and young adults might not have a fully matured brain in terms of their capacity for advanced cognitive tasks. Yet even when the brain is fully matured, neuroplasticity allows it to continually adapt to the environment. Knowing these concepts gives the instructor tools to anticipate resistance and respond effectively to promote growth, vital steps toward the development of student core intellectual and professional skills. The elucidation of the invisible nature of cognitive development and brain maturation are powerful and significant components of the integrated model of student resistance and may explain some of what students experience in the learning environment.

References

Baxter Magolda, M. (1992). *Knowing and reasoning in college: Gender-related patterns in student development.* San Francisco, CA: Jossey-Bass.

Baxter Magolda, M. (2000, Summer). Teaching to promote holistic learning and development. *New Directions for Teaching and Learning, 82,* 88–98.

Bayliss, D. M., Jarrold, C., Baddeley, A. D., & Gunn, D. M. (2005). The relationship between short-term memory and working memory: Complex span made simple? *Memory, 13,* 414–421. doi:10.1080/09658210344000332

Bowman, N. A. (2009). College diversity courses and cognitive development among students from privileged and marginalized groups. *Journal of Diversity in Higher Education, 2*(3), 182–194. doi:10.1037/a0016639

Bowman, N. A. (2010). College diversity experiences and cognitive development: A meta-analysis. *Review of Educational Research, 80*(1), 4–33. doi:10.3102/0034654309352495

Crone. E. A., Wendelken, C., Donohue, S., van Leijenhorst., L., & Bunge, S. A. (2006). Neurocognitive development of the ability to manipulate information in working memory. *PNAS, 103*(24), 9315–9320. doi:10.1073/pnas.0510088103

Dewey, J. (1997). *Experience and education.* New York, NY: Touchstone. (Original work published in 1938)

Fuster, J. M. (2002). Frontal lobe and cognitive development. *Journal of Neurocytology, 31*(3), 373–385. doi:10.1023/A:1024190429920

Geidd, J. N., Blumenthal, J., Jeffries, N. O., Castellanos, F. X., Liu, H., Zijdenbos, A., . . . Rapoport, J. L. (1999). Brain development during childhood and adolescence: A longitudinal MRI study. *Nature America, 2*(10), 861–863.

Hill, S. (2010). Troublesome knowledge: Why don't they understand? *Health Information and Libraries Journal, 27*(1), 80–83.

Hofer, B. K., & Pintrich, P. R. (1997). The development of epistemological theories: Beliefs about knowledge and knowing and their relation to learning. *Review of Educational Research, 67*(1), 88–140. Retrieved from www.jstor.org/stable/1170620

King, P. M. (2000, Summer). Learning to make reflective judgments. *New Directions for Teaching and Learning, 82,* 15–26.

King. P. M., & Baxter Magolda, M. (1996). Developmental perspective on learning. *Journal of College Student Development, 40*(5), 599–609.

King, P. M., & Kitchener, K. S. (1994). *Developing reflective judgment: Understanding and promoting intellectual growth and critical thinking in adolescents and adults.* San Francisco, CA: Jossey-Bass

King, P. M., & Kitchener, K. S. (2004). Reflective judgment: Theory and research on the development of epistemic assumptions through adulthood. *Educational Psychology, 39*(1), 5–18.

Kloss, R. J. (1994). A nudge is best. *College Teaching, 42*(4), 151–158. doi:10.1080 /87567555.1994.9926847

Linvill, D. L., & Mazer, J. P. (2011). Perceived ideological bias in the college classroom and the role of student reflective thinking: A proposed model. *Journal of the Scholarship of Teaching and Learning, 11*(4), 90–101.

Love, P. G., & Guthrie, V. L. (1999). Perry's intellectual scheme. *New Directions for Student Services, 99*(88), 5–15. doi:10.1002/ss.8801

Meyer, J., & Land, R. (2005). Threshold concepts and troublesome knowledge (2): Epistemoligical considerations and a conceptual framework for teaching and learning. *Higher Education, 49,* 373–388. doi:10.1007/s10734-004-6779-5

Pavelich, M. J. (1996). Helping students develop higher-level thinking: Use of the Perry Model. *Proceedings of the 26th Annual Frontiers in Education Conference, 1,* 163–167. doi:10.1109/FIE.1996.569935

Perkins, D. (1999). The many faces of constructivism. *Educational Leadership, 57*(3), 6–11.

Perry, W. G. (1970). *Forms of intellectual and ethical development in the college years: A scheme.* New York, NY: Holt, Rinehart and Winston.

Piaget, J. (1980). *Adaptation and intelligence.* Chicago, IL: University of Chicago Press.

Schommer, M. (1990). Effects of beliefs about the nature of knowledge on comprehension. *Journal of Educational Psychology, 82*(3), 498–504. doi:10.1037/0022-0663.82.3.498

Segalowitz, S. J., & Davies, P. L. (2004). Charting the maturation of the frontal lobe: An electrophysiological strategy. *Brain and Cognition, 55,* 116–133. doi:10.1016/ S0278-2626(03)00283-5

Shad, M. U., Bidesi, A. S., Chen, L., Thomas, B. P., Ernst, M., & Rao, U. (2011). Neurobiology of decision-making in adolescents. *Behavioral Brain Research, 217,* 67–76. doi:10.1016/j.bbr.2010.09.033

Shulevitz, J. (2015, March 21). In college and hiding from scary ideas. *New York Times.* Retrieved from http://www.nytimes.com/2015/03/22/opinion/sunday/ judith-shulevitz-hiding-from-scary-ideas.html?_r=0

Smith, A. B., Halari, R., Giampetro, V., Brammer, M., & Rubia, K. (2011). Developmental effects of reward on sustained attention networks. *NeuroImage, 56*(3), 1693–1704. doi:10.1016/j.neuroimage.2011.01.072

Thomas, J. A. (2008). Reviving Perry: An analysis of epistemological change by gender and ethnicity among gifted high school students. *Gifted Child Quarterly, 52*(1), 87–98. doi:10.1177/0016986207311422

Thompson, J. M. (1999). Enhancing cognitive development in college classrooms: A review. *Journal of Instructional Psychology, 26*(1), 56–63.

Touchton, J. G., Wertheimer, L. C., Cornfeld, J. L., & Harrison, K. H. (1977). Career planning and decision-making: A developmental approach to the classroom. *Counseling Psychologist, 6*(4), 42–47. doi:10.1177/001100007700600417

Twain. M. (1885/2002). *The adventures of Huckleberry Finn*. New York, NY: Penguin Classics.

van Duijvenvoorde, A. C. K., Zanolie, K., Rombouts, S. A. R. B., Raijmakers, M. E. J., & Crone, E. A. (2008). Evaluating the negative or valuing the positive? Neural mechanisms supporting feedback-based learning across development. *Journal of Neuroscience, 28*(38), 9495–9503. doi:10.1523/JNEUROSCI.1485-08.2008

Ward, H., Shum, D., McKinlay, L., Baker-Tweney, S., & Wallace, G. (2005). Development of prospective memory: Tasks based on the prefrontal-lobe model. *Child Neuropsychology, 11*(6), 527–549. doi:10.1080/09297040490920186

West, E. J. (2004). Perry's legacy: Models of epistemological development. *Journal of Adult Development, 11*(2), 61–70. doi:068-0667/04/0400-0061/0

Widick, C. (1977). The Perry scheme: A foundation for developmental practices. *Counseling Psychologist, 6*(4), 35–38. doi:10.1177/001100007700600415

9

HOW PROMOTING STUDENT METACOGNITION CAN REDUCE RESISTANCE

Rob Blair, Anton O. Tolman, Janine Kremling, and Trevor Morris

Student resistance to learning and principles for overcoming resistance are closely related to the concepts of cognition and metacognition. *Cognition* generally refers to knowledge or knowing and the mental processes through which knowledge is acquired (Cacioppo & Petty, 1982). In contrast, *metacognition* involves *self-awareness* of cognition and regulation of cognition (Vrugt & Oort, 2008), or the overseeing and control of cognitive processes—that is, knowledge about cognitive processes and control of cognitive processes (i.e., acquiring knowledge) (Allen & Armour-Thomas, 1991). In addition, *metacognition* has also been defined as "people's abilities to predict their performances on various tasks and to monitor their current levels of mastery and understanding" (Bransford, Brown, & Cocking, 2000, p. 13). The goal of promoting metacognition is to increase students' responsibility for their own learning and to encourage them to become more active in the learning process (Flavell, 1979).

Flavell (1979) defined four classes of *metacognitive phenomena*. First, *metacognitive knowledge* is defined as "your (a child's, an adult's) stored world knowledge that has to do with people as cognitive creatures and with their diverse cognitive tasks, goals, actions, and experiences" (Flavell, 1979, p. 906). For instance, a person may believe that he is better in learning a new language than in math. The term also refers to beliefs about cognitive differences between individuals. Some students may believe that they are not as capable in writing as other students. Second, people have *metacognitive experiences*—that is, "any conscious cognitive or affective experiences that accompany and pertain to any intellectual enterprise" (Flavell, 1979, p. 906). An example of a metacognitive experience is a situation in which a person is reading a book and is aware that she doesn't understand the content. Another example is a student feeling that he will likely fail the upcoming exam. Third, *goals* or *tasks* refer to the "objective of a cognitive enterprise" (Flavell, 1979, p. 907). A student may have the goal to pass a class she feels will be very difficult but get an A in another, easier class. Fourth, *actions* or *strategies* are cognitions or behaviors to achieve the goals. Actions or strategies may include behaviors such as studying more effectively and/or attending tutoring sessions. This chapter will focus primarily on metacognitive goals and actions or strategies.

Metacognition and cognitive development have a shared and potentially reciprocal relationship. To develop better metacognition, more advanced cognitive development (chapter 8) is important, and to advance cognitive development, metacognition is necessary (Bransford, Brown, & Cocking, 2000; Flavell, 1979). Cognitive strategies are important to improve cognitive skills, and metacognition is important to monitor improvement and recognize strengths and weaknesses (Flavell, 1979). Without cognitive processes students would not learn; without metacognition, students would not know how much they have learned and where they need to improve. Stated differently, a cognitive strategy is to read about a certain topic to increase knowledge; a metacognitive strategy is to ask yourself questions to test your knowledge.

For instructors it is imperative to understand why students resist learning and how metacognition can be used as a tool to overcome student resistance. Students who are able to think and evaluate their behavior via metacognition may understand that they are resisting and what causes their own resistance. They may also understand that their resistance is a behavior that hinders learning and developmental growth (Flavell, 1979) and thus be moved to change it.

Mindsets and Resistance to Learning

One psychological theory useful for understanding student resistance describes the self-theories of students. Dweck's (2000) research into "self-theories" evaluated how students perceived themselves, the structuring or implicit beliefs that influence major aspects of one's identity. Dweck called this structuring belief a "self-theory" or, in the literature released for the general population (Dweck, 2006), a "mindset." A mindset is a collection of ideas and beliefs about how the world works and how we, as individuals, work within it. Given these structuring beliefs, students' perceptions about learning opportunities can vary significantly, and these beliefs can have a dramatic influence on how a student views risk taking, learning itself, or the definition of *success*—or *failure*.

Dweck (2006) explored two primary self-theories or mindsets: the *fixed mindset* and the *growth mindset*. According to her research, people with a fixed mindset believe that their "qualities are carved in stone" and that "people only have a certain amount of intelligence, a certain personality, and a certain moral character" (p. 6). Therefore, putting forth effort or struggling to learn something would be an acknowledgment of a lack of innate intelligence or talent. Thus, when students with a fixed mindset are challenged to do things that they believe they cannot do effortlessly, this challenge will be met with resistance (Dweck, 2006), primarily related to self-preservation. Challenging work is a risk to the self-identity of a person with a fixed mindset because it could demonstrate that he is not as smart as he thinks; it generates anxiety and the possibility of failure. Conversely, tasks that he believes are straightforward and in which he will do well validates and supports his self-identity, making him feel good about himself.

On the contrary, people with a growth mindset believe that "your basic qualities are things that you can cultivate through your efforts. Although people may differ in every which way—in their initial talents, aptitudes, interests, or temperaments—everyone can change and grow through application and experience" (Dweck, 2006, p. 7). Students with a growth mindset tend to see challenges as opportunities and are more open to putting forth effort to learn. These students are less likely to resist learning because they believe that a person's true potential is unforeseeable and that they can improve and overcome deficiencies (Dweck, 2006). To these students, failure on a task is not failure as a person; it is a chance to learn something new.

Mindsets and Teacher Behaviors

Studies on Dweck's "mindset model" have demonstrated the value of her self-theories. Mueller and Dweck (1998) looked at the mindset of students given praise in the classroom. Two groups of students were given a problem-solving test and were then praised on their scores either by giving trait-oriented praise (e.g., "You must be really smart at these"), effort-oriented praise (e.g., "You must have worked hard"), or generalized praise (e.g., "This is a good score"). The groups were then given the chance to do a harder set of problem-solving questions. The trait-praised group was less likely to take on this greater challenge. What's more, their lower score on the second test was more likely to cause negative emotion, lower enjoyment, and lower persistence. Perhaps the most interesting outcome, however, is that these students performed significantly worse than both the effort-praised group (which did the best) and the control group. Students in the trait-praised group were also surprisingly likely to lie, with 40% of them misrepresenting their scores when such an opportunity presented itself compared to almost none of the effort-praised students. Mindsets extend beyond isolated incidents like those created by this study. The mindset of students also has a substantial impact on the performance goals those students hold (Dweck & Leggett, 1988). Students with a fixed mindset, when given a choice, would select a task that documents their competencies or abilities, whereas students with a growth mindset would select a challenging task, a task that increases their competencies. In addition, multiple studies have demonstrated that achievement levels themselves are heavily influenced by mindset during both adolescent education and the college years. For instance, Blackwell, Trzesniewski, and Dweck (2007) found that students' math achievement could be significantly improved for those who had a growth mindset. In sum, studies on contingent self-worth have found that those who feel bad about doing something wrong are less likely to change the problematic behavior or aim to resolve the negative outcomes (Tangney, 1995). These studies have implications not only for student learning but also for instructors as it relates closely to resistance to learning. To better understand why some students happily embrace new challenges and others resist those challenges, one must understand where the mindset comes from. This understanding will aid in overcoming resistance and helping students develop their potential.

Where Does a Mindset Come From?

A mindset doesn't come from a single place, nor is it a consistent and immutable trait of an individual's personality (Dweck, 2006). According to Dweck, mindset is also not a trait someone is born with, or else some children would never learn to walk or talk. Mindset develops via interaction with others and is influenced by a large number of factors, all of which are part of the integrated model of student resistance. Some of the most salient factors are socialization via parenting and experiences in school (Dweck, 2006). For instance, as described previously, studies have shown that praise for ability rather than effort can lead to the development of resistance toward challenges because of children's fear that not being able to complete a more challenging task would be met with negative feedback (Dweck, 2006). Contrarily, children who were praised for effort rather than ability were motivated to work harder and chose more challenging tasks. They were not afraid to fail because completing the task wasn't about their ability but about their effort. Thus, as long as they put forth their best effort, they would receive praise (Dweck, 2006). Effort, in most cases, also resulted in successful completion of the task, which then served as a motivator to continue seeking challenges.

Furthermore, a person can have a fixed or growth mindset in some categories but not in others (e.g., "I get better at math by practice, but I'm just not a writer") and can even have different mindsets within individual categories (e.g., "I get better at playing basketball by practicing, but I'm just terrible at football no matter what I do") (Dweck, 2006). The origin of those self-theory beliefs is no less complicated.

Some portion of one's self-theory beliefs undoubtedly come from prevailing cultural beliefs about certain skills. For example, many people who otherwise subscribe to a growth mindset adopt a fixed mindset with traits like creativity or mathematical ability, in which social discussions revolve around the skills as if "you have them or you don't." The term *talent* is often used to express this idea of an innate, almost genetic ability that someone possesses or does not, especially in artistic fields, athletics, or areas like math or writing. These beliefs can also form self-fulfilling prophecies in which persons act on these beliefs, lowering effort and avoiding opportunities for development in areas in which they feel they "have no talent" and then see those beliefs confirmed by poor results or else expending significant effort and learning in areas in which they believe they are talented and seeing positive results. Such experiences can only make these self-theories stronger. For some students, fixed mindsets may focus on intelligence, and the effects may be more general (e.g., "I am smart" or "I am not very intelligent") and will influence effort, persistence, and willingness to participate in active learning.

It is also possible to observe the self-blame, risk aversion, lowered persistence, damaged self-esteem, and general helplessness of children who are faced with priming situations that place them in a fixed mindset position (Cain & Dweck, 1995; Kamins & Dweck, 1999; Smiley & Dweck, 1994). This helplessness seems to come mainly from harsh criticism (Heyman, Dweck, & Cain, 1992). For instance, Heyman and colleagues (1992) found that children whose teachers said they were "disappointed" in them because of the quality of a submitted project were more likely to show signs of helplessness, had higher degrees of negative affect, and were less likely to develop constructive problem-solving strategies to overcome obstacles. However, not all criticism has the same impact. Research has shown that it is the meaning of the criticism that influences mindset: When criticism is about the person, it instills a fixed mindset; when criticism is about the product or outcome, it has a roughly neutral impact on mindset; when criticism is about the strategies used to reach the product and includes suggestions on those strategies, the growth mindset is instilled (Kamins & Dweck, 1999; Mueller & Dweck, 1998). But how children react to criticism is determined by more than the mindset of the child. Some people persist in their endeavors despite facing criticism. Professor Ellen Pollack shared a story that might explain why some girls still believe that they cannot excel in hard sciences:

> As one of the first two women to earn a bachelor of science degree in physics from Yale—I graduated in 1978—this question concerns me deeply. I attended a rural public school whose few accelerated courses in physics and calculus I wasn't allowed to take because, as my principal put it, "girls never go on in science and math." Angry and bored, I began reading about space and time and teaching myself calculus from a book. When I arrived at Yale, I was woefully unprepared. The boys in my introductory physics class, who had taken far more rigorous math and science classes in high school, yawned as our professor sped through the material, while I grew panicked at how little I understood. The only woman in the room, I debated whether to raise my hand and expose myself to ridicule, thereby losing track of the lecture and falling further behind.
>
> In the end, I graduated summa cum laude, Phi Beta Kappa, with honors in the major, having excelled in the department's three-term sequence in quantum mechanics and a graduate course in gravitational physics, all while teaching myself to program Yale's mainframe computer. But I didn't go into physics as a career. At the end of four years, I was exhausted by all the lonely hours I spent catching up to my classmates, hiding my insecurities, struggling to do my problem sets while the boys worked in teams to finish theirs. I was tired of dressing one way to be taken seriously as a scientist while dressing another to feel feminine. And while some of the men I wanted to date weren't put off by my major, many of them were.
>
> Mostly, though, I didn't go on in physics because not a single professor—not even the adviser who supervised my senior thesis—encouraged me to go to graduate school. Certain this meant I wasn't talented enough to succeed in physics, I left the rough draft of my senior thesis outside my adviser's door and slunk away in shame. Pained by the dream I had failed to achieve, I locked my textbooks, lab reports, and problem sets in my father's army footlocker and turned my back on physics and math forever. (Pollack, 2013, para. 1–3)

Even though the hard sciences and education overall have become more welcoming toward females, social biases against women's "abilities" in the

STEM fields continue to exist and negatively affect their professional development and their judgment of others, including their children ("the revolving door of fixed mindsets"). Once the mindset is instilled, people seem to perpetuate it for themselves and those around them. Studies have found that people judge others according to their own mindset. Those with a fixed mindset tend to engage in rapid trait-based judgments of other individuals (Molden, Plaks, & Dweck, 2006) and other groups (Rydell, Hugenberg, Ray, & Mackie, 2007). People who apply such trait-based labels have difficulty in accepting information that the label may be incorrect and are even willing to underemphasize or disregard contradictory information (Erdley & Dweck, 1993). This is important because students with a fixed mindset who label their teachers as being too harsh, expecting too much, or exhibiting unfair or unlikable characteristics may not be open to arguments or proof to the contrary—and vice versa. Resistance to the teacher influences resistance to the class and content, resulting in a lack of learning. An instructor would have great difficulty convincing the student that her resistance is self-damaging and that the instructor actually has her best interests in mind.

In comparison, those with a growth mindset tend to give more effort-oriented evaluations of their peers' performance (Heyman & Dweck, 1998). Stated differently, people with a growth mindset tend to evaluate the behavior of others in the situational context and on the basis of psychological processes, such as beliefs, needs, emotions, and goals (Molden et al., 2006). A change in behavior or new information would likely lead to a different evaluation. For example, students with a growth mindset may resist an expectation by a teacher, but when the teacher explains the assignment, its importance, and its relevance, they may embrace it.

Even though Dweck (2006) uses the term *fixed mindset*, it is important to realize that the mindset can be changed. The growth mindset did not grow in a vacuum but was shaped by experiences. Aronson, Fried, and Good (2002) conducted a rigorous study with mixed black and white college students involved in three one-hour workshop sessions in which the experimental group was asked to engage in advocacy in favor of a growth mindset position. After they had been informed about neural plasticity and brain development, students were asked to write two letters of encouragement to fictional middle school children who were struggling in school and, ultimately, to write and video-record a speech encouraging the younger students to think of intelligence as malleable. Although this intervention did not reduce their actual perception of stereotype threat (see chapter 5), black students in the experimental group, compared with black students who were not in the group, showed lasting improvements in their enjoyment and perceived value of academics and had higher grades. White students also benefited from the intervention, although not to the same degree. The authors suggested that combining this type of simple and quick intervention with other interventions shown to reduce stereotype threat might produce even more powerful results. This study demonstrates that helping students to understand the malleability of intelligence and developing a growth mindset can have significant benefits. Our brains do not stop developing at some specific point; learning continues as long as we live and make the effort to learn (Fuchs & Fluegge, 2014), an important message for students to hear.

Mindsets and Neural Plasticity

Neural plasticity is the field of research into how, when, and why the brain develops (Stiles, 2000). The findings of that field go against the prevailing cultural narrative of fixed intelligence. Rather than reaching our intellectual potential in our mid-20s and simply staying there, our brains continue to develop in the areas that correspond to the skills we practice (Fuchs & Fluegge, 2014; Stiles, 2000). In other words, the field of neural plasticity provides strong scientific support of the core beliefs of the growth mindset. This is not to say that all mental abilities are the result of mental training. Recognizing limitations and differing rates of growth is also important for setting realistic expectations. Studies about happiness, physical fitness, and intelligence have found similar results regarding the contributions of genetics as opposed to training (Seligman, 1993). Some people will respond to training far more quickly than others, receiving double the impact from the same routine. Some people have a higher or lower "baseline" that determines where their abilities will settle with little or no training.

However, rather than thinking of students as having certain traits, it's more useful to think of intelligence and skills (e.g., critical thinking, writing) in terms of proclivity and potential. All students share the potential to learn challenging topics and perform strenuous mental tasks, but some students may be able to reach a milestone with less effort than their peers (Seligman, 1993). In any given set of students, we can expect a range of intelligence types and proclivities. Variation in intelligence and proclivities will yield an approximately normal curve, and students at the top and bottom of that curve (consistently reaching new milestones before or after their peers) are likely to become frustrated, disinterested, and resistant. Although it doesn't simplify the question of how to structure a class, it's useful to think of students learning course content and key skills in the same way they might learn a complicated dance routine. Some will simply need more time and help than others, but all of them can make significant improvement.

Rob Blair

When I took a racquetball course, my general fitness was worse than that of my peers, so I began with a weak level of play. My peers picked up the new techniques quickly, while I found myself struggling to get the moves down; no matter how often I told my body how to position itself for the backhand swing, I couldn't seem to get the motion down. When I indicated my inability to perform techniques we'd just been taught, the coach was frustrated with me. He repeatedly told me I was overthinking things. For him, it may have simply been as natural and fluid as allowing his body to do what seemed right (curse of knowledge).

I am tempted to say my slow growth was simply due to having never done something with similar movements, but the same was true of many of my peers. What's more, I had faced similar struggles in dance. While the other dancers saw and repeated movements without issues, I tripped over myself. But I also knew from those experiences that my body, while slower to figure out certain movements, could pick them up eventually. For my racquetball course, I came in during free hours to keep practicing, eager to teach my bones how to make these unfamiliar movements. As hours of bonus training allowed me to pick up the core techniques, I caught myself smiling. "See," I told myself. "You don't stay bad forever."

And here's what I discovered: I am not a bad racquetball player. True, I'm slow to pick up swing styles, and my court movement required conscious effort. But after I had picked up the basics, my athletic proclivities started to show. I intuitively snapped my body into swings that made for fierce returns. My ability to hit complex multiwall shots, once I knew how to get my swing in a straight line, won grunts of frustration from my opponents. I have a strong intuitive awareness of how my strength will correspond to ball positions, which makes my serves deadly.

This came up again when I served as a teaching assistant (TA) during the poetry segment of a creative writing class. As experts, we often become frustrated, simply telling students they're over- or under-thinking an issue instead of offering support for someone who learns at a different rate and in a different way than we do. How often do we give up on students who haven't mastered the basics, assuming that a weakness in the narrow scope of intelligence involved in those basics indicates a weakness for the overall topic. In working with students unfamiliar with poetry, I have been astonished at the strengths demonstrated by initially "terrible poets." Once they learn to hear lyricism and rhythm, as they learn what to look for in powerful images and metaphor, their natural proclivities emerge: a student's rich ability to express sensory experience, a knack for using alliteration and assonance, an intuitive grasp of how others will respond to certain images, or an aptitude for syncopating poetic rhythm like a New Orleans jazz musician. Had I written students off when they showed a weakness for the basics of poetry, I would never have seen their strengths.

Existing Instruments to Assess Metacognitive Awareness

It is one thing for instructors, to be aware of the vital role of metacognition in learning and the influence of mindsets on student resistance and response to learning challenges. It is another to figure out how to use those ideas to improve the learning environment. Although astute instructors may be able to evaluate and determine the degree to which students are using metacognitive goals and strategies in the classroom and to determine student mindsets, this process is surely facilitated by consideration of metacognitive assessment tools.

The main purpose of these assessment tools is to enhance students' process metacognition and learning. The contention that student learning across the curriculum will be enhanced by inclusion of process metacognitive assignments is supported by findings that key differentiators between high- and low-performing students are study strategies and motives (Yip, 2009). Process metacognition assessments increase student self-awareness of their own learning approaches and strategies. For example, using a limited sample of secondary students, Ibe (2009) found that asking students to complete metacognitive reflection questions before class discussion was a more effective method to help students retain information and improve success than think-pair-share or non-metacognitive assignments. Downing, Ho, Shin, Vrijmoed, and Wong (2007) have argued that metacognitive strategies teach students to handle a changing world and "successfully cope with new situations and the challenges of lifelong learning" (p. 11). Thus, enhancing student metacognition of their own learning patterns can help them develop a personal template for becoming successful problem solvers, regardless of course content.

Instructors may seize opportunities to enhance student process meta-cognition through a variety of strategies. The first is an emphasis on student learning *styles*. There are at least two major perspectives on learning styles. The Learning Styles Inventory (LSI; Kolb, 2011) emphasizes learning as a reflective process. A second approach to learning styles sees learning as the interaction of individual preferences for specific sensory modalities (e.g., visual, auditory, kinesthetic; Fleming, n.d.). Multiple instruments, both commercial and free, are available on the Internet for each of these approaches. The largest drawback to this approach is the concern about the validity of the underlying concepts. Pashler, McDaniel, Rohrer, and Bjork (2008) noted in their review of the literature that the central meshing hypothesis, the idea that teaching should be adapted to students' preferred learning styles in order to maximize learning, has suffered for lack of evidence. These authors argued that although plentiful data suggest that people may actually differ in their aptitudes for learning, there are almost no experimental studies explicitly testing the meshing hypothesis, and several studies using an appropriate method found results contradictory to the hypothesis. They concluded that at this time, there is insufficient support in the literature to consider the meshing hypothesis as sufficiently valid to justify the cost of assessing learning styles and to increase the complexity of instructional methods to match students' learning styles.

Another approach to process metacognition is self-regulated learning (SRL). Multiple instruments have been developed to assess various aspects of SRL, including cognitive strategies to encode information (e.g., Learning and Study Strategies Inventory [LASSI; Weinstein, 1987]); student motivational issues (perceptions of the classroom environment, self-beliefs related to confidence or anxiety); the use of cognitive strategies such as rehearsal, elaboration, or organization (e.g., Motivated Strategies for Learning Questionnaire [MSLQ; Pintrich, Smith, Garcia, & McKeachie, 1993]); and students' knowledge of their own cognitive processes and their ability to be aware of how they monitor, plan, and evaluate their cognitive efforts (e.g., Meta Cognitive Awareness Inventory [MAI; Schraw & Dennison, 1994]). Muis, Winne, and Jamieson-Noel (2007) evaluated the convergent validity of these scales, concluding that they measured different aspects of the self-regulated learning construct. Instructors using these scales should carefully consider what aspects of self-regulated learning they are interested in assessing and pick the appropriate instrument.

Although all of these instruments appear to tap important elements of metacognitive activity, most inventory items ask students to evaluate *generalized* statements that are reflective of stable traits (Muis et al., 2007). For example, an item on the LASSI asks students to rate themselves as to how descriptive or "typical" a statement is of themselves, such as "I find it hard to stick to a study schedule." The other instruments function similarly: "Compared with other students in class, I expect to do well" (MSLQ) or "I know what information is most important to learn" (MAI). Thus, these instruments are not directly focused on helping students change. By taking these inventories, students may begin to self-reflect on their own attitudes and thoughts about learning, which is helpful, but they do not necessarily provide the instructor or the student a map or blueprint of areas that need change and direction in *how* to implement that change. For the instructor, working to directly assist students in improving their learning, metacognitive instruments that help to identify students' readiness to change or become more effective learners and that suggest proximate forward steps might be more helpful.

Another well-established and useful area of process metacognition involves three distinct approaches to learning: surface, deep, and strategic (e.g., Atherton, 2010; Bain & Zimmerman, 2009; Biggs, Kember, & Leung, 2001; Blumberg, 2009; Felder & Brent, 2005; Rhem, 2009/2010). The surface approach learner is motivated primarily by fear of failure and relies on memorization, manipulation of formulas, or rote exercises in order to pass the class. The deep approach learner is motivated more by curiosity and a quest for mastery; the student questions, probes, and explores the information, seeking to understand how to apply the material. Strategic learners are motivated primarily by competition, the desire to win and to look good to themselves and others, using whatever strategies achieve these aims. Learners will change their approach according to their interest in the subject, its applicability to their planned profession or personal development goals (Felder & Brent, 2005; Kember, Leung, & McNaught, 2008), what they will be assessed on, and the teaching and learning environment.

Many educators and psychologists promote a deep approach to learning out of the belief that this develops student intrinsic motivation, enhances lifelong learning skills, and improves mastery of course content (Blumberg, 2009). Millis (2010) suggested that instructors can enhance student use of a deep approach through class activities that involve active learning and peer interactions. Other authors have noted that the approach used by students while they study significantly affects how well they learn and their academic success (Entwistle, Tait, & McCune, 2000; Spada, Nikcevic, Moneta, & Ireson, 2006). One measure of students' approach to learning was described by Biggs and colleagues (2001), who simplified Biggs's original Study Process Questionnaire (SPQ). The Revised SPQ (R-SPQ) helps learners self-evaluate their learning approach preference. The R-SPQ assesses both the surface and deep approach to learning and can be completed using a minimal amount of class time, making it a practical tool for informing the instructor of student learning. For instance, Wong and Lam (2007) used the R-SPQ to examine the learning approaches of their students and to help them shift to a problem-based learning style in their social work course. These existing approaches have value, may assist students in recognizing their current attitudes and approaches, and may help instructors identify the needs of the students and design more effective activities and interventions.

However, as noted previously, existing approaches focus on generalized patterns more than on specifically helping students to shift their motivation to adopt effective cognitive/learning strategies. Making students aware that such strategies even exist as well as helping them, and the instructor, to assess whether they are making progress in using these strategies to improve would be a valuable addition to the field. Also important are the *interactions* that exist between significant aspects of student learning. For instance, Kember and colleagues (2008) found that participants in their workshop were more likely to use a deep approach for their major classes but might switch to a surface approach when working on a disliked subject. These results demonstrate that students' approaches to learning are markedly influenced by context and other factors related to student motivation. Thus, assessing student motivation to *change*, to implement new and better learning strategies as part of becoming an effective lifelong learner, seems like an important direction to explore.

A New Approach to Metacognition in Education: The Transtheoretical Model of Change

The transtheoretical model of change (TTM) was originally developed to identify the stages of change through which individuals advance in order to successfully overcome an addiction (Prochaska, Johnson, & Lee, 1997; Prochaska & Prochaska, 1999). The model has since been extended to a variety of other settings where behavior change is essential, including health-related behaviors and mental health problems (e.g., depression, anxiety; see Prochaska & Prochaska, 1999, for more details). Thus, the transtheoretical model of change proposes a set of stages requisite for human beings to successfully achieve *any* meaningful and lasting change in behavior. It also describes the interactive roles of self-efficacy beliefs (beliefs that one is capable of change) and decisional balance (personal evaluation of the pros and cons of changing) and the way these influence a person's readiness to change. The model also describes a set of change processes specific to each stage; awareness of a person's readiness stage suggests the change processes most useful to help the person move forward and sustain new behaviors. Thus, both instructor and student self-awareness of readiness to use more effective learning strategies or work in teams or alter writing behaviors may be facilitated through use of this model.

Researchers have noted that in attempting to change behavior, it is normative to relapse back into previous stages; most individuals move through a stage several times before they are successful, an important consideration for professors in working with students both at the classroom and curricular levels (Prochaska et al., 1997; Prochaska & Prochaska, 1999). Rob Blair's racquetball story is a good illustration of this process. The stages of the TTM include *precontemplation* (denial, lack of awareness of need to change, or demoralization), *contemplation* (ambivalence to change and lack of commitment to new behaviors), *preparation* (intention to change, testing ideas, gathering information), *action* (active use of effective change processes), and *maintenance* (consolidation of gains, relapse prevention).

Surprisingly, given the emphasis that most educators place on the concept of education as producing change in how students think and behave, there is little evidence to date of the use of the TTM in educational settings. This is a significant deficit because the practical value of the TTM lies not only in helping to assess a student's readiness to change but also in understanding how to facilitate that change and identifying *what* needs to change for both the student and the instructor. For example, students in the precontemplation stage may not realize that there are more effective ways to study and learn; they have been using basic methods they learned in high school for years and have done reasonably well until college. For such students, recognizing that some of their study habits are ineffective or not optimal may be a challenge. However, an instructor aware of a student's stage could design class discussions, activities, or other methods such as a personal conference to raise the student's consciousness of the options that might help improve performance. Encouraging student self-assessment and reflection about why he or she is in this stage and whether he or she is ready to change might also further an objective of improvement.

In order to move toward just such an objective, Tolman, Kremling, and others have been utilizing a TTM-based instrument (TTM Learning Survey; Tolman, 2009b) specifically designed to assess student readiness to change as part of a metacognitive course assignment. In addition, Tolman created another instrument, the Learning Strategies Self-Assessment (LSSA; Tolman, 2009a), designed to measure the frequency with which students use effective learning strategies and to ask them to self-reflect on their learning goals and progress across the term.

Unlike the other SRL instruments previously described (LASSI, MSLQ, MAI), the LSSA might be considered more of a *state* measure than a *trait* measure. It does not ask students to indicate level of agreement with general statements about themselves; it asks them to report on their *behavior*, specifically the frequency with which they make use of a set of established and effective learning strategies that could be taught in any class and used by most students. The LSSA consists of 22 quantitative questions that are consistent over the semester and are answered using a Likert scale indicating the frequency with which a specific learning strategy is used (e.g., active reading, meeting with a study group). The complete survey also includes five to seven qualitative questions that change to match three time points in the semester (beginning, midpoint, and end). The qualitative questions ask students to self-assess their personal learning goals, progress across the semester, and achievement of course objectives. Studies evaluating the results of these instruments and comparing them to existing instruments such as the established R-SPQ (Biggs et al., 2001) show positive results for reliability and validity (see Kremling & Tolman, 2011; Kremling, Tolman, & Radmall, 2012; and Tolman & Kremling, 2011) and a manuscript is in preparation to report the psychometric results of two studies involving almost 800 students (Tolman, Biggs, & Johnson, 2016). Because the LSSA asks students to evaluate themselves across the semester, it encourages them to reflect on changes in their use of effective learning strategies over time. See the appendix for examples of the TTM Learning Survey and the LSSA as well as related course assignments.

Constructive Strategies

The following is a non-exhaustive short list of several strategies instructors could adopt in addition to or together with the assessment activities discussed previously. At a panel at an annual conference for Scholarship of Teaching and Engagement (SoTE) at Utah Valley University, most authors of this chapter were asked how much time should be spent on these sorts of activities. The underlying anxiety—that there wasn't enough time to cover the materials they were already teaching—was apparent. Although this is a legitimate concern and the balance involved must be decided by each instructor, Blair emphasized that these activities do not necessarily take up a great deal of an instructor's or student's time. Most students can complete Tolman's TTM survey in five minutes or less, for example. The R-SPQ may take 10 minutes per student. Interpretation of these instruments and student reflections on their meaning can be a homework assignment (see appendix for details). Discussions of mindsets can take place in short bursts across a term to take advantage of moments when students may be struggling. These activities are often well placed early as the semester begins with occasional reminders across the semester about their value. Some argue that an important learning outcome in higher education is to help students learn how to learn (Fink, 2005). Developing metacognitive strategies will help achieve that learning outcome. If similar discussions are reinforced across a program, students will be more likely to develop and maintain effective metacognition and mindsets.

Teach Students About Mindsets Directly

As noted previously, many students have adopted social or cultural beliefs about intelligence as innate or fixed; thus, early class discussions briefly reviewing the literature on neural plasticity and exploring how these concepts apply to students' own lives may be very useful. For instance, a brief discussion about how neurons make connections to each other and how *all* learning results from neural plasticity coupled with student contributions of new skills they have developed in the past two years may help to drive this point home. The study by Aronson and his colleagues (2002) confirms the potential value of even quick interventions designed to encourage students to adopt a growth mindset. Instructors could follow Aronson and his colleagues' example by asking students to write a letter to an imaginary or real person about a class they struggled with in the past, why they experienced difficulty, how they overcame the struggle, and what they learned from it.

As another approach, Tolman uses a tongue-in-cheek class discussion in his upper division courses called "Einstein Was an Idiot." He asks students to name the finest minds that the human race has produced; inevitably, someone mentions Einstein. Tolman then begins to critique Einstein in an exaggerated way, pointing out his many failures and repeated lack of success, noting he never completed his final unified field theory. As this happens, students begin to voice contrary opinions and to point out successes. This leads to a productive discussion of the role of persistence and effort versus innate talent and a focus solely on outcomes or grades. Videos and animations of neural plasticity are also plentiful in TED talks and on YouTube; these could be shown in class and discussed or given as a quick homework assignment early in the semester with a reflective short paper.

Instructors can also teach students about mindsets directly in a class workshop. There have been multiple "mindset workshops" set up at universities around the country (Dweck, 2006). YouTube and other videos of Carol Dweck discussing her work and its implications are also plentiful and would make good source material for class discussions and assignments. Additionally, in her summary of her own and her colleagues' studies, Dweck (2000) provided an appendix with copies of instruments used in several of these studies. These could be adapted or used as in-class surveys; the value in asking students to complete surveys is that they typically have an intrinsic desire to know the meaning of the results. Coupling a survey assignment with a brief reflection paper or in-class discussion with an end point of asking students to describe what they can do to change their mindset (fixed to growth) or maintain it (growth) can be very productive. An instrument for adults is also available online (at www.mindsetonline.com).

Because many of our students will not go on to graduate school, and even if they do, another way to make this material relevant is to engage students in a discussion about the value of understanding mindsets in teaching their own children and/or others, the role of praise, and so on. This makes the material personally relevant because parents or future parents naturally want their children to succeed and to learn. Dweck (2007/2008) published an article on mindsets specifically for parents that may be useful for class reading and discussion.

Promote Self-Reflection and Metacognition Regarding Learning Strategies

The benefits of helping students develop metacognitive skills and improve their learning strategies or approaches do not result from merely asking them to complete the assessments mentioned previously (including Tolman's instruments). The results of these instruments may be very useful for the professor in creating collaborative learning teams, designing class activities, and deciding what types of discussions on these topics would be most useful. However, for students, the real value in doing these assessments comes when they are asked to reflect on the *meaning* of their scores; this activity can open up a new framework, a new perspective on their own learning behaviors. Many students may not think very often about *how* they are learning or their level of mastery and areas in which they need to improve; instead, they are largely focused on *what* they are learning, what their grades will be, and how to remember the material. In our opinion, if instructors decide to use any of these assessment tools, then follow-up discussions, feedback, and a reflective assignment are necessary to solidify gains. For example, students completing one of Dweck's (2000) surveys and learning the meaning of the results might be surprised to realize that they have largely been operating from a fixed mindset. Together with class discussion, self-reflective writing, or further readings, this might prompt them to begin reconsidering their view of education, its purpose, and their own view of themselves as they think about how to move toward a growth mindset.

Even a simple reflective writing prompt such as "How would accepting the benefits of a growth mindset change how you study or the study methods you use?" might be very useful. This example also demonstrates the interactions that occur between elements of the IMSR; helping students develop metacognitive skills furthers cognitive development and vice versa. Similarly, asking students who take Tolman's TTM survey to identify their readiness to improve their learning strategies or to work collaboratively with others may cause them to reassess their own attitudes and behaviors and to perhaps acknowledge that they have been stalled in making changes; the next step is to ask students to specifically describe what they need to do in order to move forward, encouraging reflection and awareness of how they could improve. Nuhfer (2002), in his review of the literature and best practices for how to develop student critical thinking skills, focused on metacognition. He described the "imperative" to use open-ended problems, those that do not have a clear answer and require higher levels of

Bloom's taxonomy to work through, so students can practice developing both their skills and their awareness of the process they are using to reach a conclusion. Studies cited by Nuhfer suggest that development of metacognitive self-assessment follows acquisition of at least basic competence in the skill being assessed. He also noted, "If we want students to be able to distinguish their own metacognitive level, we must give them some framework to do so" (p. 7). By framework, Nuhfer (2002) was referring to such tools as Bloom's taxonomy itself, or disciplinary frameworks for how experts or professionals approach problems with the field; these frameworks can be built into rubric criteria for grading. Nuhfer gave an example of asking students whether common levels of radon are dangerous for homeowners and suggested rubric criteria such as "distinguish tested hypotheses from advocacy statements" (p. 8).

We agree with Nuhfer; lacking a framework, students may feel like they are thrown off the boat without a life preserver. A conceptual framework of some kind gives students a pathway or steps to follow as they use the data at hand to reach a conclusion on their own, similar to the value of the IMSR in understanding resistance. Follow-up discussion or exploration helps students recognize that peers or other groups may have used the same framework to reach similar or different conclusions. In addition, because many students are unaware of best practices in learning strategies or approaches, it may be useful to specifically teach them how to learn. There are many great examples in the literature of how to do this. For instance, McGuire and McGuire (2015) combined metacognitive exercises that help students become aware of whether they are using "study mode" versus "learning mode" for their class, with specific instruction on how to use what they call the *study cycle,* involving elements of active reading and other information-processing steps to help students to learn better in their classes. The authors also suggested ideas for faculty and students to assist with motivation, replacing negative emotions with positive ones, and suggestions for working with underprepared learners.

Teach the Benefits of Failure and Normalize Struggle

Because students often view the professor as an expert, possibly even a genius in the field, and because they lack an understanding of the long road to develop that expertise, it can be important to help students understand our own struggles and failures. Sharing with the class personal stories of our own difficult struggles in specific courses in college or painful moments in graduate school, teaching, research, or performance can be very helpful in demonstrating to students the value of persistence and effort, especially if we emphasize the benefit and learning that resulted. It illustrates that success is not an innately driven automatic process and that the struggle to grasp complex material is a normal part of learning.

Stories of how we developed our own metacognitive awareness of our mastery, or lack of it, in a specific course or for a specific exam or outcome (e.g., dissertation defense, scholarly work, professional writing) and how we used that awareness to drive our efforts to improve may also be very useful as a reinforcement of prior discussions of mindsets. Class discussions could also encourage students to share moments when their own failures resulted in learning or improvements; student stories may be followed by a brief discussion or lecture on mindsets. Care should be taken with these stories to ensure they are focused on a learning objective and are not long personal ramblings; the more relevant or related these discussions are to course assignments or content the better.

Use Productive Criticism, Formative Feedback, and Reflection

The need to avoid attacking morale when students fail should already be apparent. Dweck's studies on praise and criticism show that the worst outcomes resulted from labeling a person on the basis of his or her performance. However, what is striking is that the most common sort of labeling in academia is the *global* variety: This *product* is wrong; this isn't what the *paper* should look like; this isn't the *answer* you should have gotten. Global feedback proved neutral in effectiveness for establishing a growth mindset. The best results came from the strategy orientation of criticism (Kamins & Dweck, 1999). Rather than focusing on whether something is right or wrong, this approach looks at the process of work and makes suggestions on what seems to be working and what seems to be going wrong. Furthermore, it looks at questions of *why* ("I'm not sure what you're saying in this sentence." "I'm not sure what 'it' means in this context." "It would be clearer for readers if you specified what you meant here."), which naturally points students to what they *can* do rather than what they've failed to do. Clearly, there is also value in providing students with relatively low-cost early assignments (such as paper outlines, annotated bibliographies, basic performances) that can be used to provide formative feedback and help students orient to course expectations and that provide a developmental framework for later, more complex assignments. Feedback that does not overwhelm students with details of every mistake but that highlights key things done well and notes a few major areas for improvement with specific suggestions, especially in the context of a course that has already focused on student metacognition, is likely to produce better results. Enhancing student metacognition of their own work can also be fostered by requiring later assignments or revisions to incorporate a reflective element. For example, Tolman encourages students to turn in a draft research paper in his abnormal psychology course and provides formative feedback to students. They can revise their papers and turn them in again (usually significantly improving their scores), but the revisions must be accompanied by a brief reflection in which the students describe the changes they made and why they made them, evaluating their own papers against the grading rubric that incorporates elements of Bloom's taxonomy. This reflective pattern, replicated across several assignments in the course, helps students to think not just about *what* they are saying or producing but *how* they are doing it.

Conclusion

The aim of this chapter has been to explain how self-theories relate to student resistance and how metacognition and metacognitive instruments can be useful tools in reducing student resistance. If we do not help them develop metacognitive skills, students are likely to continue using their previous approaches and strategies, many of which are likely ineffective or counterproductive. This can lead to instructor frustration as students struggle to learn as well as student frustration that can only accelerate their resistance. Moreover, without the development of metacognitive skills to evaluate their own mastery, approaches to learning, and skill development, students often see their education as "jumping through hoops," working to complete arbitrary performance goals set by some external authority (institution or professor).

Through the use of effective metacognitive exercises and assessment instruments, instructors can facilitate student recognition of their own patterns and approaches to learning, creating an opportunity for them to become more intentional and motivated to learn. The dawning awareness that metacognition brings is that students are partners in learning. They start to realize that their own behaviors shape their success or failure to learn and that choices they make, the methods they use, and the behaviors they engage in are, in many ways, more important to their learning than what the instructor does. Their education is no longer imposed on them; it is something that they help to forge.

This development, however, takes time and effort; the more instructors understand metacognition and learning approaches and strategies and the more instructors are willing to work with students to overcome a fixed mindset and previous habits, the more students will learn and the more rewarding the learning environment will be for everyone. Creating time for these activities and efforts in our classes can create a lasting legacy for students.

References

Allen, B. A., & Armour-Thomas, E. (1991). Construct validation of metacognition. *Journal of Psychology, 127*(2), 203–211.

Aronson, J., Fried, C. B., & Good, C. (2002). Reducing the effect of stereotype threat on African American college students by shaping theories of intelligence. *Journal of Experimental Social Psychology, 38*, 113–125.

Atherton, J. S. (2010). Approaches to study "deep" and "surface." *Learning and Teaching*. Retrieved from http://www.learningandteaching.info/learning/deep-surf.htm

Bain, K., & Zimmerman, J. (2009, Spring). Understanding great teaching. *Peer Review: Emerging Trends and Key Debates in Undergraduate Education, 11*(2), 9–12.

Biggs, J., Kember, D., & Leung, D. Y. P. (2001). The revised two-factor Study Process Questionnaire: R-SPQ-2F. *British Journal of Educational Psychology, 71*, 133–149.

Blackwell, L. S., Trzesniewski, K. H., & Dweck, C. S. (2007). Implicit theories of intelligence predict achievement across an adolescent transition: A longitudinal study and an intervention. *Child Development, 78*(1), 246–263.

Blumberg, P. (2009). *Developing learner-centered teaching: A practical guide for faculty*. San Francisco, CA: Jossey-Bass.

Bransford, J. D., Brown, A. L., & Cocking, R. R. (2000). *How people learn: Brain, mind, experience, and school*. Washington, DC: National Academies Press.

Cacioppo, J. T., & Petty, R. E. (1982). The need for cognition. *Journal of Personality and Social Psychology, 42*(1), 116–131.

Cain, K. M., & Dweck, C. S. (1995). The relation between motivational patterns and achievement cognitions through elementary school years. *Merrill-Palmer Quarterly, 41*(1), 25–52.

Downing, K., Ho, R., Shin, K., Vrijmoed, L., & Wong, E. (2007). Metacognitive development and moving away. *Educational Studies, 33*(1), 1–13.

Dweck, C. S. (2000). *Self-theories: Their role in motivation, personality, and development*. New York, NY: Psychology Press.

Dweck, C. S. (2006). *Mindset: The new psychology of success*. New York, NY: Ballantine Books.

Dweck, C. S. (2007/2008, December/January). The secret to raising smart kids. *Scientific American Mind, 6*, 36–43.

Dweck, C. S., & Leggett, E. L. (1988). A social-cognitive approach to motivation and personality. *Psychological Review, 95*(2), 256–273.

Entwistle, N., Tait, H., & McCune, V. (2000). Patterns of response to an approaches to studying inventory across contrasting groups and contexts. *European Journal of the Psychology of Education, 15*, 33–48.

Erdley, C. A., & Dweck, C. S. (1993). Children's implicit theories as predictors of their social judgments. *Child Development, 64*, 863–878.

Felder, R. M., & Brent, R. (2005, January). Understanding student differences. *Journal of Engineering Education, 94*(1), 57–72.

Fink, L. D. (2005). *Integrating course design* (Idea Paper No. 42). Retrieved from http://ideaedu.org/wp-content/uploads/2014/11/Idea_Paper_42.pdf

Flavell, J. H. (1979). Metacognition and cognitive monitoring. A new area of cognitive-developmental inquiry. *American Psychologist, 34*(10), 906–911.

Fleming, N. (n.d.). *The nature of preference.* Retrieved from http://vark-learn.com/wp-content/uploads/2014/08/THE-NATURE-OF-PREFERENCE.pdf

Fuchs, E., & Fluegge, G. (2014). Adult neuroplasticity: More than 40 years of research. *Neural Plasticity, 2014*, 1–10. doi:10.1155/2014/541870

Heyman, G. D., & Dweck, C. S. (1998). Children's thinking about traits: Implications for judgments of the self and others. *Child Development, 69*(2), 391–403.

Heyman, G., Dweck, C., & Cain, K. (1992). Young children's vulnerability to self-blame and helplessness: Relationship to beliefs about goodness. *Child Development, 63*, 401–415.

Ibe, H. N. (2009, December). Metacognitive strategies on classroom participation and student achievement in senior secondary school science classrooms. *Science Education International, 20*(1/2), 25–31.

Kamins, M. L., & Dweck, C. (1999). Person versus process praise and criticism: Implications for contingent self-worth and coping. *Developmental Psychology, 35*(3), 835–847. doi:10.1037/0012-1649.35.3.835

Kember, D., Leung, D. Y. P., & McNaught, C. (2008). A workshop activity to demonstrate that approaches to learning are influenced by the teaching and learning environment. *Active Learning in Higher Education, 9*(1), 43–56. doi:10.1177/1469787407086745

Kolb, D. A. (2011). The Learning Styles Inventory [Online inventory]. Retrieved from http://learningfromexperience.com/tools/kolb-learning-style-inventory-lsi/

Kremling, J., & Tolman, A. O. (2011, April). *Assessing the validity of three metacognitive instruments: TTM Learning Survey, R-SPQ, and LSSA.* Paper presented at the 14th CSU Symposium on University Teaching, California State University, Channel Islands.

Kremling, J., Tolman, A. O., & Radmall, R. (2012, March). *Improving students' learning strategies by utilizing metacognitive instruments.* Workshop presented at the 24th Annual Conference of the International Alliance of Teacher-Scholars (Lilly West), Pomona, CA.

McGuire, S. Y., & McGuire, S. (2015). *Teach students how to learn: Strategies you can incorporate into any course to improve student metacognition, study skills, and motivation.* Sterling, VA: Stylus.

Millis, B. J. (2010). *Promoting deep learning* (Idea Paper No. 44). Retrieved from http://www2.humboldt.edu/institute/workshop_materials/Millis/IDEA_Paper_47_Deep_Learning.pdf

Molden, D. C., Plaks, J. E., & Dweck, C. S. (2006). "Meaningful" social inferences: Effects of implicit theories on inferential processes. *Journal of Experimental Social Psychology, 42*, 738–752.

Mueller, C. M., & Dweck, C. (1998). Praise for intelligence can undermine children's motivation and performance. *Journal of Personality and Social Psychology, 75*(1), 33–52.

Muis, K. R., Winne, P. H., & Jamieson-Noel, D. (2007). Using a multitrait-multimethod analysis to examine conceptual similarities of three self-regulated learning inventories. *British Journal of Educational Psychology, 77,* 177–195.

Nuhfer, E. (2002). Using what we know to promote high level thinking outcomes. *National Teaching and Learning Forum, 11*(3), 6–8.

Pashler, H., McDaniel, M., Rohrer, D., & Bjork, R. (2008). Learning styles: Concepts and evidence. *Psychological Science in the Public Interest, 9*(3), 105–119.

Pintrich, P. R., Smith, D. A. F., Garcia, T., & McKeachie, W. J. (1993). *A manual for the use of the Motivated Strategies for Learning Questionnaire.* Ann Arbor: University of Michigan.

Pollack, E. (2013, October 13). Why are there still so few women in science? *New York Times Magazine.* Retrieved from www.nytimes.com/2013/10/06/magazine/why-are-there-still-so-few-women-in-science.html?_r=0

Prochaska, J. O., Johnson, S., & Lee, P. (1997, September/October). The transtheoretical model of behavior change. *American Journal of Health Promotion, 12*(1), 38–48.

Prochaska, J. O., & Prochaska, J. M. (1999). Why don't continents move? Why don't people change? *Journal of Psychotherapy Integration, 9*(1), 83–102.

Rhem, J. (2009/2010). Deep/surface approaches to learning in higher education: A research update. *Essays on Teaching Excellence: Toward the Best in the Academy, 21*(8). Retrieved from http://podnetwork.org/content/uploads/V21-N8-Rhem.pdf

Rydell, R. J., Hugenberg, K., Ray, D., & Mackie, D. M. (2007). Implicit theories about groups and stereotyping: The role of group entitativity. *Personality and Social Psychology Bulletin, 33,* 549–558.

Schraw, G., & Dennison, R. S. (1994). Assessing metacognitive awareness. *Contemporary Educational Psychology, 19*(4), 460–475. doi:10.1006/ceps.1994.1033

Seligman, M. E. P. (1993). *What you can change . . . and what you can't.* New York, NY: Fawcett.

Smiley, P. A., & Dweck, C. S. (1994). Individual difference in achievement goals among young children. *Child Development, 65*(6), 1723–1743. doi:10.1111/1467-8624.ep9501252902

Spada, M. M., Nikcevic, A. V., Moneta, G. B., & Ireson, J. (2006). Metacognition as a mediator of the effect of test anxiety on a surface approach to studying. *Educational Psychology, 69*(5), 615–624. doi:10.1080/01443410500390673

Stiles, J. (2000). Neural plasticity and cognitive development. *Developmental Neuropsychology, 18*(2), 237–272.

Tangney, J. P. (1995). Recent advances in the empirical study of shame and guilt. *American Behavioral Scientist, 38*(8), 1132–1145. doi:10.1177/0002764295038008008

Tolman, A. O. (2009a). Learning Strategies Self-Assessment [Unpublished instrument]. Retrieved from http://bit.ly/u3rmnh

Tolman, A. O. (2009b). TTM Learning Survey [Unpublished instrument]. Retrieved from http://bit.ly/u3rmnh

Tolman, A. O., Biggs, B. L., & Johnson, B. A. (2016). *New metacognitive instruments to advance student learning.* Manuscript in preparation.

Tolman, A. O., & Kremling, J. (2011, March 12). *Using metacognitive instruments to reduce student resistance to active learning.* Workshop presented at the 23rd

Annual Conference of the International Alliance of Teacher-Scholars (Lilly West), Pomona, CA.

Vrugt, A., & Oort, F. J. (2008). Metacognition, achievement goals, study strategies and academic achievement: Pathways to achievement. *Metacognition Learning, 30*, 123–146. doi:10.1007/s11409-008-9022-4

Weinstein, C. E. (1987). *LASSI user's manual.* Clearwater, FL: H&H Publishing.

Wong, D., & Lam, D. (2007). Problem-based learning in social work: A study of student learning outcomes. *Research on Social Work Practice, 17,* 55–65. doi:10.1177/1049731506293364

Yip, M. W. (2009). Differences between high and low academic achieving university students in learning and study strategies: A further investigation. *Educational Research and Evaluation, 15*(6), 561–570.

10

CREATING A CAMPUS CLIMATE TO REDUCE RESISTANCE

Anton O. Tolman, Janine Kremling, and Ryan Radmall

Although this is the last chapter in our book, it is not a summary of everything that has already been said. This chapter is different than the other chapters in a couple of ways. First, most chapters have been written to assist instructors in recognizing student resistance, and the elements that contribute to it as visualized in the integrated model of student resistance (IMSR) and to suggest strategies to reduce resistance and increase student motivation to learn. This material is also helpful for department chairs, administrators, and others involved in the process of working with students because it can increase their understanding and perspective concerning these complex interactions. However, this chapter is aimed primarily at those in administrative positions: presidents, chancellors, vice presidents in academic or student affairs, and deans and professionals working in faculty development. Nevertheless, we hope faculty who have been reading will stick around because faculty voices in institutional decisions and policies are very important, and many faculty will spend some time in administrative positions, as directors of important campus centers or institutes; department chairs; chairs of various important committees, including tenure, curriculum, and general education; and positions such as officers or members of faculty governance. This chapter, we hope, will be useful to all of you in thinking about student resistance through another lens; we hope it can add to a common vocabulary for exploring campus problems and concerns from a new perspective for everyone.

Second, this chapter does not focus on a specific element of the IMSR. Instead, this chapter takes a step backward to look at the IMSR and student resistance from a more holistic administrative perspective and to consider how administrative policies and practices could be shaped or tuned to reduce student resistance on campus, improve learning, and enhance the university's standing with the public. After all, resistance is not something that is limited to the classroom, as recent and vigorous student protests over rising tuition costs and institutionalized racism have demonstrated. Resistance, arising from the various elements described by the IMSR, affects a student's relationship with the institution as a whole; it can shape student attitudes, expectations, and motivation in ways that affect all aspects of campus life. It is linked to important institutional outcomes of concern to everyone, including student recruitment, retention, persistence, grades, graduation rates in specific fields (e.g., STEM), and tuition. It can also influence alumni and community support. At the same time, we recognize that although resistance is a common central discussion among faculty, it may not be as central in administrative planning or assessment discussions. We are suggesting that it should be, that looking at resistance through an administrative lens can perhaps create new synergies of thought and spur new innovations and ideas for improvement.

With that in mind, we suggest that the IMSR, as well as our preparatory discussions about human biases that distort our understanding (chapter 3), might serve as practical tools for institutional planning and assessment. For instance, in reviewing campus outcomes and progress, perhaps it could be useful to ask: What are the strongest sources of resistance to learning in our students? What interactions occur on our campus between the different elements of the IMSR that build or exacerbate resistance, and how might we intervene to alter those patterns? What courses on campus demonstrate the strongest student resistance, and where is that resistance coming from? Which departments are using effective strategies to reduce resistance to active learning, and how do we share and encourage other departments to learn from their example? How do the answers to these and other questions shape our thinking about institutional priorities and funding?

A quick set of potentially useful outcome indicators, some of which are probably already being examined at institutions, could include courses with high drop or high fail rates (counting drops, perhaps, disentangled from federal or state reporting deadlines), courses that engender the highest rates of student complaints to chairs or deans, courses or faculty who may receive high rates of negative student evaluations (with consideration that, perhaps, this is not just a signal of a professor who is not teaching well), the measurement of actual student learning outcomes in different courses using empirical instruments such as the Collegiate Learning Assessment (CLA; Council for Aid to Education, 2016), the engagement indicators on the National Survey of Student Engagement (NSSE; Center for Postsecondary Research, 2016) and others. Thinking of these assessment tools and outcomes as indicators or windows into student resistance adds a new dimension to how they are typically thought of in administrative discussions. Used together with the IMSR, an institutional focus on resistance might enable a new mapping or understanding of students, faculty, and departments to help inform planning.

We will proceed in this chapter by describing six major areas that we consider to be useful overall targets for interventions to reduce student resistance. We will describe each area briefly, explain its connection to resistance, and then offer a few suggestions that may be useful in promoting discussion or that may lead to other ideas that can be customized to specific institutions. In proposing these solutions, we acknowledge that many institutions may already be working on these targets or similar interventions; what is new is consideration of student resistance and the IMSR as a coherent framework for looking at this work. We also acknowledge that institutional change is culture change and that this can be a difficult process. We suggest that sustaining intentional effort at more than one entry point and building on existing momentum is more likely to produce long-term change. We also suggest that improvement efforts that rally the strengths of students, faculty, and administrators to reduce resistance will have the best chance to improve student learning and benefit our institutions and society.

Encourage, Support, and Reward Innovative Teaching Strategies and Mentoring

Busteed (2014) has stated that half of U.S. colleges and universities will be out of business in the next 15 years because they fail to deliver on the fundamental value and core mission of institutions of higher education. According to Busteed (2014), these core values include teaching students in ways that lead to success in their chosen profession and to productive citizenship. Busteed described a relevant study conducted as a partnership between Gallup and Purdue University using a representative sample of 30,000 college graduates examining the link between college experiences and long-term success in their careers and lives after college.

They found that, regardless of age and year of graduation, graduates who felt "supported" by professors who cared, made them excited about learning, and encouraged them to pursue their goals were twice as likely to be engaging in productive work and thriving in their well-being. Three elements were also crucial for "experiential and deep learning" experiences: participation in internships, involvement in extracurricular activities and organizations, and completion of a long-term project. Participation in these areas doubled the odds of graduates being engaged at work. Another factor that related strongly to long-term success was having a mentor who encouraged them to pursue goals and dreams.

Unfortunately, only a small percentage of students indicated that they experienced opportunities in these success areas. About 14% of college graduates strongly agreed they were "supported" by professors in the three areas of caring, excitement, and encouragement; 6% of college graduates participated in "experiential and deep learning" as measured by all three elements; 22% of college graduates strongly agreed that they had the support of a mentor; and 29% of graduates participated in an internship in which they could apply what they learned. Even more disheartening, only 3% of college graduates noted that they benefited from all six areas of support and experiential and deep learning during college.

This target area for institutional action is not new. Innovative teaching strategies include a wide range of active learning strategies, many of which have been developed and implemented in the past two decades both inside and outside the classroom. In an active learning pedagogy, the instructor is not a sage but a mentor, guide, or facilitator, and class time is more often spent on participatory activities and collaboration than it is on lecture delivery or content review. The focus in these courses is more on student learning than on teaching or conveying ideas or concepts (see Barr & Tagg, 1995), and the emphasis is on skill development (including communication, teamwork, problem-solving, and critical thinking skills) rather than on acquisition of facts or concepts. Why is this important? Because active learning environments and courses using innovative teaching strategies tend to be "hot spots" for student resistance because they violate student expectations and increase student anxiety about performance in a new environment. This is significant because as elaborated by Tolman, Sechler, and Smart in chapter 3, these "new" approaches to teaching promote achievement of the very outcomes that Busteed (2014) referred to and that are being demanded of higher education, including in national goals and concerns. These innovative teaching approaches also generate the "support" elements that Busteed (2014) reported as being so influential in the Gallup-Purdue study.

However, there are several obstacles to widespread implementation of innovative pedagogies that continue across the country. Although there are significant data on the increased value of active learning approaches (see

Freeman et al., 2014) in promoting student learning when compared with traditional lecture approaches, these are not "cookbook" pedagogies that can be immediately and easily dropped into a course. They must be learned, adapted, and improved over time by the faculty using them in order to be successful. Similarly, mentoring is not a "natural" process that just happens; there are best practices and models that can be adapted to increase the chances of success (see Pfund, Branchaw, & Handelsman, 2015). This process benefits, some might say depends on, faculty development, including faculty mentors or coaches and professors who have previously learned and successfully implemented these approaches with students; at least, the development of a faculty learning community new to using an active learning pedagogy can also assist with implementation as they share experiences and strategies. These pedagogies involve taking a proactive approach to student resistance and seeking to improve student "buy-in" from the very beginning, which can also make them valuable as campus tools in the process of shifting student expectations and instilling an understanding of the meaning of academic performance.

In addition to the significant need for faculty development, there is a need for enhanced consistency in the curriculum across instructors, programs, and departments. If only a few sections of a course are implementing active learning pedagogies, the clear signal to students is that this form of teaching is an aberration, an unusual type of class that involves more work and effort on their part. This tends to drive students who are the most resistant to sections taught in a more traditional manner, only reinforcing resistant attitudes and behaviors that affect all courses taught on campus. It may even have this effect on students who otherwise would be self-motivated for deep learning. However, if departments and programs review their curricula and implement a consistent pattern of active learning pedagogies regardless of instructor, course level (specific methods would vary by course level and class size), and status (full-time/part-time instructors, graduate instructors), students are more likely to come to see this form of learning as common and expected in the institution. This is especially true if this pattern continues across departments because as students take their general education coursework, they will be exposed to various forms of active learning in multiple settings. In contrast to seeing active learning as unusual, and therefore a cause for resistance, active learning could actually reduce resistance in ways that help to further the institutional and societal goals.

Active institutional support for these types of mentoring and teaching efforts could begin by targeting poor retention courses, but it should not stop there. Active learning pedagogies could be a key institutional lever for poor retention courses and bottleneck prerequisite courses and should be a regular part of all courses related to high-impact practices (see Kuh, 2008), including but not limited to service-learning courses, freshman seminars, internships, and writing-intensive courses. Active support would include making financial and priority decisions regarding funding of centers for teaching and learning, staff to develop and carry out programs, and financial incentives or rewards for faculty who participate. Additional considerations might include course buy-out time for faculty, even small faculty teams, to redesign existing high-priority courses to implement active learning methods; stipends to encourage faculty to participate in long-term development; and support for faculty to travel and participate in professional conferences dedicated to faculty development and active learning. Without effective supports and follow-through by top administrators, many faculty are unlikely to participate for the reasons outlined in chapter 4; if institutional values and priorities denigrate teaching or relegate it to "second-class citizen" status, most faculty will see participation in these efforts, even if marketed to them by administration, as a threat to their careers. This is especially important for research institutions where graduate assistants may be involved in teaching many of these high-priority courses. Few of these graduate assistants receive professional development in active pedagogies; they should be rewarded for participating in faculty development and applying what they learn to the classroom.

Tenure policies speak louder than presidential speeches, and institutions that are serious about reducing student resistance and improving student outcomes need to carefully review and examine tenure and promotion policies to ensure that student mentoring and use of active learning methods is a clear expectation that will be rewarded. Similarly, institutional policies that permit faculty to "bank" workload credits for mentoring students in undergraduate research or creative activities may see increased faculty participation in these high-impact practices (see Malachowski, Osborn, Karukstis, & Ambos, 2015, for other practices). In research institutions that may have a separate category for professors hired mostly to teach, retention and tenure policies should likewise be clear on the importance of using active learning pedagogies and the value of this approach to the institution. Part of this shift involves how institutions assess quality of teaching in the tenure and promotion process.

As explained by Kremling and Brown in chapter 4, many institutions still overrely on student ratings of instructors as a primary measure for teaching quality—a situation that is problematic. However, if institutions choose to continue using student ratings as a component of a larger evaluation system, they should ground their rating instruments and methods in the best available research and practices (see Hativa, 2014a, b). We suggest there are better ways of assessing teaching quality. Some examples include observing teaching methods, studying student learning outcomes, and conducting student interviews; also helpful are faculty portfolios and teaching scholarships, awards, or ratings (Berk, 2005; Van Note Chism, 1999). For a comprehensive evaluation it is important to have several of these methods. For instance, a combination of self-evaluation, student interviews, and peer ratings would provide a better measure of teaching quality. This is referred to as *triangulation* because the "multiple sources build on strength of all sources, while compensating for the weaknesses in any single source" (Berk, 2005). Institutions that are serious about improving teaching quality and signaling to faculty that excellence will be rewarded should ensure that review policies consider triangulation.

There are also important roles for staff in student affairs (see Kuh, 2009). Some of the high-impact practices described previously use staff rather than faculty, especially for freshman experiences and similar programs. These staff should also have access to effective professional development in the area of active learning pedagogies. Other staff, involved in advising and guidance for students, should be actively encouraged to steer students toward active learning courses and support them if they struggle, assisting them with effective learning strategies and encouraging them to persist. Staff working on student and parent orientation can also emphasize the role of active learning on campus and the value and relevance of these types of experiences for students' future lives and careers.

By prioritizing institutional efforts to shift the culture through curriculum redesign and faculty development, rewarding faculty and graduate assistant efforts to use active learning strategies, and designing a coherent system to reward engaged teaching on campus, institutions can help to reshape student expectations and attitudes and create situations that will reduce negative classroom experiences and enhance student cognitive development and metacognition. Resistance is likely to decrease in such an environment while outcomes improve.

Create an Inclusive Campus Environment That Welcomes All Students

One of the most significant changes in higher education continuing to shape and also challenge institutions is the continued emphasis on access for students who are not part of the "elite" cohorts of society. This has resulted in an increased presence on campus and online of students of various ethnicities, religions, races, sexual orientations, nationalities, and ages, many of whom will be first-generation college students. This shift toward increasing the benefits of higher education to all of society is of vital national importance, but sometimes the experience does not live up to the promise.

At the institutional level, these changes are not solely about promoting improved retention of underrepresented or first-generation students, which are common institutional goals. As Lee, Lindstrom, Sechler, and Smart explained in chapters 5 and 6, identity affects students' thoughts about themselves and their capabilities and shapes the way that students interact with each other and professors. Particularly important is Lee and Lindstrom's note in chapter 5 that these students desire a deeper understanding and conversation about diversity than a superficial and offensive attempt to promote "tolerance." Through subtle mechanisms such as this that mimic societal patterns, an institution may affect a student's identity by reinforcing existing stereotypes or their effects in ways that contribute directly to resistance. Although institutions of higher education cannot change society at once, administrators and campus leaders, including student leaders, are responsible for shaping the campus environment and climate toward *inclusion*, defined as

> how organizations, groups, their leaders, and their members provide ways that allow everyone, across multiple types of differences, to participate, contribute, have a voice, and feel that they are connected and belong, all without losing individual uniqueness or having to give up valuable identities or aspects of themselves. (Ferdman, 2014, p. 12)

Without intentional use of inclusion practices, some students may feel alienated or dismissed as a result of their identities and the stereotypes inherent in such identities, may perform poorly as a result of autonomic threat activation (e.g., stereotype threat), and may even withdraw from using effective learning practices because of stress and health issues. This type of resistance is self-protective, but it also damages student motivation and learning and reduces student participation in the classroom and campus communities. These effects ripple outward, depriving other students of the chance to hear the perspectives, experiences, and voices of people different from themselves. Of particular interest to college educators and administrators is that institutional policies and procedures and the enactors of these procedures—professors and administrators—play a vital role in how a climate of inclusion is fostered (Ferdman, 2014). In education, inclusion involves changing content, approaches, structures, and strategies with a common vision to responsibly educate all students (Ferdman, 2014).

There are multiple strategies and approaches that may help create a more inclusive campus environment. Efforts described in the last section to create, support, and sustain faculty development efforts toward active learning pedagogies and high-impact practices can be dovetailed nicely with efforts to sustain inclusion. Faculty, staff, and teaching assistants can participate in learning opportunities to better understand the cultural and social barriers faced by underrepresented and first-generation students and learn ways that they can mitigate these effects in their classes. The use of high-impact practices and active learning methods has been shown to have a positive differential effect on student learning (partially through reducing resistance), especially for underrepresented students (Freeman et al., 2014; Kuh, 2008). In this way, institutions can integrate key foundational support for multiple ways to reduce resistance and enhance learning.

Other institutional efforts are fairly well-known but are still useful to mention, such as emphasizing diversity in marketing materials, especially materials aimed at new students and their families. Institutional outreach efforts should focus on communities of underrepresented students and include more than marketing or recruitment; these efforts should also give practical strategies and tips for how to be successful in higher education as well as useful information about how to manage the financial stress of college. Institutions can also seek to create safe spaces on campus that signal, both in intent and design, acceptance of a variety of viewpoints and practices. For instance, Utah Valley University recently opened a Reflection Center in the Student Life and Wellness Building. This center consists of a space for silent prayer, meditation, and reflection; a space for verbalized prayer and other forms of religious expression; and a space for lectures, student club meetings, discussion groups, and so on. The location of the Reflection Center, the purpose of the spaces, and the acknowledgment of the need for education and dialogue about differences are all useful in promoting inclusion.

An institutional emphasis on dialogue, the value of multiple viewpoints, and the contributions of people of all backgrounds could also be built into mission or values statements and should be backed up with actions, including in the classroom. For example, selection of invited campus speakers together with an emphasis on discussion and dialogue concerning a range of ideas and cultural values is also important. Institutions should ensure that there are channels, both verbal and nonverbal, such as e-mail or social media, through which the diversity of student voices can be heard and expressed. One of the most difficult challenges to institutions is to ensure that hiring practices and recruitment efforts encourage formation of a diverse population of faculty and graduate students. Otherwise, students hear claims about the value of diverse perspectives, but they do not see it when they look around.

Many institutions have already committed to creating support structures for students who may be underprepared for higher education; it is vital, to both the institution and to the students, that these students be perceived as valuable to the institution and worth the resources to help them be successful. Likewise, counseling support, including financial counseling, is increasingly important for first-generation and underrepresented students who may struggle to resolve academic expectations with work and school commitments and whose families may not have the background to effectively help them.

For example, in trying to improve graduation statistics mostly due to outside pressures, some colleges have exacerbated student stress by emphasizing graduation in four years at the potential cost of significant debt. Americans currently owe $1.3 trillion in student loan debt, with the average student losing 30% of income after graduation to loans and interest rates (Squires, 2016). About 70% of students have loans, and the average debt of the class of 2015 was $35,051 (Berman, 2016). One in four student borrowers are in delinquency or default. Worse, more than 36,000 borrowers have lost part of their social security income due to failure to pay off federal student loans. Especially for women and minorities, who have lower earning power, repaying student loans may result in fewer opportunities to secure their future and retirement (Berman, 2016). It may be beneficial, especially for first-generation and underrepresented students, to work during school, even if it takes longer to graduate. Actively making financial counseling available and promoting those services can help students potentially avoid the crushing debt that could drive many of them out of higher education. Efforts such as these signal a campus culture of concern and support that can help reduce alienation and decrease resistance.

Use Technology to Increase Student Engagement

Few would argue that technology is playing an increasing role in higher education. The fast pace of technological change and innovation is a challenge to faculty, staff, and administrators, and both the underuse and overuse of technology may create stress for students and potentially increase resistance. We will emphasize here the general point that there are many ways to use technology to enhance student motivation to learn and to boost learning outcomes, from classroom response systems (see Bruff, 2009) to learning management systems (LMSs) for managing course content (e.g., Blackboard, Canvas), to flipped classroom environments in which students watch lecture/ content videos outside class and then work on experiential active learning assignments in class (see Bretzmann, 2013). The institutional concerns here are to manage technology in ways that are financially viable, establish consistent standards across campus, and ensure that faculty are up-to-date with those standards and are familiar enough with technology to use it effectively in their courses.

Another key aspect of faculty development is helping students understand the role of technology in the classroom and the way it will facilitate their learning and assist them in taking responsibility for their own learning. Shifting responsibility for content acquisition to students instead of the instructor and convincing them of the value-added elements of interactive coursework requires dedicated time to address these issues (see Smith, 2008). This is especially true in online courses, in which resistance to this change may be even more pronounced. The California State University (CSU) provides an interesting example of a long-term project to address enrollment bottlenecks through innovative course redesigns and "technology-enhanced delivery methods." The approach is faculty-development intensive, using "lead" faculty who share their course designs and provide input and feedback in professional learning communities for adopting faculty. Instructors are compensated for their time, and course redesigns are evaluated for effectiveness (Christie & Bayard, 2015; see also California State University, 2015). Although not all institutions have the resources to launch as comprehensive a program as CSU, many of CSU's ideas could be adapted and customized to other institutions.

Technology use, such as regular use of the campus LMS or social media, can help students connect to content and the instructor, discover increased relevance for what they are learning, and facilitate communication, but unapproved platforms or demands for technology or devices that are not common on campus can increase students' costs and frustration in trying to comply with unique instructor demands. Consistent standards and effective faculty development, like the use of active learning pedagogies, that occur across disciplines and from general education through program courses help students feel less frustrated and more competent in navigating their classes and enhancing their skills.

Another source of technology infusion is *online courses*, which, by definition, are grounded in technology. One of the major contradictions in online learning is that although this type of course potentially increases access to classes that otherwise might be limited by geography, available seating, or time slots, it can actually reinforce an individualistic, isolated learning pattern. Students do not often work together in online courses and may be highly resistant to doing so, claiming that they took an online class precisely because they wished to avoid working with others or because they think of the course as a type of "independent study" opportunity (Smith et al., 2011). Furthermore, many online courses exist primarily as content-delivery systems with little direct interaction (other than commenting on a discussion board) between students or with the instructor. Instructors often post lecture slides or videos of lectures filmed in a studio and involve students with quizzes and discussion boards. However, there is significant research demonstrating the value of empirically supported best practices, which include methods that increase instructor "presence" or a sense of connection between instructor and students (Boettcher & Conrad, 2010). Active learning methods including problem-based learning, semester-long projects, and team-based learning are possible in an online environment, but resistance is higher than in typical face-to-face classes (Smith et al., 2011). Smith and his colleagues have also pointed out that the use of student journals may be helpful in mediating negative feelings about teamwork in online courses and recommended that instructors provide "explicit, succinct recommendations" for how to operate in an online group environment.

The implication of fostering online courses is that institutions carry an ethical burden, given the higher levels of resistance in this environment and institutional goals of increasing participation, for supporting faculty use of best practices, providing effective technical and instructional support systems to faculty and students, and putting in place practices that can help shape student expectations for active learning in online courses. To focus mostly on increasing online participation without consideration of these ethical realities is to contribute to student resistance in ways that may carry forward into other aspects of student interactions with the institution.

Foster Student Engagement and Responsibility From the Beginning

One of the main ways that institutional culture contributes to student resistance is through mechanisms (recruitment, marketing, advising) that reinforce or contribute to expectations for superficial learning or a consumer mentality. These patterns interact with environmental forces and can lead to negative classroom experiences and even inhibit the development of metacognitive skills in students. A strong way to address this issue from the beginning that also begins to shape student expectations and behaviors in ways that reduce resistance is to foster a sense of self-responsibility for student learning and education from the very beginning. In contrast to marketing campaigns that trumpet the economic value of a degree, institutions can focus on campaigns that emphasize student skill development, competence, and mastery and that prepare students for classrooms and online courses that are interactive, engaged, and focused on application rather than just "learning" things and that build on relevance through genuine relationships with local and national communities.

In 1970, the Carnegie Foundation for the Advancement of Teaching established a continuously updated classification system for identifying the many different types of higher education institutions (Center for Postsecondary Research, 2015). One of these changes included a new elective classification (released originally in 2006) for community engaged institutions. As of 2010, earning this classification requires an institution to make a substantial commitment to both curricular integration and outreach and community partnerships (New England Resource Center for Higher Education, n.d.). The most recent classification involved hundreds of institutions across the United States of varying types, from community colleges to research universities. Making an institutional commitment to become publicly identified as a community engaged university is one example of how an institution can shift the paradigm and perspective of students as well as local, state, and national communities about the goals and mission of the institution.

A public institutional commitment to something like the community engaged classification would incorporate that information into marketing materials, outreach, student and parent orientations, and use of high-impact practices (Kuh, 2008) such as freshman seminars, common readings, learning communities, and service-learning. Students joining such an institutional culture, especially if faculty are involved in this process and are committed to this vision, might have a substantially different view of the purpose of education and might expect to be experientially involved in problem-solving, application, and community interactions. They would be expecting, rather than resisting, active learning environments, although faculty preparation of students for specific courses and activities would still be necessary.

Even if institutions decide they cannot commit to the elective Carnegie classification, they could shape student expectations through mechanisms similar to those previously mentioned. Other useful and important institutional commitments could involve integration of undergraduate research and scholarly activities into the curriculum (particularly introductory and general education courses; Boyd & Wesemann, 2009; Karukstis & Elgren, 2007) and robust support of student scholarly and creative activities across programs. Supplemental instruction in which focused student sections meet with teaching assistants to discuss and review course material (sometimes including laboratory sections) and lower division mentoring and advising programs, if properly organized and structured, can serve to reinforce an institutional message of engagement, skill development, and student responsibility for learning that can pay dividends in upper division courses. Campus celebrations of engaged activities such as research days, student art showcases and senior capstones, civic engagement projects, and internships highlight and punctuate the institution's commitment to active learning as well as student responsibility for designing and carrying out these projects and providing role models for entering students in how to succeed, something most important for first-generation college students. All of these programs require financial support and commitments, but they contribute to a dynamic campus culture that is at once engaging, while expecting high academic performance and emphasizing students' responsibility for their own learning in ways that reduce resistance.

Support Adjunct (Part-Time) Faculty

As noted in chapter 4, across all types of universities both the size of administration and the use of part-time instructors have increased. At the same time, tenure density has decreased (American Association of University Professors, 2015). Furthermore, universities understand that without tenure-track faculty it is difficult to provide the advising and mentoring to students that is necessary for them to succeed. Partly to solve these issues, some universities are making greater use of professional advisers to ensure student access, taking over a traditional faculty role. Universities may also take this route with a view to increasing student graduation rates by getting students through school more quickly (Selingo, 2014). This is not necessarily a problem from the view of faculty who are very busy teaching, publishing, and securing grant funding, but it reflects the trend toward a professional rather than academic workforce and may increase the probability of resistance due to fewer student contacts with full-time faculty and fewer opportunities for the type of mentoring that Busteed (2014) has linked to long-term outcomes.

The issue of increased use of part-time faculty will not be easily resolved. However, given Busteed's (2014) findings from the Gallup index, we believe it is important for institutions to constantly evaluate and consider ways to shift the balance back toward more full-time faculty. Because adjunct faculty will likely be an ongoing feature of college environments, it is vital that administrations give consideration to providing structural support to encourage adjunct faculty to create and sustain active learning environments for students. This is especially important because many, if not most, adjuncts are assigned to teach introductory and lower division courses and are therefore positioned precisely at points where they may have the most impact on student expectations and can increase or decrease resistance. Although adjuncts often have less connection to the institutions and students (given that they may work for multiple institutions), steps can be taken to improve their relationship to the institution and commitment to its mission, values, and goals such as engaged learning. Some of these steps are probably at the department level whereas others are decisions for those in higher administrative positions.

Institutional practices and policies include fair and reasonable pay for adjunct work and access to faculty development opportunities, especially in regard to curricular decisions about engaged learning and high-impact practices. Adjuncts could be provided with LMS course shells or syllabi that include built-in active learning assignments and assessments so that they do not have to expend uncompensated time and effort to find and add materials and methods to generic course designs. They also should have a voice, a way to provide input to departments and the institution regarding their concerns. Faculty development for adjuncts could be provided online to enhance best practices (including understanding student resistance) for active learning and with some reasonable incentives for them to participate. These practices and policies would help adjunct faculty to feel more a part of the campus and the institution, connect them more closely to their students, enable them to develop improved skills to encourage student learning, and consequently reduce resistance and improve student cognitive development, metacognition, and positive classroom experiences.

Other Changes to Policies and Practices

Commit to Assessment of Learning Outcomes

If teaching is an important task as stated in university mission statements, then teaching quality and student learning outcomes should play a major role in institutional assessments at the program, department, and campus levels. Elevating these concerns to the level of strategic planning and decision-making benefits the institutional culture. This promotes active dialogue about teaching and learning that moves institutions further from traditional superficial learning approaches and toward reductions in student resistance through enhanced engagement.

The importance of these issues in the national discourse is highlighted by the fact that some accreditation agencies, such as the Western Association of Schools and Colleges (WASC), are including student learning outcomes as part of institutional accreditation. Their approach requires universities to develop institutional learning objectives and redesign their curriculum to help students achieve these objectives. Other institutions may have already moved in this direction by building on other efforts, such as defining and measuring student achievement of the essential learning outcomes (ELOs) proposed by the Association of American Colleges and Universities (AAC&U, 2007). Internationally, the Organisation for Economic Co-operation and

Development (OECD) is working on the Assessment of Higher Education Learning Outcomes (AHELO; OECD, 2015). The OECD has already developed an instrument for K–12 students, called Program for International Student Assessment (PISA). The main obstacle is to secure support for a university-level study from different nation-states, especially Western nations (see Morgan, 2015). Many institutions have turned to the National Survey of Student Engagement (NSSE; Center for Postsecondary Research, 2016) and its companion instruments as tools to provide information, at an institutional level, about student engagement and participation in high-impact practices that may inform strategic decision-making. The drawback to the NSSE and similar instruments is that they are not very useful at the program, department, or course level for evaluating needs and areas for improvement.

Other ways that institutions can focus on assessing student learning outcomes include institutional deployment of student learning portfolios (e.g., Zubizarreta, 2009) linked to learning outcomes and curriculum; learning portfolios also serve as pedagogical reflection assignments that increase course relevance and student responsibility for their own learning. An institutional focus on student learning outcomes visible in course syllabi, class discussions, marketing materials, and regular conversations strengthens student motivation and reduces resistance.

Form Alliances

Addressing the challenges of student resistance at an institutional level can be difficult; many institutions may struggle to find the resources to carry out our suggestions or other ideas. One way to help reduce this burden is to form alliances or partnerships with institutions working toward similar goals. Malachowski and colleagues (2015) have described the success of different types of institutions joining together in consortia or networks to promote and develop undergraduate research, a high-impact practice. Their case examples illustrate the value of institutions working together to obtain additional resources from state systems of higher education and other sources to achieve these goals.

Similarly, the establishment of faculty development consortia involving similar institutions or those that are physically close together can reduce the burden on centers of teaching and learning to provide comprehensive services. Different centers may have different expertise that can be shared, and the examples and best practices that faculty and graduate students learn from consortium events may provoke new discussions and innovations in an institution. Opportunities exist to participate in national dialogue and consortium activities. For instance, the Lumina Foundation (www.luminafoundation .org) is dedicated to improving graduation rates in higher education through a focus on learning outcomes. One recent project is to encourage development of student transcripts that include extracurricular activities and achievement of learning outcomes as part of a student's official record. Efforts such as this leverage the knowledge, best practices, and resources of multiple institutions. Active participation in one or more of these types of alliances can generate new ideas, lead to improved practice as these ideas are implemented, and result in increased student engagement and learning.

Conclusion

In this chapter, we have presented six broad approaches that may be useful to shift institutional culture and reduce student resistance with multiple examples of what could be done in each area. In reality, these are not unitary, self-action situations. Resistance is transactional, a systemic outcome, and all six areas we have discussed in this chapter are parts of the system within an institution that interact with the other elements of the integrated model of student resistance. We believe that it is possible to achieve multiple gains in several of these areas at once by thinking and planning systemically and by giving thoughtful consideration to how faculty, staff, course designs, and curriculum are interdependent and influence each other. Students bring their own identities, prior experiences, and levels of cognitive development and metacognitive skills with them to campus, and it is through the interaction of all these elements that student resistance can either become a significant obstacle to student learning or can be ameliorated. We hope that looking at the IMSR through the eyes of a committee chair, department chair, faculty senator, dean, administrator, or faculty developer might give a new perspective and create new opportunities for innovation.

References

American Association of University Professors. (2015). *Background facts on contingent faculty.* Washington, DC: Author.

Association of American Colleges and Universities. (2007). *College learning in the new global century.* Washington, DC: Author.

Barr, R. B., & Tagg, J. (1995, November/December). From teaching to learning—A new paradigm for undergraduate education. *Change, 27*(6), 12–26.

Berk, R. A. (2005). Survey of 12 strategies to measure teaching effectiveness. *International Journal of Teaching and Learning in Higher Education, 17*(1), 48–62.

Berman, J. (2016, January 19). America's growing student debt crisis. *MarketWatch.* Retrieved from http://www.marketwatch.com/story/americas-growing-student-loan-debt-crisis-2016-01-15

Boettcher, J. V., & Conrad, R. (2010). *The online teaching survival guide: Simple and practical pedagogical tips.* San Francisco, CA: Jossey-Bass.

Boyd, M. K., & Wesemann, J. L. (Eds.). (2009). *Broadening participation in undergraduate research: Fostering excellence and enhancing impact.* Washington, DC: Council on Undergraduate Research.

Bretzmann, J. (Ed.). (2013). *Flipping 2.0—Practical strategies for flipping your class.* New Berlin, WI: Bretzmann Group.

Bruff, D. (2009). *Teaching with classroom response systems: Creating active learning environments.* San Francisco, CA: Jossey-Bass.

Busteed, B. (2014, December 1). The real disruptive innovation in education. *Gallup Business Journal.* Retrieved from http://www.gallup.com/businessjournal/179564/real-disruptive-innovation-education.aspx

California State University. (2015). *Course redesign with technology.* Retrieved from http://courseredesign.csuprojects.org/wp/proven

Center for Postsecondary Research. (2015). *Carnegie classification of institutions for higher education.* Retrieved from http://carnegieclassifications.iu.edu

Center for Postsecondary Research. (2016). *National Survey of Student Engagement: Engagement indicators.* Retrieved from http://nsse.indiana.edu/html/engagement_indicators.cfm

Christie, B., & Bayard, J. (2015, November). *Large scale course redesign efforts: Putting reflection into action.* Presentation at the 40th Annual POD Conference, San Francisco, CA.

Council for Aid to Education. (2016). *CLA+ references.* Retrieved from http://cae.org/participating-institutions/cla-references

Ferdman, B. M. (2014). The practice of inclusion in diverse organizations. In B. M. Ferdman & B. Deane (Eds). *Diversity at work: The practice of inclusion* (pp. 3–54). San Francisco, CA: Jossey-Bass.

Freeman, S., Eddy, S. L., McDonough, M., Smith, M. K., Okoroafor, N., Jordt, H., & Wenderoth, M. P. (2014, June 10). Active learning increases student performance in science, engineering, and mathematics. *Proceedings of the National Academy of Sciences (PNAS), 111*(23), 8410–8415.

Hativa, N. (2014a). *Student ratings of instruction: A practical approach to designing, operating, and reporting* (2nd ed). Seattle, WA: Oron Publications.

Hativa, N. (2014b). *Student ratings of instruction: Recognizing effective teaching* (2nd ed). Seattle, WA: Oron Publications.

Karukstis, K. K., & Elgren, T. E. (Eds.). (2007). *Developing and sustaining a research-supportive curriculum: A compendium of successful practices.* Washington, DC: Council of Undergraduate Research.

Kuh, G. (2008). *High-impact educational practices: What they are, who has access to them, and why they matter.* Washington, DC: Association of American Colleges and Universities.

Kuh, G. (2009). What student affairs professionals need to know about student engagement. *Journal of College Student Development, 50*(6), 683–706.

Malachowski, M., Osborn, J. M., Karukstis, K. K., & Ambos, E. L. (Eds.). (2015). *Enhancing and expanding undergraduate research: A systems approach* (New Directions for Higher Education No. 169). Danvers, MA: Wiley Periodicals.

Morgan, J. (2015, May 7). Teaching quality, globally. *Inside Higher Education.* Retrieved from https://www.insidehighered.com/news/2015/05/07/oecd-prepares-measure-teaching-quality

New England Resource Center for Higher Education (NERCHE). (n.d.). *Carnegie community engagement classification.* Retrieved from http://www.nerche.org/index.php?option=com_content&view=article&id=341&Itemid=618

Organisation for Economic Co-operation and Development (OECD). (2015). *Testing student and university performance globally: OECD's AHELO.* Retrieved from http://www.oecd.org/edu/ahelo

Pfund, C., Branchaw, J. L., & Handelsman, J. (2015). *Entering mentoring* (Rev. ed.). New York, NY: W.H. Freeman.

Selingo, J. J. (2014, April 11). Who advises best: Pros or profs? *New York Times.* Retrieved from http://www.nytimes.com/2014/04/13/education/edlife/who-advises-best-pros-or-profs.html?_r=0

Smith, G. A. (2008, September). First day questions for the learner-centered classroom. *National Teaching and Learning Forum, 17*(5), 1–4.

Smith, G. G., Sorensen, C., Gump, A., Heindel, A. J., Caris, M., & Martinez, C. D. (2011). Overcoming student resistance to group work: Online versus face-to-face. *Internet and Higher Education, 14*, 121–128.

Squires, A. (2016, February 8). Confused about your student loans? You are not alone. *NPR Higher Education.* Retrieved from http://www.npr.org/sections/ed/2016/02/07/465556666/confused-about-your-student-loans-youre-not-alone

Van Note Chism, N. (1999). *Peer review of teaching: A sourcebook.* Bolton, MA: Anker.

Zubizarreta, J. (2009). *The learning portfolio: Reflective practice for improving student learning* (2nd ed.). San Francisco, CA: Jossey-Bass.

Final Thoughts

Anton O. Tolman and Janine Kremling

A s we began work on this book, one of the most difficult things we struggled with was trying to help our readers understand, in an analytical way, the separate elements of the IMSR. The more we delved into any one of the five main elements, the more we became aware of the network of interactions that existed between that element and the other key elements of the integrated model. Our students often expressed this same realization through sometimes frustrated discussions as they tried to make clear and specific points about their own subject area—for example, the impact of social stereotypes on resistance or the way mindsets shape student behaviors in the classroom, without veering too far into the territory being written about by others.

For purposes of this book, we told them that it was fine to reference other chapters, to note some of the interactions, and to leave it at that while staying focused on describing how their own area contributed to student resistance. On reflection, this difficulty in explaining the IMSR is entirely appropriate. The IMSR is a transactional model, and although we can try to explain the pieces of the system separately, they cannot truly be understood until one steps back and looks at the system as a whole. The IMSR is an experience in synthesis rather than analysis. Experiences and events that occur or are shaped by one part of the model have significant influence on, and react to, other elements of the model, sometimes simultaneously.

Consider an example involving a first-generation student of some minority background. He comes to class already feeling somewhat isolated on campus. Everyone else seems to know what they are doing, and there are few people of his background visible; he is struggling to decide if college is even necessary or "right" for him and has had to bite back retorts and frustration at some of the biased or racist comments he has already experienced. He worries that he needs to perform well for his family and his group but secretly harbors serious doubts about whether he can succeed in this environment. On an early assignment, he gets a grade much lower than he expected. He shoots an e-mail to his professor expressing frustration and asking for extra credit options. The professor, who has observed this student as someone reluctant to participate and who often does not seem fully prepared, interprets the e-mail as evidence the student doesn't really care about his education and just wants an "easy A." She also has a midterm tenure review coming up and needs to really produce some significant progress on her research and grant proposal, so she sends a quick e-mail back saying she cannot violate the class policies and that he needs to step up his game and do better.

The next day in class, the instructor announces that students will form groups and discuss a controversial subject. The student becomes extremely reluctant to do this, fearing his opinions will not be welcomed by others; he sees no reason to work with students when the instructor is the expert and interprets this assignment as a form of "busywork" with no purpose. She should just tell them the facts that they need to know. Looking around the room, the instructor notices the student's behavior, which only confirms her previous suspicions. Several weeks later, after an important mini-exam, the student is further alarmed by his score and begins to worry about the status of his financial aid if this continues. He believes he is struggling because the instructor is failing in her duty to teach and/or he just is not cut out for college. He begins to demand that the instructor teach them what they need to know. Under pressure to complete her midterm portfolio and knowing teaching will be viewed in a lesser light, she interacts with him more harshly than she normally would have; in class, other students have begun to ignore him or avoid him as he draws more attention to himself.

Although this scenario is contrived to demonstrate the interacting elements of all parts of the IMSR model, we imagine that most faculty who have seen student resistance can identify with at least several elements of this description. It is easy to imagine how, if not adequately addressed fairly quickly, this situation and the student's resistant behaviors will begin to spill over into other behaviors and influence his performance in other courses. Here we observe multiple simultaneous interactions occurring, all of which could be diagnosed by reference to the relevant parts of the IMSR: an institutional environment that contributes to tension and stress and devalues teaching; environmental factors such as racism, stereotype threat, and oppositional culture that shape the student's perception and experience; negative classroom interactions with the instructor and peers (shaped in part by the instructor's and the student's own actor-observer biases and cognitive miserliness); cognitive development that sees the world as dichotomous and instructors as knowing the right answers; and a lack of metacognitive awareness by the student of how to learn more effectively and judge his own level of content mastery.

Of course, situations like this are not unique to first-generation underrepresented students; the elements of the IMSR, to varying degrees, are present in every situation giving rise to student resistance. We believe it is important for you, as our readers, to realize that it is not necessary to master the entire IMSR model and be fully conversant with the literature for each element to be able to take effective action to reduce resistance. Even the chapter authors did not fully tap the available literature in their area but selected key concepts and ideas to help illustrate how the element contributes to resistance and to suggest some strategies you might use to improve the situation. If you are familiar with one area of the model and feel comfortable with how that aspect of the model is being addressed in your courses, then select another element of the model to learn from and work on. Keep in mind the synergies and interdependencies that exist in the different parts of the model and use those to your benefit by selecting assessment strategies and interventions that might enable progress in more than one area, adapting them to your classes.

As with any aspect of excellent teaching, learning how to use the IMSR, seeing its elements happen in front of us or in our own heads, and developing effective interventions takes time and practice. In a chapter describing implementation of team-based learning (TBL), Roberson and Franchini (2014) described moving from traditional lecture-based teaching to TBL as an emotional journey. We would agree and say that this description applies to effective use of the integrated model of student resistance as well; just as Roberson and Franchini did, we advocate that you embrace the journey. As you use the IMSR in your daily work, we anticipate you will start to recognize and counteract your own human biases and tendencies and start to recognize the IMSR elements as they manifest. You can then try some of the suggestions from this book to reduce resistance or come up with and test your own. We have noted that each of the elements of the IMSR has its own literature; those fields continue to evolve and develop, and as they do, our understanding will grow and our interventions will become even more effective.

The IMSR is a work in progress. This book represents an attempt to go beyond anecdotal or single-field explanations of student resistance to a more comprehensive and integrated vision of what resistance is and how it occurs. Although we have based our explanations and suggestions on the available literature, we recognize that there is much work still to be done, especially empirical testing of the model. Recently, we (Tolman and Kremling) began some work to develop a way to directly measure the central dependent variable—student resistance—without reference to the five elements of the model. That work paused as we began this project, but it is important work that needs to move forward. The ways the IMSR elements interact with each other, the specific aspects of each dimension that are most strongly associated with resistance, and the best interventions in each area are all ripe for investigation. Tolman's metacognitive instruments (see chapter 9) also are a rich new area for exploration in terms of linking them to student outcomes and resistance. We welcome such investigations and would love to hear about your work; there may also be areas of collaboration that we would be happy to consider, so please feel free to contact us.

In his foreword, John Tagg wrote that this book addresses what may be the greatest challenge faced by higher education, noting that "students are the medium and agents of education" (p. ix). Despite statistics about student retention, despite reams of studies about the value of active learning and ongoing national conversations about the need to improve teaching and to reform of higher education, despite increasing access to higher education for all parts of our society, if students elect, consciously or not, to resist and not learn what we are teaching, then our efforts are wasted. The integrated model of student resistance presents a way forward, a chance to align our heads with our hearts, to sit down with our students and work together for their benefit and ours. We conclude with words of wisdom from Paul Lingenfelter (2015):

> Improving practice requires an appreciation of complexity, the wise use of measurement, an understanding of the surrounding systems and context of practice, and respect, not unqualified deference, for practitioner wisdom and judgment. . . . Some of the most dramatic improvements in business and in medicine have occurred through improvement science, a disciplined analysis of systems, process interactions, and outcomes in order to find pathways for improvement. Such approaches, combined with efforts to gain deeper understanding of fundamental issues, are more promising than searches for silver bullets or easy victories. (p. 213)

References

Lingenfelter, P. (2015). *"Proof," policy, and practice: Understanding the role of evidence in improving education*. Sterling, VA: Stylus.

Roberson, B., & Franchini, B. (2014). The emotional journey to team-based learning. In J. Sibley & P. Ostafichuk (Eds.), *Getting started with team-based learning*, (pp. 161–174). Sterling, VA: Stylus.

The purpose of this appendix is to provide some of the instruments described in chapter 9 that are used by Tolman and Kremling in their classes (and by some other professors as well). This appendix contains the TTM Learning Survey (the current TTM-ST version incorporating assessment of readiness to work in collaborative in-class teams), the Learning Strategies Self-Assessment 1 (LSSA1) and LSSA3 instruments, resources, and a description of how Tolman uses them in his courses. A previously published description of how Tolman uses these and some additional metacognitive tools in his abnormal psychology courses is provided in Tolman (2011).

The Tolman Approach

- Within the first two weeks of class, students are asked to turn in the TTM Learning Survey (i.e., TTM-ST), the Revised Study Process Questionnaire (R-SPQ; Biggs, Kember, & Leung, 2001), and LSSA1. Tolman does not make available the key to the instrument at this time. He informs students via the course learning management system (LMS; e.g., Canvas) of their TTM readiness stages for individual study and for teamwork. At the same time, he posts a document called "Becoming Aware of Your Approach to Learning" on the course LMS as well as one named "Interpreting the R-SPQ." These documents explain the transtheoretical model of change and the meaning of deep and surface learning to students in the context of their learning in the course.
- Students then complete a follow-up assignment called the Personal Learning Plan (PLP). The first part of that assignment asks students to reflect on what their scores on the TTM-ST and the R-SPQ mean, whether they believe they are in a position to change their study and learning patterns, and what they might need to do next or what steps they have already taken. The PLP assignment also asks students to write out a study plan for the semester, including

how they plan to avoid distractions and obstacles. The assignment also requires students to provide their thoughts on the course Objectives Map (a document demonstrating how course objectives align with assignments and assessments) and invites them to offer suggestions for changes to course policies. The assignment ends with a chance for them to ask the professor for help in any areas they are concerned about.

- Tolman provides feedback to the students on the basis of their LSSA1 scores and answers and tracks student stages and LSSA scores in a spreadsheet.

- Tolman uses the scores, particularly from the TTM-ST team section, as one of the key elements in deciding how to allocate students to teams for his team-based learning (TBL) courses.

- At the end of the semester, students retake these same instruments, except they complete the LSSA3 instead of the LSSA1 (same quantitative questions, but different qualitative questions). The LSSA3 asks students to reflect on progress or lack of it in improving their study and learning patterns across the semester and invites them to think about how to plan for improvement in the future.

For those who are interested, following preliminary testing, Tolman and colleagues presented on these instruments at conferences and are working on a manuscript that describes the psychometric properties of the instruments across two studies involving almost 800 undergraduates (Tolman, Biggs, & Johnson, 2016). The results support the reliability and validity of these tools and their relationship to deep approaches to learning, although more work is needed. Interested parties are encouraged to contact Tolman directly.

Special Notes and Suggestions

The Meaning of SQ4R

Both the TTM Learning Survey and LSSA instruments use the acronym SQ4R in the text (see TTM Learning Survey instructions). There are multiple variations of this acronym depending on where one runs across it. For example, it can stand for Survey, Question, Read, Recite, wRite, Review or Survey, Question, Read, Recite, Relate, Review, among others. In all of its incarnations, SQ4R represents six steps of active reading or reading for deeper retention of material. Other methods have also been described for active reading and given different names such as *muscle reading*, but all of these methods are built on learning research and on roughly the same framework as SQ4R. There is evidence that using the prior incarnation of this method (SQ3R; Robinson, 1946/1970) produces gains in student learning (see Carlston, 2011). Because *SQ4R* is frequently mentioned in psychology texts and in college success courses at Utah Valley University, this term was used to represent active learning strategies in these instruments.[1]

Notes Regarding the Learning Strategies Self-Assessment Instruments

There are more than three variants of the LSSA instrument. Tolman originally created three versions to be administered across the semester. The LSSA1 would be given early in the semester, the LSSA2 at or around midterms, and the LSSA3 at the end of the semester. This was not just to encourage students to think about their learning as something to be considered at the beginning of the semester and then forgotten but also to encourage them to reflect on their progress and stumbles so that they could pick themselves up and start again. However, students complained about completing the instrument three times in the semester; in recent years, Tolman has been using the LSSA1 and LSSA3 and not the LSSA2. All three instruments use the same quantitative sections and scales; they differ in the qualitative questions that are relevant to the different phases of the semester (beginning, midterm, and end).

The third quantitative area of the LSSA was created to measure student readiness to become more effective writers. In part this was because written communication is a core learning outcome across most institutions and disciplines, and thus, instructors looking at that area could determine if they needed to emphasize different aspects of writing in their course designs and classroom activities. However, that area of the LSSA was intended to be modular in the sense that other relevant learning skills or outcomes could be inserted into that same place in the instrument. For instance, for a time, Barbara Biggs (who participated in studies regarding the instrument psychometrics) removed the writing component and worked with Tolman to substitute a scale to assess student math anxiety for her math courses. This would give her a measure of the intensity of student math anxiety and would be helpful for her in deciding on interventions and evaluating student progress across the semester. Tolman would encourage other instructors to consider similar adaptations as appropriate.

Last, the LSSA instruments included in this appendix were adapted to Tolman's abnormal psychology course. For instance, question 26 on the LSSA1 (like question 25 on the LSSA3) asks students to review Bloom's taxonomy as posted on the Canvas LMS for the class. There are a few other university-related specific items included on the quantitative scales as well.

Interested readers are free to adapt or alter these to fit their own institutional or course contexts, for example, substituting "Blackboard" for "Canvas."

Anyone who has questions about the instruments or would like the key to the TTM Learning Survey, the Personal Learning Plan description, Word versions of these instruments to facilitate adaptation, or other items mentioned in this appendix are encouraged to contact Anton O. Tolman at Anton .Tolman@UVU.edu. We are especially interested in collaboration with colleagues who are considering use of these instruments in their courses or who would be interested in extending the testing and evaluation of these tools to enhance student metacognition. We are including here the interpretation documents that are posted for students to use in reflecting on their scores.

Note

1. Another common variant is SQ6R (Williams, 2005), but eight steps to active reading may provoke more student resistance than six. To reduce resistance, many faculty break up the six steps of SQ4R into three stages: (a) S&Q; (b) actively read; and (c) recite, relate, review.

References

Biggs, J., Kember, D., & Leung, D. (2001). The Revised Two-Factor Study Process Questionnaire: R-SPQ-2F. *British Journal of Educational Psychology, 71,* 133–149.

Carlston, D. (2011). Benefits of student-generated note-packets: A preliminary investigation of SQ3R implementation. *Teaching of Psychology, 38*(3), 142–146.

Draper, S., & Waldman, J. (2013). *Deep and surface learning: The literature.* Retrieved from http://www.psy.gla.ac.uk/~steve/courses/archive/CERE12-13-safari-archive/topic9/webarchive-index.html

Robinson, F. P. (1946/1970). *Effective study.* New York, NY: Harper and Brothers.

Tolman, A. O. (2011). Creating transformative experiences for students in abnormal psychology. In R. L. Miller, E. Balcetis, S. R. Burns, D. B. Daniel, B. K. Saville, & W. D. Woody (Eds.), *Promoting student engagement* (Vol. 2, pp. 136–145). Washington, DC: Society for the Teaching of Psychology. Retrieved from http://teachpsych.org/e-books/pse2011/vol2/index.php

Tolman, A. O., Biggs, B., & Johnson, B. (2016). New metacognitive instruments to advance student learning. Manuscript in preparation.

Williams, S. (2005). Guiding students through the jungle of research-based literature. *College Teaching, 53*(4), 137.

TTM LEARNING SURVEY

Study Section

Studying is defined as any planned activity (e.g., reading a textbook, reviewing vocabulary) or learning strategy (e.g., applying material to personal experience, SQ4R, creating practice questions or concept maps) performed to increase knowledge. Such activity should be performed *three or more times per week* for at least *30 minutes* per session to count as studying.

Please read all *of the following statements before answering. In regard to studying regularly, please indicate which* one *of the statements is* most *true of your situation by putting an X in the space next to the statement:*

S1. _____ I usually read assigned chapters before class, and I am making deliberate use of specific study or learning strategies when I study every week; I usually keep to my study schedule.

S2. _____ I have been thinking that it is time that I start taking more responsibility for my own learning and studying; I'm not learning as effectively or performing as well as I think I should.

S3. _____ Learning to study better is a good thing, but due to work, family, or other things, I don't have time or energy to study regularly; some instructors demand too much of busy students.

S4. _____ I have decided to find out about some new study strategies or skills that I can use this semester to improve my learning; I also have decided that I need to write out a specific study plan and am going to start following it soon.

S5. _____ Six months ago or more, I decided to really get serious and improve my study skills and learning strategies; I picked several new skills to learn and have been using them since then; I also worked out a study schedule and have stuck to it for at least a semester.

S6. _____ I believe it is the instructor's job to teach me, not my job to teach myself; setting up a study schedule and learning new study skills are not worth the time they take.

Team Section

A collaborative team is defined as a group of three or more students who work together in class on assigned projects or activities. These groups may be the same across a semester or may vary depending on the day.

Please read all *of the following statements before answering. In regard to participating on a collaborative team, please indicate which* one *of the statements is* most *true of your situation by putting an X in the space next to the statement:*

T1. _____ I have been involved in collaborative teams in several courses *or* across more than one semester; they are great ways to learn *and* I look forward to the chance to participate.

T2. _____ I think collaborative teams are a waste of time; I want to hear from the expert, not other students.

T3. _____ I appreciate collaborative teams; I think I learn well in a team, and I work hard to be a good team player.

T4. _____ I have been thinking that maybe I need to put more effort into learning and working on a collaborative team.

T5. _____ I think the idea of collaborative teams is okay in theory, but they annoy me and are overused.

T6. _____ I think collaborative teams can be useful; I am looking for ideas of how I can use them to learn better and to improve my teamwork skills.

Note: In Tolman's classes, he uses a form adapted to fit entirely on a single page.

LEARNING STRATEGIES AND SELF-AWARENESS ASSESSMENT 1

This first assignment is designed to help you think about your attitudes and past learning-related behaviors as you begin this class; it gives you a baseline assessment to compare yourself to in the future. There are no right answers—the more honest you are the more likely this assessment will be useful to you.

Section 1: Learning Strategies

Think of a class you took last term at UVU or another institution. Please indicate how often you used any of the following study or learning strategies in that class. Please indicate a number in the space provided.

1	2	3	4	5
Did not use	Used once or twice in the semester	Used at least once monthly	Used it at least once weekly	Used it daily or several times a week

Effective Strategies I Use to Learn the Material

_____ 1. Set up a study schedule, adapted it as necessary, and stuck with it

_____ 2. Used SQ4R (Survey, Question, Read, Recite, Relate, Review) or another specific strategy (e.g., muscle reading) for reading the textbook

_____ 3. Used underlining (*sparingly*) or wrote personal notes in the margins or on sticky notes/in my notebook as I read

_____ 4. Made use of concept maps or some other graphical way of recording information from lecture or the text

_____ 5. Read my assigned readings *before* the first day of class on the assigned topic

_____ 6. Identified unfamiliar vocabulary or terminology from text or lecture; asked in class about it or learned and reinforced meaning in another way

_____ 7. Came to class prepared with questions about things I needed clarification on or wanted examples of

_____ 8. Reviewed (*not* just reread) material from each chapter assigned at least two additional times, comparing my understanding with lecture notes and other sources

_____ 9. Reviewed any materials available for this course on Blackboard or other sites, regularly kept up with online quizzes, and chapter summaries, and read assignment requirements and grading criteria

_____ 10. Reviewed notes from class or the textbook within four hours of the end of class

Enhancing and Enriching My Understanding of the Material

_____ 11. Participated in a student study group to discuss/review class concepts and lectures

_____ 12. Prepared for exams by studying with another student or group of students

_____ 13. Shared what I thought or what I had learned with others either in class discussion or outside class

_____ 14. Came up with examples of how the concepts I was reading about or discussing in class linked or applied to the real world or my own/family's/friends' life/lives

_____ 15. Took time to help or explain concepts to other students who were struggling in class

Effective Strategies for Improving Papers/Writing Skills and for Other Assignments

_____ 16. Wrote multiple drafts of papers that were due for a class before I turned in my papers

_____ 17. Asked for help on papers or other assignments from my professor or other professionals

_____ 18. Went to the Writing Center for help with papers

_____ 19. Asked a friend or peer to read my paper drafts out loud to me while I evaluated areas I needed to improve

_____ 20. Made use of online materials to help me better understand grammar, appropriate formatting, or effective writing

_____ 21. Reviewed any criteria posted or handed out by the professor on how to write papers effectively and how to avoid common mistakes

_____ 22. Reviewed and carefully considered feedback I received from the professor or others in order to understand the types of mistakes I was making and to define areas in which I could do better

Section 2: Self-Assessment for This Course

Please answer the following questions

23. Why are you taking this course? Explain how you think the course might be useful to you or to those around you (family, spouse, friends, clients) in the future.

24. Please describe *your own* personal learning goals in the class (not the class objectives). What do *you* hope to learn from the class?

25. Please look at your answers to the questions in Section 1 (items 1–22). What patterns do you see? Describe your strengths and weaknesses as a learner.

26. Review the Bloom's taxonomy document on Canvas. Where do you think you are right now with your mastery of the material related to this course? What would help you move further up the taxonomy during this class?

27. What ideas or suggestions do you have about how *you* can maximize your learning in this class? What ideas or suggestions do you have for how your instructor can help you do that?

LEARNING STRATEGIES AND SELF-AWARENESS ASSESSMENT 3

This is the last of the LSSAs. You should review *your own* PLP and your LSSA1 before you complete this assignment. This assignment asks you to think about your learning for this entire semester and reach some overall conclusions for your future.

Section 1: Learning Strategies

Please indicate how often you used any of the following study or learning strategies for this course. *Please indicate a number in the space provided.*

1	2	3	4	5
Did not use	Used once or twice in the semester	Used at least once monthly	Used it at least once weekly	Used it daily or several times a week

Effective Strategies I Use to Learn the Material

_____ 1. Set up a study schedule, adapted it as necessary, and stuck with it

_____ 2. Used SQ4R (Survey, Question, Read, Recite, Relate, Review) or another specific strategy (e.g., muscle reading) for reading the textbook

_____ 3. Used underlining (*sparingly*) or wrote personal notes in the margins or on sticky notes/in my notebook as I read

_____ 4. Made use of concept maps or some other graphical way of recording information from lecture or the text

_____ 5. Read my assigned readings *before* the first day of class on the assigned topic

_____ 6. Identified unfamiliar vocabulary or terminology from text or lecture; asked in class about it or learned and reinforced meaning in another way

_____ 7. Came to class prepared with questions about things I needed clarification on or wanted examples of

_____ 8. Reviewed (*not* just reread) material from each chapter assigned at least two additional times, comparing my understanding with lecture notes and other sources

_____ 9. Reviewed any materials available for this course on Blackboard or other sites, regularly kept up with online quizzes and chapter summaries, and read assignment requirements and grading criteria

_____ 10. Reviewed notes from class or the textbook within four hours of the end of class

Enhancing and Enriching My Understanding of the Material

_____ 11. Participated in a student study group to discuss/review class concepts and lectures

_____ 12. Prepared for exams by studying with another student or group of students

_____ 13. Shared what I thought or what I had learned with others either in class discussion or outside class

_____ 14. Came up with examples of how the concepts I was reading about or discussing in class linked or applied to the real world or my own/family's/friends' life/lives

_____ 15. Took time to help or explain concepts to other students who were struggling in class

Effective Strategies for Improving Papers/Blogs/Writing Skills and for Other Assignments

_____ 16. Wrote multiple drafts of papers that were due for this class before I turned them in

_____ 17. Asked for help on papers or other assignments from my professor or other professionals

_____ 18. Went to the Writing Center for help with papers

_____ 19. Asked a friend or peer to read my paper drafts out loud to me while I evaluated areas I needed to improve

_____ 20. Made use of online materials to help me better understand grammar, appropriate formatting, or effective writing

_____ 21. Reviewed any criteria posted or handed out by the professor on how to write papers effectively and how to avoid common mistakes

_____ 22. Reviewed and carefully considered feedback I received from the professor or others in order to understand the types of mistakes I was making and to define areas in which I could do better

Section 2: Review of the Semester

23. Summarize your own assessment of how well you achieved each of the *class* objectives listed in the syllabus. Did you meet or partially meet all or

some of the objectives? Did you feel you did not achieve some of them? What kind of a plan could you devise to improve in those areas you struggled with for other classes or in your future learning?

24. Summarize how well you achieved your personal objectives described in LSSA1 (item 24). Did you get out of class what you had hoped to? What kind of a plan could you devise to improve in those areas you struggled with for other classes or in your future learning?

25. How far did you advance on Bloom's taxonomy? What level are you currently on in regard to psychopathology? Explain your answer or justify it.

26. Review your responses to Section 1 (items 1–22) and compare them with the same items on LSSA1. What do you notice? How well would you say you did in making use of effective study strategies this term?

27. Please describe the top two to three aspects of the course that most assisted your learning during this term. How did they help you?

28. Please describe one or two things in the course that seemed like obstacles to you or made it more difficult for you. How could they have been changed to improve your learning?

29. Look at your PLP and review your stage of change and your approach to learning (surface, strategic, or deep) at the beginning of the semester. Did either your individual study or team readiness stage (TTM Learning Survey) change during this term? (For example, did you move from contemplation to action? Did you recycle backward?) Did you alter or change your approach to learning? How do you plan to apply what you learned to future classes or future learning?

BECOMING AWARE OF YOUR LEARNING APPROACH

Completing the R-SPQ gives you the chance to evaluate what approach to learning you tend to use the most. The questionnaire usually demonstrates that people use more than one approach depending on circumstances. The R-SPQ focuses on contrasting a deep approach (DA scale) and a surface approach (SA scale) to learning.

Read the following about the surface and deep approaches to learning. In addition, the literature also describes a third approach that is not currently covered by the R-SPQ: the strategic approach. Review the description of each approach and honestly evaluate how much you may use each style. Keep in mind that you may use one approach for certain classes and another approach for other classes (e.g., nonmajor courses). Then read the instructions at the end for how to evaluate your own development.

→ **If your scores are more than eight points apart, then you may have a significant *preference* for one approach or the other (whichever is highest), although most learners use some of both from time to time. The characteristics of these approaches (not the person) are described.**

Surface Approach (SA Scale)

Learners using this approach tend to

- Be motivated to avoid failure rather than focused on doing their best; use performance avoidance (such as procrastination) to help reduce anxiety; give a good "reason" or excuse for not doing well
- Have low self-confidence in their abilities as learners
- Focus on "survival" or "getting through" the class
- Focus on memorization; "what does the professor want to hear?" or "will this be on the exam?"; will probably avoid use of more advanced study skills (e.g., SQ4R, concept maps, study groups)
- Avoid personally investing themselves in the material, completing assignments with the least degree of involvement necessary to ensure a passing or reasonable grade

Deep Approach (DA Scale)

Learners using this approach tend to

- Focus on intrinsic or internal motivation; even with required courses may say to themselves, "I have to take this class, so I want to learn as much as I can"
- Be motivated by the sense of satisfaction of mastering complex materials and ideas
- Actively want to understand the world around them, to participate in events
- Seek out challenging courses and assignments and focus on *mastering* the material required in the assignment rather than just completing it or getting a good score
- Relate course content and assignments to their own lives and future careers, leading to enhanced memory for the material and thus more success in the course

A deep approach is often the source of vitality in a professional career and generally produces higher quality services and more ethical service delivery.

→ **If you find that you tend to be using the surface approach more than the deep approach, ask yourself why. Why do I resist engaging with the material? What would happen if I did engage or if I were to accept the challenge of using more advanced skills and seeking to master the concepts? If you scored higher on the deep approach, then look at your individual items, particularly those related to deep learning or mastery of the material and see if there are still areas in which you could improve how you approach learning.**

→ **If you fall "in between" with a score that suggests you may use both strategies roughly equally (scores are within eight points of each other), you may want to consider that perhaps you are actually using a strategic approach. Alternatively, if your difference is close to eight, you may use one approach more than the other but may not have a consistent preference.**

Strategic Approach

Learners using this approach tend to

- Be motivated primarily by competition (wanting to win, do well, come out better than others)

- Argue points or minor issues in order to gain more points or improve a grade; are more concerned about the grade than about learning or mastery of the material
- Feel good about themselves when they are "winning" or looking smarter than others
- Be "bulimic" learners, doing enough for success on exams or assignments but then purging it out and forgetting about it
- Not really want to know the material or to be challenged to think or evaluate their own assumptions, attitudes, or behaviors
- Not want the course material to have any impact on their lives but see courses as "jumping through hoops" to get where they want to go or just as requirements to get done

Those who adopt the strategic approach often see school and the courses they take as requirements made up by someone else, and so they are not *personally* engaged. Alternatively, they may see the course as a type of game they are playing and they want to "win." They do not yet understand that the people who designed the requirements have more experience and a perspective on future careers and the development of skills that will lead to success in future careers than they do. They also may not yet understand that learning is not a game or that learning is something that happens outside the college as well as within it. In today's complex world and economy, every field requires ongoing and constant learning. College is a place where one learns skills for *how to learn* that will be useful throughout one's career.

→ **If you believe you use the strategic approach frequently, ask yourself: What am I trying to win? Is feeling smart or competent more important than mastering important skills? What skills and knowledge am I working to develop? How can I shift my focus from seeing grades as trophies to feeling smart and competent when I master and retain complex skills and information?**

You may also find the discussion of surface versus deep approaches by Draper and Waldman (2013) useful.

Self-Evaluation

Steps for evaluating your own approach and level of development (use this process to help you with the first section of your Personal Learning Plan [PLP] assignment):

1. Examine your own scores on the R-SPQ, especially the size of the difference between your DA and SA scores.
2. Do you have a consistent or significant preference for one approach or the other? What has led you to develop that preference? Are you happy with where you are?
3. If your scores are fairly close together (within eight points), what does that mean? Do you use both approaches almost equally? Do you go back and forth? What determines which approach you use when? Might you be taking a strategic approach rather than one of the others?
4. Examine the survey items that contributed to your scores on the R-SPQ. Which items did you agree with most strongly? What do those items tell you about your approach to learning?
5. Compare your scores with your classmates' scores by looking at the data that will be posted on Canvas. You will get some idea of how you tend to approach material in your courses and your current course in particular compared with your peers. Were your scores higher than average? Lower than average? What does that mean for each of the scales?
6. Write down your thoughts for your PLP.

INTERPRETING THE TTM LEARNING SURVEY

The TTM Learning Survey you took is an experimental instrument that I created to help students; research is ongoing with the instruments, but the results are looking both reliable and valid. The instrument is based on the transtheoretical model of change (TTM), which describes behavior change as resulting through a series of changes over time. According to this theory, adopting permanent changes in our lives requires consistent effort; recycling or sliding back into earlier stages is a very common result. In fact, the creators of this model believe that long-term change may only be accomplished in many cases by a type of spiral in which we move forward through the stages, then cycle backward (hopefully not all the way back to precontemplation), and then move forward again, but at a "higher level" of effort. This is an important concept: if we recycle, or slide backward, it does *not* mean that we are failures or that we should give up. This is just how change happens in human beings.

Read the following description of the TTM stages of change; following the description are the instructions to help you interpret your survey so that you can write about it in your Personal Learning Plan.

The Transtheoretical Model Stages of Prochaska and DiClemente

There are five key stages of change:

1. *Precontemplation* (PC1 and PC2). No intention to change in the foreseeable future. Persons may be unaware of their problems or are referred by others for help, but they disagree that they need to do anything or even do not acknowledge that there is a problem. In my scale, PC1 describes "hard core" precontemplators—they do not see any need or reason to change and, in fact, may argue *against* the need to change. PC2 describes persons who may acknowledge that some change might be useful, but they do not want to put the time or effort into changing. To move forward the persons need to acknowledge or "own" the problem (take responsibility), increase their awareness of the negative aspects of the problem, and accurately evaluate self-regulation abilities; this may require consciousness raising, input or feedback from others.

2. *Contemplation* (CN). People at this stage are thinking about working on the problem but have not yet made a commitment (emotional or cognitive) to do so. They are evaluating options; they can remain in this stage for *long* periods (think about someone deciding when to quit smoking). To move forward people must avoid chronic contemplation; they need to make a decision to take action. This may require looking at the pros and cons of making a decision and increasing their belief that they are capable of change.

3. *Preparation* (PR). Persons intend to take action in the immediate future; they begin not with large significant changes but by making small behavior changes ("baby steps"; e.g., gathering information, talking with others, looking at ways or plans for changing, taking small steps like dropping from smoking a pack a day to eight cigarettes per day). To move forward persons need to set goals and priorities. They need to select a plan of action and dedicate themselves to the plan. They may need to actively reward themselves for taking positive actions and work out some personal punishment for not achieving their goals.

4. *Action* (AC). Persons are currently actively modifying their own behaviors or their environments to overcome their problems. This usually takes dedicated time and energy, especially if they are trying out new behaviors. The measure of action is if persons have actually completed or reached a significant step such as abstinence or consistency in the new behavior (e.g., exercise plan, studying) for a sustained period (i.e., more than a few weeks). To move forward persons must make use of active change-oriented processes such as counterconditioning (replacing negative behaviors with healthy ones), stimulus control (changing the environment to reduce or eliminate cues for negative behaviors), and contingency management (rewarding self-change and punishing relapsing behavior). These skills help to disrupt habitual patterns of behavior. Also important is to identify situations or stimuli that might undermine success and act to prevent these triggers.

5. *Maintenance* (MN). Persons need to work on maintaining gains made and preventing relapse. For some problem behaviors, the maintenance stage may last the rest of a person's life and require ongoing vigilance (e.g., think about how to prevent procrastination from happening again or how to permanently give up smoking or drinking). To continue progress persons need to continue to make use of action-oriented processes. Remaining free of problem behaviors or continued use of new behaviors for six months signals the maintenance stage. Persons must work to prevent relapse.

Recycling or relapse is a consistent issue. It is quite common and a natural part of learning; many (maybe most) people require multiple efforts before they move forward. A person may relapse back to an earlier stage or may even give up and move back to precontemplation, although this may be avoidable with planning and awareness that this spiral cycle of change is normal and should not be interpreted as failure or lack of ability to change. If you slide backward, recognize what happened (do not *avoid* recognizing it in order to not feel like a failure), figure out what led to the backward slide, and make a new plan and stick with it.

Steps to Take to Interpret Your TTM Learning Survey

Follow three steps:

1. Look at my comment about your stages in the Canvas Speedgrader. The "key" for interpreting what this code means is at the end of this step. This instrument is designed to measure your degree of willingness or "readiness" to adopt new effective learning behaviors (e.g., SQ4R, concept maps, participating in collaborative teams, taking personal responsibility for your own learning) and leave behind ineffective behaviors (e.g., procrastination, ineffective study strategies). This instrument assesses your "readiness to change" in two areas: individual study strategies and willingness to engage with a collaborative team of your colleagues in enhancing your learning. *Please comment on both areas in your PLP.* Here are the codes:

   a. PC1 = Precontemplation: not willing to change or take responsibility, or argues against change
   b. PC2 = Precontemplation: believers, accept need for change, but do not think it is possible for a variety of reasons
   c. CN = Contemplation stage: thinking about change, weighing pros and cons
   d. PR = Preparation: investigating ways to learn more effectively
   e. AC = Action: taking steps right now
   f. MN = Maintenance: have made changes in the past and kept them going for at least one full semester

2. Look up your stages and then use those terms to describe yourself in your PLP and explain what you would need to do to make a change (that information is in the previous discussion of the stages). You will use this information throughout the semester and also in your Learning

Strategies Self-Assessment (LSSA), so do not delete the survey! You will also compare it to where you are at the end of the semester.

Good questions to ask yourself:

Why did I pick the item that I did? What would I need to do to move to the next stage? What does my stage suggest about how I may react to things in this class and in other classes? What would it take for me to move forward in adopting new strategies? Is there an advantage to me in doing so (e.g., preparing for graduate school or a professional career)?

3. Once you have looked at your study skills stage of change, then look at your team stage. Your team stage in regard to collaborative work may be different or the same as your stage in regard to study skills. Describe your stage and how it affects the way you work with teams or groups.

EDITORS AND CONTRIBUTORS

Editors

Janine Kremling completed her doctorate in criminology at the University of South Florida. She is an associate professor in the Department of Criminal Justice at the California State University, San Bernardino. Her research in regard to student learning has focused mainly on metacognition and the impact of institutional culture on the learning environment.

Anton O. Tolman is a professor of behavioral science at Utah Valley University. He received his PhD from the University of Oregon in clinical psychology and worked in clinical and forensic settings before joining the academy. He is past director of the Faculty Center for Teaching Excellence, where he served for almost eight years, and his recent work and publications have focused on student metacognition, power dynamics in the classroom, and student resistance. He lives in Orem, Utah, with his wife, Patricia, and is an avid boardgamer.

Contributors

Matthew Andersen graduated from Utah Valley University with a bachelor's degree in behavioral science. He previously coauthored with Matthew Draper a chapter in *The Routledge Handbook of International Crime and Justice Studies* (Routledge, 2014) and has presented at several conferences. Currently, he works as a science curriculum writer at www.shmoop.com, designing online neuroscience, psychology, biology, and other classes for high school students. He plans to achieve a PhD in neuroscience to study neurological aging diseases.

Rob Blair is a creative writer and community builder. He received his degree from Utah Valley University in integrated studies, which allowed him to explore the overlap between creative writing and psychology, especially as it concerns the psychology of creativity and the methods we can use to effectively teach composition. He is also the founder of the website CreativeWriting Guild.com, which shares articles and essays on the writing craft.

Erikca DeAnn Brown is a science teacher of 18 years at Rancho Cucamonga High School in Rancho Cucamonga, California. She received her MA in teaching from Grand Canyon University, another MA in education from Claremont Graduate University, and her PhD in education from Claremont Graduate University. Her research interests include microaggressions, organizational culture, cultural competency, diversity, and inclusion. She lives in Upland, California, with husband, Dave, and daughter, Ana. In her leisure time, she loves to read and teach Zumba.

Averie Hamilton is a New Mexico native and industrial/organizational psychologist. She was first introduced to this book project while she completed her undergraduate behavioral science honors degree at Utah Valley University. She currently is finishing her master's in industrial/organizational psychology at Purdue University, Indianapolis. She now extends her research on learning into the workplace via employee training, learning, and development. When she's not computing statistics, she enjoys long-distance running and occasional trips to Disneyland.

Christopher Lee is a Southern California native who holds a graduate degree in American studies with an emphasis in folklore and rhetoric and composition. He is currently a lecturer at Utah Valley University, where he teaches composition and literature courses and enjoys aiding undergraduates in research and publication. His research interests include composition pedagogy and educational psychology.

Amy Lindstrom is a 38-year-old nontraditional student. She has been married to her husband, Ryan, for 18 years. Together they have three children: Jakob, Dawson, and Mallory. She has transferred from Utah Valley University to Brigham Young University and plans to complete her PhD in clinical psychology there. Her goals include creating a practice for clinical and recreational therapy, with a special focus on strengthening family relationships.

Trevor Morris is program coordinator for the Office of Teaching and Learning at Utah Valley University with five years of experience in faculty development. He holds a master's degree in psychology from Palo Alto University and taught as adjunct faculty in the Department of Behavioral Science for over four years. His research interests include cognitive and noncognitive factors in student success and learning.

Ryan Radmall is a graduate student and adjunct faculty member at California State University, San Bernardino where he is pursuing a degree in industrial-organizational psychology. His research interests include metacognition, determinants of police turnover and use of force, and flow. He lives in San Bernardino with his cat and enjoys motorcycle riding and snowboarding.

Colt Rothlisberger graduated from Utah Valley University with a bachelor's degree in behavioral science with an emphasis in psychology. He currently works as a special education teacher at an elementary school. Working on this book was, in a way, the culmination of his undergraduate experience.

Andy Sechler graduated from Utah Valley University with a bachelor of science degree in behavioral sciences with an emphasis in psychology. He is presently working on an interdisciplinary master's degree in consciousness studies at John F. Kennedy University in the San Francisco Bay area of California. His research interests include psychology, education, and Eastern philosophy. When he is not reading or writing, he can usually be found hiking or biking in the mountains.

Shea Smart graduated in 2015 with an undergraduate degree in behavioral sciences from Utah Valley University. While at UVU he was involved in several different research groups and projects and was able to travel and present research at domestic and international conferences. He currently conducts research and analysis at an independent health care IT company.

John Tagg is coauthor, with Robert Barr, of the seminal *Change* magazine article "From Teaching to Learning: A New Paradigm for Undergraduate Education." His book *The Learning Paradigm College* (Jossey-Bass, 2004) expands on and develops the learning paradigm idea. In more than a dozen other articles and in presentations at over 100 colleges and universities, he has advocated reform of higher education to better promote student learning. He is currently at work on a book on barriers to change and levers for improvement in higher education. He is emeritus professor of English at Palomar College in San Marcos, California.

The New Science of Learning
How to Learn in Harmony With Your Brain

Terry Doyle and Todd Zakrajsek

Foreword by Jeannie H. Loeb

"This is a path-breaking book. Faculties have been learning about how the mind works, and this book spreads the message to students, who need it just as much. More sophisticated and empirically grounded than any study skills manual, this book addresses all the major research findings on how the human brain learns. And it does so using language and examples that students can easily understand and immediately apply to enhance their attention, depth of processing, retention, retrieval, and far-transfer abilities. Plus, each chapter ends with excellent summaries and scholarly references. It deserves to be required reading for all college students—really, anyone interested in learning."—*Linda B. Nilson, Director, Office of Teaching Effectiveness and Innovation, Clemson University*

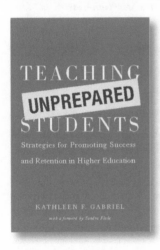

Teaching Unprepared Students
Strategies for Promoting Success and Retention in Higher Education

Kathleen F. Gabriel

Foreword by Sandra M. Flake

"Though written with undergraduate institutions in mind, most of what she offers can easily be applied to other educational settings. It is a very readable and practical book."—*Teaching Theology and Religion*

"Teaching is a tough job, especially when your pupil is underprepared. *Teaching Unprepared* Students is a guide for this all too common situation where a student is dangerously in over his or her head in the class they are in. Aiming for students to get the resources they need to turn a subpar student into a superb one. . . . *Teaching Unprepared Students* is an invaluable manual for when traditional methods just aren't good enough."—*Midwest Book Review*

22883 Quicksilver Drive
Sterling, VA 20166-2102

Subscribe to our e-mail alerts: www.Styluspub.com

Also available from Stylus

Creating Self-Regulated Learners
Strategies to Strengthen Students' Self-Awareness and Learning Skills

Linda B. Nilson

Foreword by Barry J. Zimmerman

"Linda Nilson has provided a veritable gold mine of effective learning strategies that are easy for faculty to teach and for students to learn. Most students can turn poor course performance into success if they are taught even a few of the strategies presented. However, relatively few students will implement new strategies if they are not required to do so by instructors. Nilson shows how to seamlessly introduce learning strategies into classes, thereby maximizing the possibility that students will become self-regulated learners who take responsibility for their own learning."—*Saundra McGuire*, *Assistant Vice Chancellor (Ret.) & Professor of Chemistry, Louisiana State University*

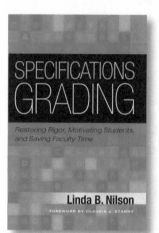

Specifications Grading
Restoring Rigor, Motivating Students, and Saving Faculty Time

Linda B. Nilson

Foreword by Claudia J. Stanny

"This book will change your life! Every instructor should buy it now. Nilson shows us how to make grading easier, more logical, and more consonant with research on learning and motivation. A practical, time-saving, and student-motivating system of grading. A major advance in our thinking about how we grade and how students learn."—*Barbara Walvoord*, *Professor Emerita, University of Notre Dame*

"Faculty who struggle with the challenges of managing time for grading student work and collecting meaningful assessment data from assignments and projects embedded in their courses will find much to interest them in *Specifications Grading*. Nilson proposes a new approach to rubrics that simplifies the task of grading, maintains standards for consistency and validity of assessments, and aligns grades with specific learning outcomes."—*Claudia J. Stanny*, *Director, Center for University Teaching, Learning, and Assessment; and Associate Professor, Department of Psychology, University of West Florida*

(Continues on previous page)